Luminos is the Open Access monograph publishing program from UC Press. Luminos provides a framework for preserving and reinvigorating monograph publishing for the future and increases the reach and visibility of important scholarly work. Titles published in the UC Press Luminos model are published with the same high standards for selection, peer review, production, and marketing as those in our traditional program. www.luminosoa.org

D1599168

Being Single in India

ETHNOGRAPHIC STUDIES IN SUBJECTIVITY

Tanya Luhrmann, Editor

1. *Forget Colonialism? Sacrifice and the Art of Memory in Madagascar*, by Jennifer Cole

2. *Sensory Biographies: Lives and Deaths among Nepal's Yolmo Buddhists*, by Robert Desjarlais

3. *Culture and the Senses: Bodily Ways of Knowing in an African Community*, by Kathryn Linn Geurts

4. *Becoming Sinners: Christianity and Moral Torment in a Papua New Guinea Society*, by Joel Robbins

5. *Jesus in Our Wombs: Embodying Modernity in a Mexican Convent*, by Rebecca J. Lester

6. *The Too-Good Wife: Alcohol, Codependency, and the Politics of Nurturance in Postwar Japan*, by Amy Borovoy

7. *Subjectivity: Ethnographic Investigations*, edited by João Biehl, Byron Good, and Arthur Kleinman

8. *Postcolonial Disorders*, edited by Mary-Jo DelVecchio Good, Sandra Teresa Hyde, Sarah Pinto, and Byron J. Good

9. *Under a Watchful Eye: Self, Power, and Intimacy in Amazonia*, by Harry Walker

10. *Unsettled: Denial and Belonging among White Kenyans*, by Janet McIntosh

11. *Our Most Troubling Madness: Case Studies in Schizophrenia across Cultures*, by T. M. Luhrmann and Jocelyn Marrow

12. *Us, Relatives: Scaling and Plural Life in a Forager World*, by Nurit Bird-David

13. *The Likeness: Semblance and Self in Slovene Society*, by Gretchen Bakke

14. *The Anatomy of Loneliness: Suicide, Social Connection, and the Search for Relational Meaning in Contemporary Japan*, by Chikako Ozawa-de Silva

15. *Being Single in India: Stories of Gender, Exclusion, and Possibility*, by Sarah Lamb

Being Single in India

Stories of Gender, Exclusion, and Possibility

———

Sarah Lamb

UNIVERSITY OF CALIFORNIA PRESS

This publication was made possible in part by a grant from Carnegie Corporation of New York. The statements made and views expressed are the responsibility of the author.

University of California Press
Oakland, California

Suggested citation: Lamb, S. *Being Single in India: Stories of Gender, Exclusion, and Possibility*. Oakland: University of California Press, 2022. DOI: https://doi.org/10.1525/luminos.125

Library of Congress Cataloging-in-Publication Data

Names: Lamb, Sarah, 1960– author.
Title: Being single in India: stories of gender, exclusion, and possibility/ Sarah Lamb.
Other titles: Ethnographic studies in subjectivity ; 15.
Description: Oakland, California: University of California Press, [2022] | Series: Ethnographic studies in subjectivity ; 15 | Includes bibliographical references and index.
Identifiers: LCCN 2021051585 (print) | LCCN 2021051586 (ebook) | ISBN 9780520389427 (paperback) | ISBN 9780520389434 (ebook)
Subjects: LCSH: Single women—India—West Bengal. | Single women—India—West Bengal—Social conditions. | Gender identity—India—West Bengal. | Marriage—India—West Bengal. | Kinship—India—West Bengal.
Classification: LCC HQ800.2 .L344 2022 (print) | LCC HQ800.2 (ebook) | DDC 306.81/53095414—dc23/eng/20211201

LC record available at https://lccn.loc.gov/2021051585
LC ebook record available at https://lccn.loc.gov/2021051586

31 30 29 28 27 26 25 24 23 22
10 9 8 7 6 5 4 3 2 1

I dedicate this book to
Madhabi—
friend and colleague extraordinaire,
one of the most brilliant, strong, and remarkable women I know.

CONTENTS

LIST OF ILLUSTRATIONS

FIGURES

TABLES

NOTE ON TRANSLITERATION

Most conversations reported in this book took place in Bengali, although sprinkled as is common with English terms. Bengali is transliterated into the Latin alphabet in diverse ways depending on the context, from literary publications to WhatsApp messages. I have chosen to use phonetic spellings for Bengali language terms, to enhance readability for readers unfamiliar with Sanskrit-derived transliteration systems. I use single quotes to indicate English words, such as 'patriarchal' or 'unmarried,' inserted into otherwise Bengali dialogue.

Introduction

Thinking Outside Marriage

It is difficult to convey just how prevalent and taken-for-granted are perceptions in India that it is normal and right to marry. Yet, "single" people have always existed—that is, people living outside marriage, whether by choice or circumstance—and single living appears to be on the rise.

Medha Manna was the first girl in her village to complete and pass grade ten, and she possessed a keen drive for more education and seeing the world. She ultimately received a PhD and became a professor of Bengali in a provincial city several hours by train from Kolkata, the bustling cultural and intellectual capital city of the Indian state of West Bengal. Busy pursuing an education and career, Medha became rather "too qualified" for grooms who might share a similar rural background. She also eventually passed the age of 28, then 30, then 35, by which most Indian women marry. Along the way, her natal kin had failed to really work hard to arrange her marriage, enjoying access to her generous professor's salary. In some ways, Medha herself had also resisted marriage, coming to see herself as a feminist and adamant that girls and women in India should not view marriage as every woman's ultimate goal. Life as a single woman had often been difficult, though. Now in her fifties, Medha remarked, "I have to fight with hostility in every step of my life due to my not being an ordinary person."

Aarini Guha received a fellowship to pursue a PhD in computer engineering at a prestigious US university and then worked in Silicon Valley for several years before returning home to Kolkata in her late thirties. She complained that people both in the United States and then even more so in India were continually astonished that she was single and unmarried. "As if there is only one way to live! And that is to have a hubby!" "There's a distinct hierarchy in Indian society and Bengali families," Aarini remarked. "The son is topmost, then married women, and then single women come last."

Ajay Nag fell in love with their partner, Anindita, when they were both school-girls and had never heard of the concept of lesbian. Same-sex marriage is not legally recognized in India, and gay and lesbian partners face many social barriers to living together. Yet, Ajay and Anindita managed to convince their parents not to arrange their marriages to men—a difficult task—each feeling that they could not live without the other. Now in their forties, Ajay and Anindita both reside in their natal homes with their widowed mothers, spending a lot of time at each other's places, while together running a printing business. Ajay now identifies both as a single lesbian woman and as transgender, having assumed a chosen male name and preferring masculine-style clothing. As the Bengali third-person pronoun, *se*, is gender neutral, I never asked Ajay what pronoun they would prefer in English, but I choose *they* in my English prose as most in keeping with Ajay's gender expression. Ajay has an outgoing and magnetic personality and a vibrant sense of humor, the light of any social gathering. They remarked, "Single women, many of whom choose to be alone, contend with problems and hassles every day: disrespect, sexual harassment, and huge discrimination within society. Marriage for women in any 'patriarchal' society is compulsory. If not married, then she is not considered a full person."[1]

My fieldwork with never-married women in West Bengal, India, over the past seven years has revealed both the immense challenges and the exclusions faced by women living outside marriage, as well as the expanding of possibilities for people to imagine and pursue other worlds. Not only in India, but around the world, single living and opting out of marriage are on the rise. In many countries today, unmarried individuals are the fastest-growing demographic group.[2] The trend is particularly dramatic for women: one of the largest social phenomena of our time, one might argue, is the increasing number of women who are avoiding or outright rejecting marriage in places where it has long been mandatory.[3] This book probes the gendered trend of single living, asking: what makes living outside marriage in India so challenging for women and at the same time increasingly possible?

If one takes a quick glance at India's public media, opting out of marriage does seem suddenly possible for women. A 2019 *India Today* cover story, "Brave New Woman," celebrates "a demographic fact that is fast becoming an economic and political force to reckon with—the single woman." This woman is reported to be "single by choice" and to represent "the rise of the unattached, independent woman, who has rejected the socially sanctioned default setting of married life" (Sinha 2019). Other upbeat news stories feature portraits of the new single women as "happy with their status and not wanting the burden of marriage on them,"[4] and of single women celebrities conceiving and adopting children on their own.[5] The Happily Unmarried consumerist marketing company celebrates single lifestyles with a sense of humor, featuring jokes like "Old people at weddings always poke me and say, 'You're next.' So, I started doing the same thing to them at funerals."[6]

Even ordinary individuals are voicing their support for the trend of being single. An Amazon.com reader from India commented as follows on Kalpana Sharma's 2019 anthology *Single by Choice: Happily Unmarried Women!*: "Young girls [reading this book] would learn marriage is something they can choose or opt out of, not a fate they have to be resigned to."[7]

At the same time, it is difficult to convey in a few words just how powerful is the sense in India that marriage is a compulsory norm, particularly for women. Historically, marriage has been the only familiar path for women to achieve kinship and economic security, respect, and a socially legitimate way of being sexual. Primarily only the most privileged, city-educated, and cosmopolitan elites are the ones who can now embrace single lifestyles by choice; and even then, many battle to make their singlehood accepted in their families and wider society.

Globally popular media depict the enormous importance of marriage in India, with hits such as Netflix's 2020 *Indian Matchmaking*, BBC's 2020 television drama miniseries *A Suitable Boy*, and the 2019 romantic-drama web series *Made in Heaven*. Advertisements featuring radiant brides adorned with glittering gold jewelry rise above Kolkata's thoroughfares and fill women's magazines, declaring how "the bride donning magnificent gold jewelry is a vision to celebrate."[8]

Blogs posted by young single Indian women facing the immense pressure to marry populate the internet. Penned under the name Rutu, one post on the blog *beyourself* opens with a cartoon figure screaming, "For the $%&^#Nth time, getting married is not the ultimate goal of my life!!!!"[9] The essay is titled "I'm 29. Single. Woman. Indian" and begins: "Not that any of it matters, unless, of course, you're 29 and single in India. If you are, you know what I'm talking about. Ever since I've turned 20, all my billion brothers and sisters have a new goal in their life: to get me married. . . . I've been born, raised, and spoiled in India, so I know I cannot escape the three ultimate litmus tests for being a *true* Indian: Bollywood, cricket, and marriages."[10] Rutu provides a collection of "eye-roll responses to people accusing me of committing the crime of being single." The list includes the following:

"You won't find a guy like him; he is a prized catch." "I know, but I'm not fishing."
"You have to get married." "Why?" "Because you have to get married."
"Your friend is getting married. Don't you want to?" "If your friend jumps off a bridge, then would you, too?"
"So, are you planning to get married?" "Not right now, mom." "Okay, so would you be finding him yourself, or should we set to work?"

Rutu's blog post also calls to mind Maria Qamar's comic-strip-style parody survival guide for young South Asian women in the diaspora, *Trust No Aunty*. Dressed in a sari with large, dark eyebrows and a concerned glare, the young protagonist's mother asks, "Why aren't you married yet?!!" The girl replies, "I'm only 12, mom, WTF" (Qamar 2017: 11).[11]

By exploring the lives of women who do not or cannot marry, this book makes its first contribution simply by pointing out that single women exist. Before I began my fieldwork on single women, I had come across plenty of anthropological and sociological representations of singlehood in India, all giving the impression that never-married single women barely exist, and that foregoing marriage for a woman in India is unthinkable. Susan Seizer reflects on how—although in India's large economic centers of Mumbai and Delhi she found some lesbian women leading "new-fangled lives" as single women—in the Indian state of Tamil Nadu where she conducted most of her fieldwork, "single, independent women are almost unheard of; the prospect of survival—loose from the net of kinship relations that are the basis of social and economic stability—is daunting, and to pursue such an uncharted course seems both foolish and suspect" (1995: 98). Linda Stone and Caroline James comment in a similar vein on "one clear fact of Indian life: the unacceptability of the unmarried adult woman" (1995: 130). Susan Seymour writes that in the eastern Indian town of Bhubaneswar, "to be unmarried and childless is considered a tragedy for a woman" (1999: 200) and that "without exception, the young women whom I have watched come of age in Bhubaneswar have accepted marriage as both inevitable and desirable" (213). N. S. Krishnakumari also remarks disparagingly on the status of single women in Bangalore: "Socially they are boycotted and victimized, psychologically they are subjected to innumerable mental tensions, sexually they are totally vulnerable, and added to this if they are economically dependent they find themselves doubly abused and exploited" (1987: 166). Exploring the lives of women living in a Delhi slum, Meenakshi Thapan writes that women "attain respectability and status through marriage and childbearing" and that "marriage is essential to their sense of self-worth" (2003: 77). Leela Fernandes notes how, as they look for housing and apply for jobs, "single working women must contend with strong gendered ideologies that construct them as a potential threat to the social order" (2006: 165). Lucinda Ramberg writes of how, to her Karnataka neighbors, "a single unmarried woman constitutes a moral liability" (2014: 29). As Sarah Pinto points out, wider assumptions in the public media and in psychiatry persist that the "unattached woman is a problem to be fixed" (2014b: 247). This collective scholarship reports on prevailing ethical imaginaries of a normal, moral life and valued subjectivity—that women will be firmly located, constrained, and contained within families and marriage. The scholarship also suggests that women themselves prize marriage above all else, viewing marriage as central to their sense of identity, self-worth, and security.

As an exception, Peter Phillimore (1991) examines a rare yet respectable alternative to the married role for women living in the Himalayan Kangra region: the role of the *sadhin* (feminine version of *sadhu*, holy man or ascetic). A *sadhin* renounces marriage and sexuality while remaining in her natal village. The decision to become a *sadhin* should be the girl's own choice, commonly because she did not wish to marry. A *sadhin* tends to wear the everyday clothing of men and may act in some contexts like men (such as by smoking publicly with men). Phillimore reports that she is still socially classified as female, however, and is bound to celibacy.

In the course of doing research on other projects in India since 1989, I had myself encountered quite a few single, never-married women, of a range of class, caste, rural and urban, life stage, and sexuality backgrounds. Some of these women were in their eighties and nineties, so I knew that remaining unmarried could not exclusively be a modern trend.

What motivated much of my ensuing fieldwork was the puzzle of why, in India, it is so incredibly challenging for most women to not marry. Marriage in varied forms, of course, has been highly common in human societies throughout history, serving often as a foundation for crucial social phenomena like reproduction, kinship, property rights, sexuality, intimacy, and sociality.[12] Yet the rising trend of global singlehood suggests that in many national-cultural contexts, to live outside marriage is becoming quite commonplace. The question facing me was, why is it so very challenging to be a never-married single woman in India?

The book argues that an easily overlooked feature of Indian patrilineal kinship systems that makes being single so challenging for women is that women have essentially no secure kinship without marriage—and in India, secure kinship is crucial for life. Such kinship precarity plays out in various ways. First, some women do not marry because they want to support natal kin—but, even if they make that choice, their brothers often feel no obligation to reciprocate the support. Further, few nonfamily housing alternatives can be found, especially for unattached women beyond the most elite. In addition, despite the current popularity of solo living in places like North America and Europe, living singly is not a familiar or desirable way of being for most people in India. Unless one can land a secure, well-paying job, supporting oneself economically while single is also challenging. Similarly, in a society where taken-for-granted visions see old age as a time for naturally needing, deserving, and enjoying care from kin, single women with tenuous kin connections and no children can feel particularly vulnerable. Regarding sexuality, widespread social ideologies press women to contain sexuality within marriage, and therefore to never be sexually active at all if unmarried. Further, to conceive a child sexually out of wedlock is extremely stigmatized; and although single women in India are legally permitted to adopt and to conceive children through IVF, in practice, they face enormous uphill challenges to be approved for parenthood, while still needing later to continually demonstrate that they acquired these children in sexually chaste, that is, in asexual, ways. The experiences of never-married mothers raising children without a father also reveal the critical importance of the father's name in accomplishing bureaucratic legitimacy and legibility before the state in all sorts of contexts, further highlighting the concrete force of normative marriage-based patriliny in Indian society.

Forces of heteronormativity vis-à-vis marriage crucially impact and constrain men's lives and subjectivities as well, of course, as I also probe in this book. However, it is very often women who face the most significant social and economic consequences for being single. The layered reasons for *why* being a single woman in India is so extremely challenging, and how women negotiate these challenges, unfold over the book's chapters.

At the same time, my research asked, *are* there increasing possibilities for women in India to craft lives outside marriage, despite and amidst such challenges? The book's chapters highlight several contemporary trends that help answer this question in the affirmative. First, educational and employment opportunities are expanding for many women, allowing more girls and women to support themselves and find value beyond marriage. Second, novel nonfamily housing arrangements are on the rise, particularly in urban centers, including single-person flats, working women's hostels, and old age homes, helping make it possible to live outside marriage. Further, India is witnessing expanding paradigms for sexual and love relationships beyond conventional marriage, most pronouncedly among the cosmopolitan elite, involving what many perceive to be "modern" ideals of sexual freedom and agency, and increased recognition of feminist and LGBTQ+ rights.

The book argues that, positioned outside the norm on roads less traveled in both daily life and ethnographies of gender, never-married single women are able to recognize and speak penetratingly about their society's broader social-cultural values and structures—offering what could be considered a queer critique of prevailing systems of gender, sexuality, kinship, pleasure, propriety, respect, social class, and social belonging. In so doing, the book offers a theoretical exploration of how gendered subjectivities are forged and rich ethnographic insight into the conditions of everyday life in contemporary India making singlehood for women both challenging and increasingly possible.

MEANINGS OF "SINGLE"

In India, "single" has been emerging as an emic, local category, referring to adult women and men who are not married. The category can be used to signify people with quite distinct marital statuses, including young cosmopolitan adults in their twenties and thirties who are dating and likely still to marry; formerly married widowed and divorced individuals; and those who have never married.

A social movement called Ekal Nari Shakti Sangathan (ENSS), or the Association of Strong Women Alone, has organized low-income "solo" (*ekal*) women in northwest India in a collective struggle for access to land, property, dignity, and legal rights, including in its mission widows, separated and abandoned women, and women over 35 who have never married (Berry 2014). Naisargi Dave examines Indian feminist and lesbian activists who, beginning around the 1990s, chose "single women" as a category both to informally organize around lesbianism and to "address the widespread discrimination that all unmarried women face at the hands of family, society, and the state" (2012: 107). Ajay, Anindita, and several others in my study had formed a "single women's" support group welcoming of all single (as in non-married or not currently married) women of any sexual orientation, while catering especially to lesbians.

In my fieldwork, I chose to focus on women who have never married and who are unlikely to marry—being over age 35, generally the age at which women are no longer regarded as marriable in India. Although public discourse and scholarship on singlehood tends to group together people with highly distinct marital statuses, I discovered through my fieldwork how the *condition of never marrying* puts women into a unique social category, outside standard heteronormative visions of kinship, reproduction, adult personhood, and the life course. It is this condition of being never married that has received the least scholarly attention, in India or anywhere.

In contrast, widows have long been a favorite topic of anthropologists, including within India. One could argue, though, that widows are in many contexts not so "single" after all and retain quite a lot of their married status. Conventionally in West Bengal, widows are expected to remain in their in-laws' home, especially if they have children, and refrain from remarrying. Although Bengali widows face some of the same hassles and stigmas confronting never-married single women, such as being regarded as sexually vulnerable and threatening, conceptualizations and symbolism surrounding Bengali Hindu widows define them in important respects as still married, simply to a deceased rather than living husband (Lamb 1999, 2000: 213–238, 2001). Further, although inauspicious, widows in India are not a highly anomalous social category. Widowed women can be easily socially understood, having followed a normal life-course trajectory of being married. They are also common numerically, "constituting as much as 25 percent of the adult female population in many societies" (Potash 1986: v).

For this project, I wanted to understand the very different experiences of never-married women. Beth Eck similarly wonders, in her study of never-married US men: "Given the declining rates of marriage, . . . it is curious that so little attention has been paid to those who do not marry" (2013: 32). I came to find that the condition of never marrying in West Bengal puts never-married single women into an anomalous social category, different from separated, divorced, and widowed women, as if the act of once having achieved marriage transfers one into (a comparatively) normal adult personhood, even without the man's current presence. I came to see never-married singlehood as a significant social and demographic category, and I wanted to learn more.

Among my interlocutors in West Bengal, people commonly use "single" in English, as well as "unmarried" in English, to refer to women who have never married. The use of the English terms can signal a category's perceived unfamiliarity.[13] To refer to older men who have never married, people commonly use the

English term "bachelor." People also use Bengali phrases to signify being unmarried, including *abibahita* (unmarried) and references to those who "did not marry" (*biye kore ni*) or whose marriage "had not happened" (*biye hoy ni*). Gender identity penetrates the phrasings here, as Bengalis generally use the passive "marriage has not happened" (*biye hoy ni*) to refer to women—articulating that girls' or women's marriages "happen," boys or men "do" marriage, and parents "give" marriage.[14] However, some of my single women interlocutors assertively preferred the active *ami biye kori ni*, "I did not marry"—conveying purposeful agency.

Importantly, local understandings of "single" convey not being married, rather than anything necessarily about a person's (sexual-romantic) relationship status. We will learn how prevailing social mores pressure single women not to have any serious sexual or romantic relationships at all. Nonetheless, some of my single interlocutors did maintain long-term intimate relationships, and some among the young "singles" crowds in India's metros are enjoying quite a lot of expanded sexual freedom in what Ira Trivedi portrays as a sexual revolution sweeping through urban India (2014). Since marriage itself or its absence is so very important to configurations of identity, sociality, kinship, residence, and even often friendships—to be "single" as in *not married* is highly significant within everyday life, whether or not a person happens to be participating in an amorous partnership outside marriage.

Noting the dearth of scholarship on singlehood and how privileging marriage can skew knowledge, Bella DePaulo (2017b) and colleagues have called for a singles studies discipline. Perspectives rooted in marriage dominate the academy, DePaulo argues, suggesting that "people who approach their scholarship from a singles perspective have . . . a different set of questions to pose, and a fresh way of analyzing and understanding the relevant issues" (2017b: 1015).[15] To meaningfully understand experiences of singlehood in single studies scholarship, one must delve into the particular meanings and experiences of being single situated within time and place.

STORIES AND SUBJECTIVITY

As part of the call to explore singlehood in local context, *Being Single in India* features the stories of never-married women from their thirties to nineties, stories which illuminate the intricacies of not only particular subjectivities but also broader social processes. The book also draws on film and fictional stories to illuminate compelling representations of the subjective experiences and broader social processes constituting singlehood in India today.

Anthropologists have used the term "subjectivity" to refer to senses of self and the lived experiences of particular subjects as they forge their lives in relationship with the other beings and social forces of their worlds.[16] The notion of subjectivity includes both the personal and the structural (social, cultural, political, and economic) as mutually arising (e.g., Jackson 2012: 6). Work on subjectivity can highlight affect, emotion, ethical strivings, individual experiences, and visions of possible lives, "as people grapple with questions of what they are, can be, and must be in the course of living" (Parish 2008: ix). Michael Jackson reflects on how "human existence involves a dynamic relationship between how we are constituted and how we constitute ourselves, between what is already there in the world into which we are born and what emerges in the course of our lives within that world" (2012: 8). In these ways, subjectivity involves the interplay between agency and constraint, or between individual experience and the constellation of cultural, ethical, socioeconomic, and political circumstances that shape, confine, and inspire people's lives.

Autobiographical and other stories provide an illuminating window into people's intricate subjectivities as they strive to find fulfillment in life amidst constraint.[17] Stories are valuable in conveying emotion, aspirations, and senses of self—what really matters to persons as they grapple with what they are, must be, and aspire to be as they make their lives. Stories are also valuable in helping both the anthropologist and their readers recognize the variety and complexity in people's life experiences, resisting easy typification. Through telling life stories, speakers also engage in the making sense of, and often the critiquing of, the broader social and cultural systems that impinge upon and shape their lives (see Lamb 2001). Further, by using stories to insistently focus on the particularities of individual lives, we can better understand the nuance and common humanity in all lives. As Lila Abu-Lughod writes: "The particulars suggest that others live as we perceive ourselves living—not as automatons programmed according to 'cultural' rules and acting out social roles, but as people going through life wondering what they should do, making mistakes, being opinionated, vacillating, trying to make themselves look good, enduring tragic personal losses, enjoying others, and finding moments of laughter" (2008: 27).

In these ways, I use the stories shared here to elucidate socially and culturally mediated subjectivities—single Bengali women's experiences of hope and struggle, laughter and fear, pleasure and disappointment, friendship and isolation, respect and stigma, care and abandonment, belonging and exclusion—as they negotiate singlehood within the contemporary Indian social context.

A LENS FROM OUTSIDE

The book also argues that single women, positioned outside the norm, offer a uniquely insightful perspective and sharp new lens on their society's values and institutions. Just as anthropologists argue that we can see the familiar more perceptively when we step outside to make it strange, so those who depart from the conventional path of marriage in India are situated outside of a familiar social identity, and from that position speak penetratingly about their society's socialcultural norms. In this way, single women's stories may be considered queer in the sense deployed by queer theory and offer a compelling portrait of compulsory heterosexuality and patriliny as seen from the margins.[18]

A queer stance stems not from any particular or necessary gender or sexual identity, but rather from a position of externality to heteronormativity.[19] Whether my interlocutors expressed themselves as heterosexual, or as lesbian, or as quite asexual, never-married single women were unique in their positionality as outside their society's prevailing models of marriage-centered heteronormativity. For instance, there were many single women who worked rather than married (chapters 2, 3), and who experienced forms of nonnormative sexuality—such as by having sexual relations with women, or not at all, or with a male lover outside marriage, or by pleasuring oneself (chapter 5). These practices positioned single women as queered subjects in queered situations vis-à-vis conventional systems of gender, sexuality, adulthood, kinship, old age care, reproductive futurity, and sociality.[20] This queered positionality often put single women in situations of social limbo and uncertain belonging. Their identities were often confusing to others, who did not know how to place them. For instance, Medha would say that people with whom she interacted casually in public, such as rickshaw drivers and vegetable vendors, seeing her as an adult, middle-aged woman but without the visible signs of being married (e.g., having *sindur*, vermilion, in the part of the hair), would assume she must be a widow and go so far as to ask sympathetically when "he" had gone.

From their position of externality to a "normal" body, sexuality, kinship, and marriage, many women were able to recognize, make visible, and critique prevailing ideologies that essentially tie feminine value to marriage. Sanjaya Dey, a middle-class woman in her forties, was one who would offer up powerful, piercing social critiques, as I would rush to turn on my recorder or pull out my notebook to capture her insights. Sanjaya was successful in leading an internationally recognized NGO focused on disabled women's rights, had a vibrant circle of both straight and lesbian friends, and was charismatic and eloquent. She had survived polio as a toddler and was left with a slight limp. For this reason, she was deemed unworthy to marry.[21]

"I may be worth a lot in certain respects—work, salary, profession, even decent beauty, if I may say so," Sanjaya articulated. "But in fact I'm worthless, because no one wants to marry me."

It pained me to hear Sanjaya say this; she is a beautiful, magnetic, brilliant person.

"Because ultimately the value of me as a woman," Sanjaya continued, "is in marriage. These are common people's perceptions. My family won't say this exactly to me, in front of me, but this is what they think."

Anthropologist and queer studies scholar Brian Horton articulates how the project of queer critique has centered on denaturalizing normality, with special attention to gender and sexuality (2017). Tom Boellstorff writes of the affinity between the lenses of anthropology and queer studies, commenting that "anthropology has always been a bit queer, and queer studies has always betrayed an anthropological sensibility." With their "shared analytical agendas," both anthropology and queer studies aim to question and destabilize notions of the normal (Boellstorff 2007: 2). Queer studies and anthropology both do what many in anthropology have called "making strange"—"unsettling assumptions and showing that what counts as 'common' sense depends on time and place" (Boellstorff 2007: 19).

With the standpoints of anthropology and queer studies in mind, I gradually came to realize that this project is not only about single women—although single women are its main interlocutors. Rather, the narratives of single women were allowing me to recognize and make visible systems of gender and sexuality, kinship and marriage, personhood and the life course, and social class more broadly—systems that often felt so "normal" and taken-for-granted to other Bengalis that they had trouble seeing what was going on. I came to realize, for instance, that in some ways maybe single women were not the real or primary problem of my research, but rather marriage was—or the ways gender inequality is so intertwined with the institution of marriage in Bengali Indian society. In this way, my project also contributes to the emerging field of critical heterosexuality studies, aimed at examining the taken-for-granted assumptions that surround dominant heterosexual institutions such as marriage, shaping gender and sexual identities.[22]

Here, Lila Abu-Lughod's (1990) argument in "The Romance of Resistance" is useful to consider: examining resistance to, for example, conventions of "normal" femininity and marriage can illuminate or serve as a diagnostic of the hidden contours of power. Single women's stories help us recognize the structures surrounding gender, sexuality, kinship, marriage, and social class that operate so powerfully in everyday life.

Queer studies, like feminism, is also useful in my thinking for emphasizing visions of possibilities for change. Central to queer critique is not only the problematizing of existing norms, but also the imagining and aspiring toward new possibilities (e.g., Dave 2012: 8; Muñoz 2009). José Esteban Muñoz writes that we can feel queerness as "the warm illumination of a horizon imbued with potentiality. . . . We must dream and enact new and better pleasures, other ways of being in the world, and ultimately new worlds. . . . Queerness is essentially about the rejection of a here and now and an insistence on potentiality or concrete possibility for another world" (2009: 1). Anthropologists, too, have emphasized the importance of moving beyond the "suffering subject" of the "dark anthropology" so prominent since the 1980s, to explore the ways people not only contend with inequality and oppression but also strive for well-being through practices such as pleasure and care, hope and change (e.g., Ortner 2016; Robbins 2013).

To envision and work toward a better world was very important to many women in my study, who appealed to me to write not only about their challenges but also about the ways they were achieving new forms of value and pleasure in their lives and envisioning more equitable futures.

SINGLEHOOD, INDIVIDUAL FREEDOM,
AND THE PROBLEM OF CHOICE

As single women in India seek to actualize new imaginaries of gender, sexuality, and personhood beyond marriage, their stories complicate understandings of the autonomous, free individual at the heart of much public and scholarly discourse on the rise of singlehood in modern societies. By thinking through single women's stories, I underscore how a celebratory model of autonomous singlehood—unfettered free subjects able to choose their life paths—is neither ethnographically nor theoretically convincing. An ethnographically situated and person-centered approach is called for.

According to prevailing public and scholarly imaginaries of singlehood, it is the ideal of freedom of choice that is driving the steep decline in marriage rates around the world. For example, Elyakim Kislev announces that his book *Happy Singlehood* "charts a way forward for singles to live life on their own terms" (2019a: back blurb). He advocates that societies develop a "clear and more benign image of singlehood" to "allow individuals to freely choose whatever lifestyle fits them best," in accordance with their "true feelings," as opposed to "attitudes enforced by social norms" (2019a: 5).

In *The Unexpected Joy of Being Single*, Catherine Gray declares: "Singledom is a choice" (2018: 9). Eric Klinenberg, in his best-selling *Going Solo: The Extraordinary Rise and Surprising Appeal of Living Alone*, writes: "Living alone helps us pursue sacred modern values—individual freedom, personal control, and self-realization" (2012: 17–18).

India Today's featured story "Brave New Woman" also celebrates India's new single woman as "single by choice," "celebrating her freedom." The story announces: "The urban Indian single woman is answerable to no one but herself. . . . Her life choices are her own. . . . More than economic independence, it is the freedom to be who you are that is the attraction of singlehood" (Sinha 2019).

I can certainly see why such models of freely chosen, happy singlehood are appealing to so many authors and readers. The idea of being "free from social norms," able to define one's own identity and chart out one's own life path, resonates with the "modern sacred values" of "individual freedom, personal control, and self-realization" that Kislev and Klinenberg articulate as so dear to so many people. As a North American, I know how much I and my students love to imagine that we are free to choose whatever and whoever we wish to be.

At the same time, as an anthropologist, I study how people everywhere have a hard time recognizing the ways their personal aspirations are shaped by powerful social and cultural forces. In the United States, for instance, although there is not the same pressure as in India to be legally married, most people experience a strong socially-culturally mediated sense that they "should" be coupled up, in a "relationship," with a sexual-romantic partner. Moreover, modern American society places tremendous emphasis on romantic partners, expecting the partner to be all things at once, from best friend, to erotically satisfying lover, to economic helpmate, to intellectual colleague, to soulmate with the capacity to continuously promote their partner's personal growth.[23] Relatedly, many forms of "singlism"—implicit bias against single people—persist in the United States, lurking in the workplace, in the media, in religion, in laws and policies, and in everyday lives (DePaulo 2007).[24]

So, I wish to argue that the common rhetoric of individual freedom and choice to explain singlehood is both empirically misleading and theoretically naïve. First, it tempts us to exaggerate people's freedom to shape their worlds according to their own desires.[25] How can one speak of single individuals simply "freely choosing whatever lifestyle suits them best," free from "attitudes enforced by social norms" (Kislev 2019a: 5), without paying close attention to the local social-cultural and political-economic contexts that powerfully shape people's options and aspirations?

Second, the discourse of freedom of choice tends to presume that aspirations for individual freedom and autonomy are universal desires. However, we will come to see how Indian single women's stories challenge Western-centered liberal assumptions about the normalcy, value, and universal desirability of the individual, independent subject.

On the first point, anthropologists have long scrutinized the ways agency and constraint work inevitably and intricately together in human social-cultural life. Models of contemporary singlehood that posit a notion of agency as "free will" exercised by autonomous individuals making free choices elide the pervasive influence of culture on human intentions, beliefs, and actions. If we think of agency as "the socioculturally mediated capacity to act" (Ahearn 2001: 112, 118), a core insight of anthropological practice theory is that individuals create their societies and lifeworlds just as society creates them.[26] Anthropological understandings of human social-cultural life and practice emphasize the social influences on agency: "human actions are central, but they are never considered in isolation from the social structures that shape them" (Ahearn 2001: 117). As Lata Mani articulates in her critique of the ideal of personal freedom underlying much contemporary neoliberal discourse: "We live in an interdependent world with finite resources, in obdurate sociocultural contexts that we are compelled to negotiate at every turn, and within a matrix of possibilities shaped by these constraints as well as our own personal inclinations, strengths, and weaknesses" (2014: 27).

Further, even as many strive to craft meaningful lives outside marriage, the single Bengali women I have come to know rarely articulate their aspirations in terms of a drive for individual independence. For one, most do not find it comfortable, familiar, or desirable to live completely alone or independently.

Chapter 1 explores how solo living is extremely rare across genders and communities in India, and how living independently is widely regarded as a quite peculiar lifestyle and form of personhood. As Sarah Pinto articulates, freedom and even self-determination may not always be clear indexes of the "good." Integration in family and community life does not come without constraint, and yet "what might be called 'independence' can be a lonely, sad existence" (2014a: 253).

I suggest over the following pages that what those crafting a single female life in India desire more than independence or the "rise of a singleton society" (Klinenberg 2012: 16) is belonging—to find new ways, beyond marriage, to count, to be worthy of recognition, and to be intimately connected with others as part of a social body.[27] As such, singlehood in India contrasts the thrust of the US "epoch of single women" and "invention of independent female adulthood" which Rebecca Traister depicts in *All the Single Ladies: Unmarried Women and the Rise of an Independent Nation* (2016: 7).

In my fieldwork with single Indian women, some did speak with a language of choice and individual decision making, and this is a paradigm we see featured in Kalpana Sharma's 2019 anthology of narratives by mostly elite single women from India's metros: *Single by Choice: Happily Unmarried Women!* I found, however, that it was primarily only women from highly elite cosmopolitan backgrounds who were able to embrace singlehood as a distinctive lifestyle emerging from a claim to freedom of choice; and even for these women, complex social-cultural and political-economic forces were at work behind their decisions. The common emic conceptualization that marriage "happens" to women, rather than that marrying is something a woman "does" (see note 14), also belies a theoretical model emphasizing free choice and agency. Further, a strong majority, 70 percent, of women in my study did not see themselves as having actively chosen not to marry (chapter 1). Rather, evading marriage was very often a consequence of other pressing life decisions.

Especially for those who walk on paths less traveled, making "choices" is often challenging, complicated, and painful. I aim to illuminate through the book's diverse and intimate stories how single living is not best understood as the product of simple free "choice" nor as only "happy." Scholarship intentionally focusing only on "happy" singlehood, as in Elyakim Kislev's 2019 *Happy Singlehood*, lacks the nuance and complexity that an intimate, person-centered ethnographic examination can offer.

In these ways, *Being Single in India* urges readers to rethink the notion of the autonomous, free individual foregrounded in recent singles studies scholarship, while challenging liberal assumptions that posit ideals of autonomy and freedom as universal desires.[28] The book argues that understanding singlehood can only be grasped through the thickness of cultural specificity and attention to the intertwined phenomena of freedom and constraint constituting agency in human social-cultural life. In so doing, the book opens up new approaches for understanding gender, sexuality, subjectivity, and singlehood in the world today.

ON FIELDWORK AND FRIENDSHIPS

Several years into my fieldwork, I went to stay for a weekend with Indrani and her family. Indrani (featured in chapter 6 on never-married single moms) had adopted six years earlier a wonderful baby daughter with her parents' help. The four lived together very happily in their spacious family home in the desirable Deshopriya Park neighborhood of south Kolkata. Indrani's mother smiled when I described my research topic, "What fun! You can just hang out with your friends!" She was teasing me, and we laughed. But in a way she was right. I had never before pursued a research topic where fieldwork and friendships so overlapped. That weekend, as Indrani shared experiences of being an unmarried woman and single mom, we also enjoyed chatting about other matters in both our lives, hunting for lovely folk art in a large outdoor market, strolling around a shaded park while her daughter and little friends played, enjoying tea and *dosas* in an outdoor café, and sipping whiskey in the evening while sharing more stories and confidences. It was indeed fun!

I defended myself to Indrani's mother, though, insisting that I was not merely hanging out with my former friends! Most of the women in my study—Indrani being one of two exceptions—I had met only through the research itself. Nonetheless, several of the women interlocutors in the project did become close friends.[29] I will explain more how and why in a moment. First, let me back up a little to introduce my basic research methodology.

In 2014, I began to focus my fieldwork in West Bengal, India, on the lives of never-married single women, making over the next seven years (through January 2020) eight short fieldwork trips to Kolkata and nearby towns and villages for the project, while enjoying into 2021 ongoing virtual conversations with several of my closest interlocutors. I also draw on the narratives of single women gathered over years of ethnographic fieldwork conducted in the region since 1989.[30] I combined the eliciting of life stories and formal, open-ended interviews with ethnographic research involving "hanging out" with women in daily-life contexts, what anthropologists call participant observation. Such participant observation-research included spending time with women in their homes and while talking over tea, dining out, going shopping, gathering with friends, attending single women's support group meetings, taking weekend getaways, talking by phone, exchanging WhatsApp messages and video calls, and with some of the more English-speaking elite, engaging in dialogue over email.

The book is based on the stories and experiences of fifty-four core interlocutors, never-married single women ranging in age from 35 to 92. These interlocutors include highly educated urban professionals and rural day laborers, women who evaded marriage both by choice and by circumstance, those who identify as heterosexual and as lesbian, and women living in a range of housing—with natal kin, entirely alone, in government hostels for working women, and in old age homes. My analyses are also bolstered by insights gained from everyday conversations with countless others, both married and single, in the wider community.

I chose to focus on women in their mid-thirties and older, beyond the age generally considered "marriable" in Indian social contexts. In fact, even beyond 22 or 28, depending on the social class, it becomes difficult to be considered a suitable bride (chapter 1).

I located the fifty-four core participants mainly through snowball sampling, where existing participants recruited future subjects from among their acquaintances. I would also visit villages where I had long had connections to ask about any never-married women in these communities. Most single women I encountered were very interested in the project, feeling underrepresented and misunderstood in their wider societies and eager to share their stories as part of their endeavors to "find a way to count in the social body" (Dickey 2013: 219).

During interviews and participant-observation research, I was often accompanied by one of three research assistants: Hena Basu, MA; Anindita Chatterjee, PhD; and Madhabi Maity, PhD. I chose other Bengali women as assistants who were either single themselves or, in Anindita's case, living at the time quite independently from her husband, who was working abroad. The presence of these other women researchers helped facilitate lively and intimate conversations, and ensured that I did not miss the nuances of Bengali discussions.

Recent anthologies and media stories celebrating the rise of single women in India have focused almost exclusively on the elite cosmopolitan classes.[31] Because of how important class distinctions are in India and my wish to probe the intersections of class and gender, I sought out never-married women across rural-urban and social-class contexts. The core group of interlocutors included 35 women living in the large metropolis of Kolkata, 10 from smaller towns, and 9 from rural villages. In terms of social class, the group included 9 elite, 21 middle-class, 14 working-class, and 10 poor participants. Nine participants were from Scheduled Caste and Scheduled Tribe communities, designated by the Government of West Bengal as groups facing social and economic discrimination in the past and/or present. In terms of religious identity, I focused on Hindu women—the majority group in India as in the state of West Bengal (Muslims being the largest minority)—while one participant had converted to Christianity.[32]

Class designations were based on my and my research assistants' assessments and often the participants' expressed identities. I use "elite" to refer to those who tend to prefer English to Bengali, have affluent and professional backgrounds, and have spent time both abroad and in India. Although people in India often use the broad category "middle class" to include this elite globally oriented cosmopolitan group, I prefer to reserve "middle class" to signify those falling between the elite and working classes, what some of my interlocutors would refer to as the "real," or *ashol*, middle class. Among my interlocutors in West Bengal, this "real" middle class refers broadly to those who are basically economically comfortable, with enough to eat, a large proportion of whom are salaried employees, who are able to afford core consumer household goods such as refrigerators and televisions, who speak some English but often prefer Bengali, and who see themselves as well above the rural and urban poor surviving day to day in laboring jobs. To refer to the "working class," Bengalis often use the English term "labor," a category referring to those who work hard to make a living but are not suffering from severe food and housing insecurity, unlike the rural and urban poor (*gorib lok*) struggling to get by as daily workers and landless laborers.[33]

As will become apparent as the chapters unfold, class identities tend to be tied at least as much to one's family background as to one's own individual socioeconomic circumstances, such as one's own job, income, and/or education (see Dickey 2016: 36–37). This becomes highly relevant in the stories of someone like Medha, who as an individual achieved a class position as a university professor far beyond that of her impoverished rural family background, giving her a mismatched class status in her one person, making it almost impossible to marry (chapter 2).

Readers familiar with India will easily recognize signs of class distinction in my ethnographic descriptions, knowing how to visualize the ways rural village settings are so distinct from urban ones in India, and how urban class statuses are materialized through divergent forms of housing and consumption, such as how dining on the meticulously wiped floor of a one-room urban apartment signals a working-class status as distinct from the elite status enacted through sipping green tea or whiskey in comfortable chairs on the open-air verandah of a three-story private home. To help readers less familiar with India's social class divides, I aim to indicate people's class positions as I introduce them.

Caste is one important category I did not engage with substantively. Caste is less visible to me as an outsider than are the enormously conspicuous distinctions of social class in India. Further, my interlocutors rarely brought up caste directly, while frequently highlighting how the vast divides of social class impact experiences of singlehood in profound ways. Nonetheless, caste remains a formidable social distinction in India, intersecting with both social class and gender in crucial ways, akin in some respects to how race operates in the United States.[34] Throughout, I use pseudonyms for both first and last names, and when the last name reflects a person's caste identity (as is common), I have chosen a pseudonymous surname signaling the same or similarly positioned caste group.

My most elite interlocutors often spoke with me in English, the language they also tend to use with their friends and peers. Most other conversations took place in Bengali, the primary language spoken in West Bengal and the neighboring nation of Bangladesh, although peppered as is common with English terms. I use single quotes to indicate English terms used in an otherwise Bengali conversation.

I audio-recorded and then had transcribed many of the life-story interviews and other conversations, while I also in addition, and sometimes instead, took copious handwritten and laptop notes. The book's quoted conversations and narratives come both from audio recordings and reconstructions from elaborate fieldnotes, where I aimed to capture speakers' verbatim statements as closely as possible, while then typing up the conversations from notes shortly after the events. I pored over these notes and transcriptions, searching for common as well as divergent themes. My research assistant Hena also searched out for me relevant news stories, literature, films, and other classic and contemporary media on singlehood in India.

The women whose stories I share encompass a range of life experiences and perspectives, and no one is "typical." Some saw themselves as having deliberately opted out of marrying, while for others, the life path to non-marrying was much more nuanced and complicated. Some would have been very happy to have had, or still to find, a male marriage partner if various insurmountable obstacles had not been in the way; others had no interest in marriage and all its trappings of domesticity, pursuing careers instead; while others had taken on a lesbian identity, slightly more possible for women, especially in India's metros, over the past few decades.

The women navigated a range of living situations: in solo residences, with natal kin, in working women's hostels, in old age homes, and (in just one case) with friends, an option rare for Bengalis of all social classes (chapter 1). A few had given birth to or adopted a child and were raising their children as single mothers (chapter 6). Many spoke at length of the hassles, dangers, and slander they faced due to being regarded as sexually available and potentially dangerous to the social-sexual moral order (chapter 5). Mindful of prevailing stereotypes and societal judgments, many single women foregrounded tales of carefully maintaining sexual propriety throughout their lives. Others had found ways to express sexual agency and enjoy lovers against the prevailing social grain (chapter 5). Some assented, without overt challenge, to a constrained and marginalized place in society as women outside marriage; others offered penetrating critiques.

The identity and positionality of the researcher always plays a role in the research. I sometimes found myself feeling reluctant to divulge that I am married, as if my marital status—as well as my heterosexual and cis-gender status when I was hanging out with queer-identified individuals—would erect another boundary of difference between us, in addition to the obvious differences of nationality and often social class. People seemed not to be surprised that I was married, though. Moreover, the day-to-day freedoms and autonomy I experience while conducting fieldwork in India give my sensibility and routines there some affinity with those of single women. At least it seemed that way to me. I usually travel for fieldwork without my husband or daughters. This means that I do not need to be home at a certain time, cook for a spouse or children, or check in with family before deciding whether to go out in the evening or on a weekend trip. I am also accustomed to being rather alone and often a bit lonely while doing fieldwork. Doing research on singlehood meant that I was meeting many other women in similar positions of autonomy and aloneness. This mutual singleness laid the groundwork for developing friendships. At the same time, I and my interlocutors were aware that my singleness in India was temporary, and close interlocutors like Medha and Aarini would notice and comment on the kinds of prestige my married-with-children status provided me, as people we met together in cafés, trains, and fieldwork interactions would ask for and then "ooh and aah" over photos of my family.

Not everyone became a close friend, of course. Some women I only met and interviewed once. It was Medha who became my closest friend and collaborator in the project.[35]

First appearing in this chapter's opening lines, Medha is a professor of Bengali in a small provincial city, exactly my age in her early fifties when we first met, living alone, and never married. When we met by chance in an outdoor Kolkata market purchasing tie-dyed housecoats, she eagerly volunteered, "You should study *me!*" We quickly became friends, communicating not only during my visits to India but also by email and WhatsApp messaging and video calls while I was abroad. We both happen to be fanatic about organic and healthy foods; our birthdates are just three days apart; we share similar feminist sensibilities; and we both love meeting people from all walks of life, exploring the world, growing plants, teaching our students, and enjoying tea and conversation in cafés. Most importantly, Medha's brilliance and critical insight gave me a depth of understanding about Bengali society and single women's lives I could never have achieved without her. Medha was eager to accompany me on many fieldwork excursions, not only to help me and to enjoy being out and about, but also to see if she could make some like-minded single women friends. She had a wonderful way of asking intimate personal questions that I as a foreigner and married person likely would not have been able to pose—motivated in part because she herself really wanted to know—like, "Was it really hard for you to control your sexual urges when you could never have sex your whole life?" Or, "Did you never have a boyfriend or someone you liked?" Medha's insights and stories are woven through each of the book's chapters.

I was also struck by how avidly other single women interlocutors sought me out as a friend, companion, and confidante. The eagerness of some women to spend time with me helped me see how excluded many were from ordinary opportunities for intimate social interaction. When I would ask single women if they had friends, the majority would reply that they had none or very few (chapter 7). Single women would commonly respond something like, "I did have friends in school, but they are all married now." Once women are married, they often no longer have the freedom to go out socializing with their former girlfriends. Married women might make new friends among neighbors, other mothers at their children's schools, and the wives of their husbands' friends. But it is often difficult for single women to mix in such marriage-centered circles. Some mentioned as a further deterrent that married women refrain from inviting single women to social events where husbands will be present, worrying that their husbands will be attracted to the single women, viewed as sexually alluring and available because uncontained by marriage (chapter 5).

Further, it is not common in Kolkata and its surrounding towns and villages for a solo woman to indulge in outside pleasures on her own, such as stopping at a tea stall enjoying street food snacks, dining at a restaurant, or traveling (chapter 7). I myself had often eyed with some envy groups of college girlfriends, married women with their children or husbands, or men (either solo or in groups) who could easily enjoy such public indulgences. The one year when I brought my two daughters with me for fieldwork (in 2005–2006 for a project on old age homes) ended up being so fun for me, as I could buy the girls treats in public, while then also partaking myself.[36] So, I could well understand how some women whom I first solicited as research participants would then wish to continue to hang out with me as a companion with whom to do fun things, such as having picnics; going to movies, cafés, restaurants, and art shows; and going on a Himalayan trek.

Further, many women welcomed the opportunity to talk with me about their lives, aspirations, and struggles. When I thanked her at the end of her life-story interview, Rachana Sen, a single professor of history, also thanked me, remarking that the interview had given her a chance to reflect, too. Kumkum Roy, a journalist who had given birth to a daughter through IVF (chapter 6), said that she could disclose things to me that she would not tell others in her society, because she felt I would be more accepting as a foreigner. Madhuri Saha, who worked as a domestic servant, asked with a tone of curious pride when I had turned the third page of my notebook, "Does every life take a few pages?" Others who had gathered around to listen to us (privacy was rather unavailable in urban-poor settings) remarked that she was happy that I was interested, because usually no one would think her story important.

One morning in 2015, the day after I had landed in India for a return fieldwork trip, I arrived at Medha's Kolkata apartment, eager to see her. Upon entering, I remarked regretfully that I had accidentally left behind at my guesthouse the small gifts I had brought for her from the United States. Medha laughed and exclaimed exuberantly, "I need no gifts. I am so happy inside—I have so much to say! You know that my problem is that I have no friends with whom I can really share and mix. I'm going to say it all to you, and *that* will be my gift from you!"

In the following pages, I do my best to convey the stories, aspirations, and predicaments of the single women I came to know. The stories shared here beckon us to consider diverse ways of conceptualizing what it is to live well, as single women do the hard work of striving to reimagine what is good and normal, aspiring to forge new forms of recognition and belonging within the social body in ways not tied to marriage.

On Being Single

Nayani placed an array of tempting dishes on the freshly wiped floor of the small room she used for dining, living, and sleeping. I had arrived with two other women to share lunch in Nayani's rented two-room apartment on the outskirts of Kolkata. "No one be shy while eating!" Nayani exclaimed. "Eat anything you want, and take anything you want." Three single women friends and I had gathered to socialize and share stories for my research project, sitting on brightly colored hand-sewn floor cushions. I was the odd one out here, not only as an American but also as married. Yet, the others generously welcomed interest in single Bengali women's lives.

"Why did you cook all this?" Nita scolded Nayani. "I told you on the phone not to cook a lot! Bad girl, you made so much food. You know I don't eat a lot!"

"I'm starting to eat!" Medha dug in enthusiastically. "An amazing feast—friends, food, and fun. This is our Valentine's Day!"

Everyone laughed. The date was, in fact, February 14.

"Other people celebrate Valentine's Day with diamond jewelry," Nita remarked. She was dressed in a blue, white, and magenta printed silk sari with her long black hair pulled back.

"Our friendship is worth more than diamonds!" Nayani jumped in. This group had never before or since (now seven years later as I write) gathered together liked this, constrained by the demands of their work lives and a cultural milieu of limited opportunities for adult women's friendships beyond the family (chapter 7). Still, we were happy and enjoying each other's company that afternoon.

"Others often don't have real love anyway," Nita declared. "They buy diamonds just to show off."

Nayani urged us again to eat, gesturing to the bountiful rice, fish curry, fried potatoes, vegetable dishes, and sliced cucumbers with purple onion, lime, and cilantro before us. "Everyone fill your stomachs—eat as much as you can!"

Nayani and her friend Nita had met several years back while working part time at Sachetana, a feminist charitable NGO. Nayani had first joined the NGO as a client receiving skills training for domestic workers looking to advance, and she was later hired as part-time staff. Medha had located Nayani and Nita through the same NGO while trying to expand her network of single women, wishing to help me with my research and aspiring to make like-minded friends. We all chatted as we enjoyed our meal, and the women invited me to leave my audio recorder switched on.

Nayani's lavish cooking brought to mind other delicious meals I had enjoyed in elite Kolkata households, as Nayani had been trained to cook for a wealthy family with whom she had lived as a domestic servant since the age of seven. After she left that position in her late twenties, the Sachetana organization helped Nayani secure a job as a clerk in a Kolkata office. Nayani had never gone to school, but had learned to read and write while looking over the shoulders of her employer's daughter, enabling Nayani to move beyond domestic service. She was now almost 35. Dressed in a contemporary style with maroon pants and a woolen winter kurta, Nayani told us how she loves to cook but cannot find time to do much cooking in a typical day, leaving at 7 a.m. for work and returning around 8 or 9 in the evening, enduring a one- to two-hour commute by bus and train. She also does not enjoy eating alone.

Medha spoke up, "I'm giving you a proposal. I have an apartment in Kolkata, but I don't usually live there." Medha had arranged the apartment for visits to Kolkata, enjoying the cosmopolitan lifestyle in West Bengal's capital compared to the provincial city where she lives and teaches in a regional college. "I'd be very happy if someone stays there. You wouldn't have to think much about money. . . . I want to mix with others. I suffer a lot being so alone. Give my proposal a thought."

"So you would not feel so alone," Nita added to them both. Nita herself had never moved out of her natal home, residing with her elderly mother, married brother, sister-in-law, and nephew.

"Thank you," Nayani said to Medha, although noncommittally. I gradually came to learn how difficult it is to form not only marriages but also domestic partnerships and even friendships across class lines. Nayani and Medha had both been born in villages to impoverished families, but Medha had, against all odds, achieved a PhD and university professorship, while Nayani had spent most of her life as a domestic servant.

Medha and Nayani both spoke of how it would feel better if someone lived with them. "After a day of work," Medha reflected, "I just wish there were someone I could share everything with. That is why I get depressed sometimes. . . . I want to come home to someone who would ask, 'What did you do today? How was work?' I have no one at all. I go to South City Mall to watch movies sometimes—just alone! Just to feel like I am with some other people."

Nayani commented sympathetically, "Even if living with a family, one can feel very lonely, though. Can one express all things? If you find someone like that, you are very lucky, right?"

Nita turned to tell me about Nayani's situation.

"There's a problem Nayani faces," Nita related. "The people in her village get married to others from the same or nearby villages, but since she has lived in the city, Kolkata, most of her life, her ways of thinking are quite modern (*adhunik*). She can't get along with the ways of life of the villagers. She can't marry and live with a guy from a village." Nayani's parents, unable to feed all their four children, had been the ones to bring Nayani to the city as a young girl to work as a domestic servant. We will see in chapter 2 how class mobility isolates the single woman both from the social class she left and the one she has now reached, generating a near insurmountable impediment to marriage.

"Who lives in Nayani's village home now?" I asked.

"Only her mother lives there," Nita replied. "Her father died, and her brother works and lives in Kolkata. Her sisters live in the village, because they married there and live with their in-laws and children. Nayani takes care of the finances for the family. They come to her for money when they are in need."

"That was another reason for my not marrying," Nayani explained. "I had to take care of people in the family. My sisters were not married, and I needed to get them married." She had used her domestic-servant salary to pay for their wedding expenses and dowries. "I needed also to take care of the elderly people [in my employer's family]. If I got married, I wouldn't be able to take care of them all." This—a daughter's and sister's care—is a central theme of chapter 3, how first-employed sisters in struggling families forego marriage as a way to support their own natal kin.

Medha commented to me, "This is her mind-set—she wanted to take care of her sisters and fulfill her family duties."

"It's not like they didn't want me to get married," Nayani asserted. "They wanted to get me married. . . . But anyway, now I am free—all my siblings are married."

Medha turned to Nita, "Why don't you find someone for her?"

Nita replied, "She wants to marry. If you can find someone good," Nita urged Medha, "then please do look for her."

We all spoke more about the delicious food, and then Medha volunteered, "I have another proposal. Let's go on a vacation trip together!"

Everyone spoke at once about how much they love traveling, and yet how hard it is to travel as a single woman—it is not safe, and it always costs more. "Shall we go somewhere together then?" Medha suggested eagerly.

Nita apologized, "These days I can't really go out or travel anywhere, because I have to take care of my mother." Nita had recently given up her job as a school-teacher to care for her ailing mother. She complained that her sister-in-law, her brother's wife, does not stay at home or take care of her mother at all, even though she is a 'housewife' and does not work outside the home.[1] Conventionally in Bengali families, it would be daughters-in-law who provide the bulk of care for their older parents-in-law.

Talk soon turned to the stigmas single women face in society, especially surrounding insinuations of impropriety. "Even if we are not doing anything bad, we have to hear things from people," Nayani protested. "People in the village will say, 'We know what your daughter is doing in the city.' And here in this neighborhood, when I come home late at night because of work, people won't say anything to my face, but they talk behind my back." Contending with social ideologies surrounding the dangers of unattached female sexuality is an immense problem in single women's lives, explored in chapter 5.

Medha added, "In 'Indian society,' men think they can control women. 'Indian society' doesn't think women can have their independence. When women stay out late at night, people think they have boyfriends or are doing something bad. And the women who stay inside with their families are jealous of those who are more liberal and working outside."

"I can understand [the jealousy of the housewives]," Nayani remarked, "because they are not out meeting or interacting with other people."

"No, this is not about not interacting with people," Nita jumped in. "My sister-in-law does not stay inside. Ever since my nephew was three years old, she would take him to school and wait for him there, talking with all the other mothers, and then after school she would go to her own mother's house. Around evening or night, she would return to our house, to avoid all responsibility. . . . She is always going out, with her son, and then hanging out with her friends. But no one says anything, because she has the mark of *sindur*," referring to the key sign of marriage for many Hindu women, include Hindu Bengalis—red vermilion in the part of the hair.

Nita's remarks displayed how a sexual double standard applies differently not only to the practices of men and women, but also to married women and single women. (Unmarried men, it went without saying for Nita and her friends, face no problems regarding sexual respectability if they socialize beyond the home or venture to cities for work.)

I asked Medha and Nita, who were both in their fifties, "Is it any easier now that you are older? Do people say less than when you were young?"

"When you are younger, people will say things to you," Medha replied, "but even when you're older, people will say things."

Nita agreed. "If someone is old and unmarried and going out, then people will still ask about where she is going."

"I'm 54," Medha remarked, "and people still wonder where I'm going."

"Now I'm at home," Nita said, alluding to the fact that she had recently given up her job, "but now I'm facing something new—the women who are working outside wonder if unmarried women who stay *at home* have sexual relations or affairs with people from *within the house!*"

"Right! Either way!" Nayani added. "Whether you work outside or stay at home, people will talk. Some people will say that unmarried women who stay at home are 'sick.'" Nayani uses the English term to imply someone engaging in improper or perverted behavior.

Medha went on to talk about how much rape is happening in India.[2] "It's terrible. And if an [unmarried] village girl gets pregnant, she can't even enter the village again! They won't let her enter!"

Nita explained to me, "That's why mothers marry their girls off at such a young age. They think, 'If I get my daughter married, and if she gets raped, OK, then it's not *my* responsibility (*dayitva*).'" She gave a contemptuous laugh.

The three discussed what they do to stay safe and maintain their reputations. Nita always wears a sari, the most conventional Bengali woman's dress, vigilantly performing respectability in the sartorial realm to make up for perceived inadequacies in marital status. "If I wear a sari, people may look a little. But if I were to wear tight pants and shirt, that much more would they look!"

Medha commented, "This is the condition we're living in. There's nothing we can do."

The remainder of this chapter offers background and context on singlehood in India to frame the chapters to come. *Why* does Indian society create such powerful obstacles to remaining an unattached, unmarried adult woman? And yet, how nonetheless are women increasingly opting out of marriage? Is being single best understood as a "choice," or as the unintended consequence of other pressing life situations, or as a more complex admixture of both agency and constraint? I first paint in broad strokes my interlocutors' overlapping reasons for not marrying, and I begin to explore the powerful gendered marriage imperative. I close with an exploration of living solo as an unusual form of personhood: a key reason even those who resist marriage often find singlehood challenging is that living singly apart from kin is not a familiar, unremarked part of habitus for most in India.[3]

THE QUESTION OF WHY

The question of *why* a person did not marry perpetually surrounds the single individual in India, whether male or female. My single women interlocutors were constantly asked, "Why didn't you marry?" Or "Why didn't your marriage happen?"—the latter phrasing the more commonly posed to women. As noted in the introduction, Bengalis generally use the passive "marriage has not happened" (*biye hoy ni*) to refer to women, articulating that girls' or women's marriages "happen," boys or men "do" marriage, and parents "give" marriage.[4]

Usually, I hesitated to ask directly or immediately, "Why didn't you marry?" knowing that single women have had to respond to this persistent and irritating

TABLE 1. Reasons for Not Marrying

Reason for Not Marrying	Participants (out of 54)
Purposefully chose not to	16 (~30%)
Conveying a feminist sensibility: perceiving marriage at odds with gender equality	15
Parents/kin failed to arrange marriage	13
Engrossed in education and/or work	13
Natal kin needed income and care labor	10
Stigmatized embodiment (regarded as disabled, ill, infertile, too dark skinned, and/or unattractive)	9
Too educated and/or high-achieving to find a suitable match	6
Could not (yet) find the right man	5
Uncomfortable with arranged marriage process but no real access to finding own partner	5
Preference for natal kin	4
Identifies as lesbian	4
Expresses some gender dysphoria	4
Disgusted by or uncomfortable with sex and/or men	2
"No one liked me"	1
Tarnished public sexual reputation	1
Pursuing a spiritual life instead	1

NOTE: Most participants conveyed two or more reasons, so the figures add up to more than 54.

question over and over again throughout their adult lives. I would wait until I had gotten to know an interlocutor better, or if only meeting for a single interview, I would start by asking her to tell me her life story. In the life-story context, the question of why could unfold slowly in its multilayered complexity.

Medha—my "key informant" and closest collaborator and friend in this project—gradually conveyed multiple layers of her reasons for not marrying, with which I open the next chapter.[5] But when strangers posed the question "Why didn't you marry?" as we went around together, Medha's most common response was the curt, "I didn't want to," voiced in a dismissive, conversation-ending tone. I knew I had to be less direct in my questioning if I wanted to understand my interlocutors' genuine, multilayered experiences.

Table 1 portrays in plain strokes my interpretation of the reasons for not marrying conveyed by my fifty-four primary interlocutors through their life-story narratives and our fieldwork conversations. The chapters to follow flesh out these reasons in more depth, but for now, I find a simple list of intersecting reasons for not marrying illuminating to consider.

We can see from this table that near 30 percent (16) of my participants articulated that they had purposefully chosen not to marry. This does not mean that these women never regretted some aspects of their decision. Pratima, a retired schoolteacher who had chosen not to marry, reported: "I would not advise my students now to be single—I tell them to think about it very carefully." Especially for those who pursue unconventional life paths, making the decision is not always straightforward, and often involves pain and loss. Nonetheless, many in this group expressed confidence in their decisions to evade marriage, even if single life is not always easy.

Of those who *deliberately chose* to evade marriage, their most common reasons for making this choice included the following: what I call "conveying a feminist sensibility" or feeling reluctant to be subsumed within a sexist marital family, potentially facing triviality, oppression, and/or abuse (7 people); natal kin needing one's income and feeling very attached to one's own natal kin (6 people); being too engrossed in education (5 people); identifying as lesbian (4 people); and being too busy with work (3 people). (Other women also identified with these same categories but without seeing themselves as having deliberately chosen never to marry.)

Regarding the category I label "conveying a feminist sensibility," only a handful of my interlocutors specifically referred to themselves as "feminist" using the English term, but many expressed perspectives that I would consider strongly feminist, believing that every person, regardless of gender, should be treated with respect as a full human being with equal rights. Fifteen women articulated such feminist perspectives as a core reason for being reluctant to marry, imagining conventional gendered family settings as oppressive toward in-marrying wives and daughters-in-law. Polly Chakraborty, a distinguished professor and researcher, exclaimed, "Imagine if I were to be working hard on a paper, and my husband were to ask that I make him some tea!" Others told of witnessing married female relatives and neighbors being physically abused, and of how all the trappings of married household life (*shongshar*)—including dressing up, donning gold jewelry, and wearing nice saris—seemed so trivial and confining.[6]

Bengali girls also hear while growing up all sorts of warnings about the bad things that might happen to them in their in-laws' homes (*shoshur bari*) unless they learn to behave, cook, and be docile. Hanvi, who achieved an MA and enjoyed living independently, recalled how she was "too willful, even as a child," to be suitable for marriage. "My mother used to lose her temper and say, 'I don't know how that girl will ever manage to do married/household life! Her mother-in-law will welcome her in through one door and promptly kick her out through another!'"

Sanjaya, who strongly self-identifies as feminist, criticized Bengali society and young women for continuing to believe that conventional gender and marriage systems are good for women. She explained:

During the generation of my mother, 95 percent of marriages were arranged marriages. And women had to accept every character flaw of their husbands and their husbands' families. This could range from hitting to beatings, and all sorts of bad behaviors. Everything they faced, they never had a chance to open their mouth and complain. They just had to accept that life and live it. There was no chance for personal desire.[7]

Definitely things are changing. Otherwise I would not be here speaking so frankly. Many of my friends are living very independently. More women are accepting the fact that they need to earn, and they can't just depend. They need some economic independence.

Still, the vast majority of women accept—they assume that marriage is a happy life. This is especially a problem in the middle classes. Upper-class women have wealth and will manage. Among the lower classes, everyone needs to work; all women must work. But the middle-class situation is very difficult. Women see instances of domestic violence every day. But *still* they make themselves believe that they have not seen anything bad. They see "the picture of my life" as marriage.

This is idiotic—a very stupid culture and way of bringing up daughters.

Not all who expressed such feminist sensibilities, however, saw themselves as having deliberately chosen not (ever) to marry. Although not willing to marry into an oppressive situation, many had hoped to find or still hoped to find a good partner who would be respectful of women, including their autonomy, worth, work, and desires. Sanjaya herself would still be very happy to find a suitable man, if possible. Medha, too, was one who had never deliberately chosen not to marry and still dreamed sometimes of finding a suitable match. Sanjaya was in her forties during my fieldwork period and Medha in her fifties, each beyond what would ordinarily be a marriable age. Each also expressed openness to finding a good male partner with whom to "live in" outside of marriage.[8] But neither believed such an outcome would be at all likely, given all the other personal and social contexts of their lives. Further, both identify as strongly feminist and could not tolerate the idea of being partnered with a sexist man.

Being too engrossed in education and/or work to marry, or to think about marriage at the appropriate time, was a major reason for remaining single for about 25 percent of the women in my study, as I explore in chapter 2. Education and work for women are often regarded as two pillars of a silent gendered revolution taking place around the world.[9] In India, growing recognition of the value of educating girls and fostering women's desires to work are a major factor making the opting out of marriage increasingly possible.[10]

Many who pursued education or work with passion did not in their early years, however, realize that gaining an advanced degree or professional success could mean they would never marry. Instead, for many, "age happened" gradually as they pursued their studies, or they became "too qualified" to find a suitable match. Aarini recalled, "I never thought that getting a PhD would mean I would not marry. But time passed, and then I was too old." "Too much" education and success can also lead to a dearth of qualified, eligible grooms. Medha pronounced derisively, "In Indian society, the groom must be superior to the bride in all ways, in *all* ways—except for looks!"

Table 1 indicates that the majority of women—70 percent in my study—did not see themselves as having purposefully chosen to opt out of marriage. The most common reason for being unmarried not by choice was when parents (especially fathers, according to women's narratives) failed to arrange their daughter's marriage—due to factors such as death, impoverishment, intoxication, incompetence, and/or selfishness. In rural settings, that parents and other kin failed to arrange a daughter's marriage was the only common reason for finding never-married women. This was even true for Medha, who grew up in a village. Her parents had both died, and her brother (for reasons we will learn in chapter 2) never worked hard or effectively enough to arrange his younger sister's marriage. Among my participants, the most common reasons parents failed to arrange a daughter's marriage included the following: the father or both parents being deceased (8), the family being too poor to afford marriage expenses (7), and the father being incompetent, selfish, and/or intoxicated (5). Poverty often overlapped with these subcategories, for the death or incapacity of a father due to drunkenness or drug addiction often sends a family into economic precarity.

Although self-chosen "love" marriages are on the rise, the majority of marriages in India are still arranged by kin (Trivedi 2014), and wedding expenses for the bride's family can be immense, including gold jewelry for the bride, copious gifts for the groom's family (such as furniture, a refrigerator, fancy clothing), and often cash dowries. Some of my interlocutors with knowledge of Bengali social history recalled the story of Snehalata of Kolkata's British colonial era, who in 1914 took her own life at the age of 14, reportedly to save her father the untenable decision either to sell their ancestral property to fund her marriage or, unthinkably, to have an unmarried daughter (Majumdar 2004). This event incited heated public debates and social protest against dowry, which is now technically illegal in India; yet parental incapacity to fund and arrange a daughter's marriage still leads to singlehood for women today.

For women from poor and working-class families, like Nayani's, another common reason for not marrying was that their natal kin were so dependent on their income and care labor that they did not feel they could depart in marriage—the central theme of chapter 3. Marriage in a virilocal Bengali context means that a woman's income and domestic labor belong to her husband's family rather than her natal kin. Although some married women continue to support parents and siblings through visits and gifts, the prevailing sense is that a woman cannot predict beforehand whether as a wife and daughter-in-law she will have control over her own financial decisions and ability to come and go from the marital home. This gendered kinship system drives some daughters and sisters to resist marrying in order to prioritize caring for and living with natal kin.

The force of ideologies about the value of the beautiful, sexual, fertile, fit female body within heterosexual marriage also explains why women outside prevailing standards of feminine fitness and attractiveness often cannot marry (nine persons in this study). Being "too black" (*kalo*) is a common reason Bengalis provide for why a girl or woman may face difficulty marrying, experiencing the colorism which has emerged in India as a "formidable form of discrimination" and "deep-rooted problematic practice embraced by both the oppressor and the victim" (N. Mishra 2015: 749, 725).

To be infertile or otherwise disabled or perceived as ill—such as being blind or deaf, or having once had cancer, even if perfectly fine at the expected age of marrying—can be a formidable obstacle to marrying.[11] Common assumptions are that a physically "imperfect" woman may not be adequately fit and able as a wife, reproducer, mother, household worker, and emblem of her new marital family. In some cases, concerned parents worry that their dark or disabled daughter will be treated poorly in her in-laws' home and therefore choose to keep her with them, unmarried. Men with physical imperfections do not face the same difficulty getting married, my interlocutors explained, because of how people place more emphasis on a woman's appearance than a man's. Further, since women marry into a family from the outside, a groom's kin may resist tainting the family line by bringing in a bride of perceived lesser bodily caliber. A dark in-marrying wife may produce darker descendants, for instance.

When I asked Sanjaya—who had suffered from polio as a child and now directs an NGO centered on disabled girls' and women's rights—if disabled women have a harder time getting married, she replied:

> They don't get married; it doesn't happen. No one wants to marry them. Marriage is a kind of business, if I may say. Beauty, ability, and competency—these all go together. . . . Of course, there is a love thing, but that love also has preconditions. All these preconditions—a disabled woman doesn't meet them. Or maybe we can say she's the lowest on the marriage market; she doesn't have sale-ability. . . .
>
> There are three key criteria: a bride must be fair, she must be beautiful, and she must be physically fit—so she can work from 5 a.m. to 12 at night. . . . If a woman does not give birth to a child, this is also a disability. Then in 98 percent—no, in 99 percent of the time, she will be deserted by the family, and her husband will marry another.

Sanjaya spoke with eloquence and passion about how ideas of the body, marriage, sexuality, and value are interconnected in Bengali society. "Marriage is all about how much value the bride can bring from her father's home," she declared. "How much gold, cash, beauty, and other assets. A disabled woman really can't compete. . . . The perception of a bride's body is key, the overall perception. She must look very nice! Everything must be *perfect*. Jewels, nose, fair skin color. How beautiful are the hands. Oh, what nice legs and feet. . . . Now, the legs are most important. Why the legs? Because they are 'sexy'; they connect directly to the 'vagina.' Hands are not 'sexy' in the same way, because they do not connect to the 'vagina.'"

My research assistant Madhabi, who was with Sanjaya and me as we talked in Sanjaya's office over tea, interrupted to agree, adding, "And when the groom's family comes to look at the bride for marriage, they raise the girl's sari to see if her legs have any faults—maybe a flat foot, or too dark—."

"That's right," Sanjaya continued. "So, the beauty and *perfectness* of the woman's body is paramount. And people are so ignorant. They think that if there is a disabled mother, the children will get the same disability. Of course, that's usually not true! Like in my case, my disability from childhood polio, I can't pass this on to my children. But the thing that makes me so furious is that even educated people will believe that my disability will be transferred to my children.

"And our society is so 'patriarchal' that an impaired *boy* will have no problem getting married. The male child is regarded as a gold ring. Even if the gold ring is broken or bent, it is still gold. But a mother-in-law looking for a bride for her son will *never* think that a disabled girl (*pratibandhi*) is good for him. Unless a love marriage. But even in the case of love, the family will try with all their might to stop him from marrying her. And if he does, they will try to throw her out from the home.

"And if the girl's skin is black?" Sanjaya continued. "It will be very difficult to get her married. If very fair, even if she is not educated, or if her father has no money, still she will get married. For a disabled girl like me? Marriage is not possible. Maybe one in a lakh [100,000] chance."

Regarding sexual and gender identities, the four women in my study who identified as lesbian told of growing up being unaware of gay and lesbian identities as a category, but knowing they loved women and shunning heterosexual marriage, as I explore further in chapter 5. Among the four who expressed some gender dysphoria—a conflict between a person's assigned gender and the gender with which they identify—two identified as lesbian, and one told of being disgusted by the idea of sexual relations with men as a reason not to marry. One told of feeling "kind of like a boy" when growing up, often preferring boys' games, and at times wishing they had been born a boy. Another interlocutor, a retired schoolteacher now in her eighties, told of dressing up in her brother's clothing and screaming relentlessly each time her parents arranged to have a prospective groom and his family visit, praying to God that she would not have to marry but rather "work myself, earn money myself, and eat that way." One interlocutor, Ajay, dressed mostly in masculine-style clothing, had taken on a male name, and identified both as a lesbian woman and a transgender person.[12]

Finally, one woman in my study, from a poor rural family, had become pregnant through a consensual relationship with a young man from her village neighborhood, believing they would marry. After his family rejected her for becoming pregnant out of wedlock and because her family was poor (although a higher caste than his), she raised her son in the village defiantly as a single mother. Her son's father easily married—a story I tell in chapter 6.

A sexual double standard persists across social classes and rural-urban contexts in India (as in the United States and societies around the world).[13] Many Indian parents insist that a good bride must be a virgin before marriage, although a boy may do what he pleases, a double standard portrayed in the popular 2019 Indian web television series *Made in Heaven*, centered on a wedding-planning business for the uber-rich. Depicting a potent blend of old and new, the first episode features billionaire heir Angad Roshan defending his fiancée's sexual past to his judgmental parents. His father advises his son, "It's OK to have fun with whoever you want, but the girl you *marry* should be pure." Angad responds, sarcastically: "Pure? Like ghee?" His mother exclaims, horrified: "She's not a virgin!" Angad retorts, "Nor am I!"[14]

One way that parents of "unattractive" or "undesirable" daughters might nonetheless find a respectable groom is to offer a higher-than-average dowry. The perceived deficits of dark skin, previous illness, or rumors of a previous sexual relationship, for example, can often be compensated for with a large enough dowry. However, such financial resources are out of many families' reach.

Considering my fifty-four interlocutors' intersecting reasons for not marrying, I found that it is mostly only women from highly privileged, educated, and cosmopolitan classes who are able to embrace singlehood as a distinctive lifestyle emerging from a claim to freedom of choice. Moreover, even for the elite, evading marriage is most often intertwined with other pressing life decisions and social, cultural, and economic circumstances—rarely best understood as merely a simple, free "choice."

Further, recent media stories and anthologies celebrating the rise of single women in India by choice often seem aimed more at promoting new ways of thinking about women and marriage than at describing actual widespread societal transformations taking place beyond the most elite.[15] In rural contexts, only Subhagi (chapters 2 and 3) conveyed a strong sense of personal choice and agency behind her decision to be unmarried forever—in order to keep laboring to support her natal family and to live with them forever, the way a son can. The other reasons for not marrying among the nine rural women in my study were that their (impoverished or deceased) fathers had failed to arrange their marriages (5); that they had been born with congenital dwarfism (1); that they chose to serve God instead (1);[16] and that they had become pregnant out of wedlock (Suravi of chapter 6). All nine of these rural women lived with their natal kin, as really there are no other living options in a village. Medha and Nayani were themselves born in villages and had followed diverse life paths to become solo-living urban single women. Yet neither had ever precisely chosen never to marry. We will learn much more about these two women's lives over the chapters to come.

Importantly, I also met no woman of any social class who had not faced forceful social pressure to marry. This leads to the next topic: the gendered marriage imperative.

THE GENDERED MARRIAGE IMPERATIVE

A 2019 United Nations report finds that less than 1 percent of all women aged 45 to 49 in India have never married, one of the lowest non-marriage rates in the world (UN Women 2019: 54). Marriage in India is the only familiar path toward achieving economic and social security, respect, and a socially legitimate way of being sexual. Primarily only the most privileged, city-educated, and cosmopolitan are the ones who can now embrace single lifestyles by choice, and even then, many must battle to make their singlehood accepted in the wider society. Despite online campaigns such as the Happily Unmarried project of the feminist Majlis Legal Centre, fighting "to remove the stigma attached to being an unmarried woman in society," it is still hard for most Indian women to fight the social stigma tied to not marrying.[17] Priya Satalkar recalls painfully how family and friends in India deemed that "something was terribly wrong with . . . me," for not taking "the life path I was expected to walk in my society" by marrying, even though by other measures she was successful—well-educated and with a professional career. Yet, "being 30 and not married was a defect that outweighed all my professional and other personal achievements, even for my mother" (2012: 209).

One aim of this book is to move beyond implicitly situating marriage as a normative referent in the anthropology of gender and kinship.[18] But what if the emic perspectives of so many of my single interlocutors or their community members underscore that marriage is unavoidably the normative referent in women's lives?

As in the United States, where forms of singlism (implicit bias against singles) and marital privilege often go unrecognized and unacknowledged, so in India the prevailing worldview that marriage is normal and right, especially for women, ordinarily goes unquestioned.[19] The rightness and normality of marriage is generally so taken for granted that it rather goes without saying, an excellent example of what Pierre Bourdieu terms "doxa"—"the world of tradition experienced as a 'natural world' and taken for granted" (1977: 164). But a core aim of anthropology, like feminism, queer studies, and critical heterosexuality studies, is to probe the taken-for-granted, to make visible systems of meaning and inequality in order to better invite critique. So, I begin to make visible here the underlying logics of the gendered marriage imperative—that is, the ways the marriage imperative connects to specific and distinct notions about male and female gender—one of the key concerns of my fieldwork project.

The most obvious reason behind the gendered marriage imperative in India is to control sexuality, containing and channeling sexual activity within a socially sanctioned, familial, heterosexual marital context. This goes for both men and women, although generally with an even greater sense of urgency and set of restrictions for girls and women.

Ideologies about sexuality form a core part of the "sex/gender system" in any society, to borrow Gayle Rubin's useful phrase (1975). Rubin defines the sex/gender system as "a set of arrangements by which the biological raw material of human sex and procreation is shaped by human, social intervention and satisfied in a conventional manner" (2011c [1975]: 39). These sex/gender systems "provide ultimate propositions about the nature of human beings themselves" (2011c [1975]: 60). In her germinal essay "Thinking Sex," Rubin further argues that societies create "sex hierarchies" that distinguish so-called good, normal, and natural sexuality (such as heterosexual, marital, and procreative unions) from bad, abnormal, and unnatural sexual identities and practices (2011b [1984]). Through such sex hierarchies, societies organize sexualities into systems of power "which reward and encourage some individuals and activities, while punishing and suppressing others" (2011b [1984]: 180).

In India, channeling sexuality and procreation within heterosexual marriage is central to prevailing ideas about gender and the achievement of adult femininity and masculinity. Like women, men across India face pervasive and powerful expectations that they will marry heterosexually and reproduce. This can pose an especially difficult problem for gay men (chapter 6). Scholarship on "over-aged" rural bachelors in northern and northwestern India likewise exposes challenges to masculinity faced by men unable to find brides. Because of skewed sex ratios stemming from sex-selective abortions (an illegal practice that nonetheless persists) and the increasingly popular practice of hypergamy (brides and their families aspiring for higher-ranked grooms), men in many peasant communities are facing a shortage of potential brides.[20] In the northern Indian state of Haryana, over-aged bachelors are described as "bare branches" or *chade*, "a term that not only refers to bare branches of a family tree that will not yield any fruit (offspring) but also to clubs or sticks, thereby hinting at the propensity of these men towards physical and sexual violence," behaving dangerously like "uncontrolled bulls," missing the benefits of a channelized marital sexuality (P. Mishra 2018: 34). Such studies highlight the "indispensability of marriage and procreation in defining masculinities" (P. Mishra 2018: 27).[21]

In the popular 2020 Netflix original *Indian Matchmaking*—a reality TV series about arranged marriages among both Indians and Indian Americans—we also see portrayed the enormous pressure to wed for young people of both genders.[22] The most intensely pro-marriage character in the series may be the mother of Akshay, the eligible young lad from a wealthy, Mumbai-based business family. As picky and hesitant Akshay rejects over seventy matches offered up by the matchmaker, his mother Preeti gives him an ultimatum: he must get married in the next few months, by immediately picking one of three girls she has found for him, or else she and her husband will choose for him. Moreover, Preeti blames her son's indecision for her high blood pressure and worries that Akshay's delay in choosing a bride is causing her older son and wife to delay having a baby, thus ruining the whole family's plans. Preeti's overwhelming sense of determination and urgency relaxes only after her son finally enters into a lavish pre-engagement ceremony with a chosen match. *Meet the Patels* offers another popular representation of the intense parental mandate to get one's son married (Patel and Patel 2014).

Young women, however, tend to face even more pressure to marry than men, an unequal pressure tied to ideologies of natural differences in sexed/gendered bodies and roles. First, the risk of pregnancy out of wedlock threatens the moral reputation and respectability of not only the individual girl or woman but also her family and wider community. Concerns about caste and class purity also heighten concerns about the pregnancy of unmarried girls and women outside sanctioned unions.[23]

Relatedly, marriage as a crucial foundation for reproduction and motherhood is central to prevailing ideas of adult femininity and female personhood. Medha remarked on this point in an incisive email she sent me in English after I had returned to the United States from a fieldwork trip in West Bengal: "I would like to draw your attention to some customs/conducts of Indian/Bengali society that I am facing in my everyday life and sometimes make me irritated. You know in India every Indian girl is addressed as Ma (mother) by others. They may be their family members or other persons from outside the family or even by strangers! The girl should be a mother anyhow as early as possible. Indian culture has no acceptance that women could reject motherhood!"

Medha went on to note how the various Bengali kinship terms for aunt (*kakima, jethima, pisima, masima*, and *mamima*) all include the term "ma"—mother—signifying again the ways motherhood is intimately entwined with people's conceptions about a woman's identity.[24] The corresponding terms for uncle (*kaka, jetha, meso*, etc.) contain no particle referencing fatherhood.

Further, the Bengali practice of calling people by kin terms in everyday interactions reinforces a sense of compulsory motherhood and marriage, as Medha articulated in the same email: "Another point should be noted that when I am travelling by public bus or train or meet people in the vegetable market or other places, . . . everybody addresses me as kakima (wife of father's younger brother) or jethima (wife of father's elder brother) or boudi (wife of elder brother). People do not allow the womenfolk to be unmarried even in their subconscious mind!"

Marriage, too, is the only normal way for an adult woman to establish a secure place within a family, in a society where family is key to social and economic security (chapters 3, 4; Basu 1999, 2015).

All this helps explain not only the immense pressure to marry but also the pressure for girls and women to marry young. UNICEF reports that one in three of the world's child brides live in India (2019: 4). In 2015–2016, approximately one in four young women in India had been married before their 18th birthday, and nearly half of these women were married before turning age 15.[25] In the state of West Bengal, where I centered my research, 42 percent of young women currently aged 20 to 24 were first married before age 18 (UNICEF 2019: 4, 9). This is true even though child marriage in India—below 18 for women and 21 for men—is technically illegal.

One key incentive for marrying a daughter young is to keep her peak years of fertility, sexual attractiveness, and sexual desire safely contained within marriage. Grooms and their families also value a young bride as likely to be more docile and adaptable than a mature one. The fact that grooms tend to be older than their brides by around 2 to 12 years in both rural and urban contexts in India helps maintain a naturalized male dominance within marriage. As Pierre Bourdieu articulates, the widespread desire (in France and so many other societies) that a male partner be not only older but also taller than a female partner serves to "tacitly and unarguably demand that, at least in appearances and seen from the outside, the man should occupy the dominant position within the couple" (2004: 340).

Everyday fieldwork conversations with both married and unmarried persons highlight the interconnected ideologies of sexuality, reproduction, kinship, and respectability making up the gendered marriage imperative. In my fieldwork in Bengali villages, I would commonly ask, "At what age is it good for girls or women (*meyera*) to get married?"[26] I asked this question one pleasant winter morning in a mixed-class and -caste village neighborhood where several adult women were gathered out on the central lane.

"After about age 15 or 16, you begin to think—'How is this girl's marriage going to happen? How are we going to get her married?'" Chobi replied.

"By age 18, it's a must," Subhagi added. "Girls should be married by age 18."

Bandana offered a slightly higher age. "By age 20 to 22, it's good to get a girl married."

Others quickly interrupted: "Where are people waiting until 20 or 22? No one is waiting until the girls are age 20! Still now no one is waiting until she is 20 to give a girl's marriage!"

"Where are they even letting the girls reach 18 years?" Subhagi chimed in. "Society is there, no? Boys will grab the girls and eat them!" (referring to the vulnerability of unmarried girls to sexual assault). "It is better to get them married around 15 or 16."

Among more elite social classes and in urban contexts, young women pursuing education and careers often now wait until around age 22 to 28 to marry. Above age 30, many begin to feel that a woman is getting too old for marriage, and it is highly unusual for a woman in India to marry after age 35.

Author Ira Trivedi tells of her grandfather's advice on the occasion of her 21st birthday: "He said I should get married quickly because 'women are like balls of dough. If they sit around for too long they harden and make deformed chapattis.' My grandfather believed that a good marriage [or wife?] was like a perfectly round chapatti and to achieve this perfection, the dough had to be supple, fresh, and young. It has been nearly seven years since then, and now at 28, I am unequivo-cally, by Dadaji's standards, a hardened deformed, inedible roti" (2014: 173).

On another occasion in Kolkata, Shipra Chatterjee, a mother in her fifties from an upper-middle-class family, articulated a clear biological rationale for the marriage imperative, tied to her sense of natural differences between male and female bodies. Her own daughter, Aparajita, had married late at almost age 30 while pursuing a PhD. The long years of her daughter's single status had caused Mrs. Chatterjee much concern.

"These days, many educated girls are saying, 'There is no benefit to getting mar-ried. I can earn my own income, stand on my own two feet.' But their parents worry—when they get old, what will happen?" That is, with no children, who will care for them in old age?[27] Further, Shipra Chatterjee had faced criticism from her neighbors and kin for letting her daughter remain unmarried. "People would criticize and falsely slander us, saying, 'Your daughter is wandering around here and there, coming home late.'"

Mrs. Chatterjee, Aparajita, and I were dining together in the family's apart-ment, enjoying a noon meal of rice, daal, fish stew, and delectable vegetable dishes. "We worry much more about an unmarried daughter than a son," Mrs. Chatterjee explained, "because of the 'biological difference' between boys and girls."

Aparajita asked her mother with a critical tone, "What do you mean by 'biologi-cal difference'?"

Mrs. Chatterjee blushed and hesitated to answer. I asked if she was referring to the risk of pregnancy. "Yes, that's it. In Western societies, girls may know how to protect themselves; but here they don't know all that—they could suddenly fall into trouble." Aparajita later elaborated that her mother likely was expressing her general sense that Western young women have more control over their bodies and sexuality—more sex education knowledge, more access to birth control, less vulnerability to sexual assault.[28]

In another village, I gathered with three married sisters I had known since they were girls, when I had conducted dissertation fieldwork in their natal village thirty years earlier. We were assembled for a jovial reunion at the middle sister's brightly painted brick-and-plaster house, looking out to a walled courtyard filled with a kitchen garden, papaya tree, and abundant flowers. Each sister now had daughters of her own. The oldest sister, Mithu, had arranged her daughter's marriage at age 13; the youngest, Asha, had just arranged her daughter's marriage at age 15. The family had been working on finding a suitable match anyway, but sped up the process when Asha's daughter had begun flirting with a neighborhood boy they deemed to be from a lower caste. Roudri, the only one whose husband had a reliable salaried job, raising her social class a little above that of her sisters, had two daughters ages 16 and 18 who were still unmarried and in school. These girls' increased education promised to bring them higher-ranked grooms, but still their father and aunts were becoming worried.

"He'll feel a big relief once the girls are married," Roudri said of her husband.

It was a Sunday, and Roudri's husband, Dilip, was present. He concurred: "Whoever has daughters worries greatly."

But Roudri spoke of how she feels like crying each time the subject of her daughters' marriages comes up. The girls' father is home just a few days per month, residing most of the time in a coal company housing complex several hours' journey away. Roudri and her daughters spend all their time together and have become such good pals. Roudri's in-laws live right nearby in the same village neighborhood, but she and her husband had set up their own separate household.

Mithu scolded her younger sister, "Mothers will always feel bad during their daughters' weddings, but you must gain strength." In Bengali families, sons conventionally stay living with their parents after marriage, while daughters move away.

Roudri responded, "That's what everyone says. But I don't know why—I feel like crying. I cannot live without them."

Asha, the youngest of the three adult sisters, offered sympathetically, "I also at times cry for my daughter" (her only child, gone at age 15 for just the past month). Asha laughed gently to lighten the mood. She had also seemed proud and excited by her daughter's marriage when first sharing the news with me.

Anindita, my research assistant who was present that day and getting along especially well with Roudri's two teenage daughters, asked the group, "If a *boy* would be around 26 or 27 and unmarried, would you get worried then?"

"No!" Mithu answered quickly.

Dilip replied, "Until 30 is OK for a boy. Actually, if the boys want to marry, then they can, and if they do not want to marry, then let it be. For boys there is nothing to worry about.[29] But for girls—," he paused. "For girls—," he paused again. "Well, if I die, then what will they eat?" He articulated the important matter of economic security, but I sensed that underneath his comments lay an even greater concern: that the girls could become pregnant out of wedlock, their reputations ruined.

The youngest of the two daughters jumped in to protest, "You'll see! We can look after ourselves! We can look after ourselves."

One of the largest and most important responsibilities of Indian parents, people say, is to ensure that their children, of either gender, are married, as part of ensuring economic and kinship security, sexual propriety, patrilineal reproductivity, old age care, and perceived normal adulthood. Rachana Sen, a never-married history professor in her fifties who resides in her natal home, commented at the end of her life-story narrative: "I regret one thing—that my father died with that regret of my not marrying; and my mother still worries—what will happen after she leaves."

Aarini, the computer engineer in her forties who had worked in Silicon Valley before returning to her ancestral home in Kolkata, would sometimes criticize her own parents for failing to arrange her marriage: "It is the parents' '*moral responsibility*' [she emphasized these two terms, speaking in English] to get their children married, and to a *good person*, too." According to Aarini, over the years her parents had only ineffectively suggested a few matches, thinking that their independent, PhD-pursuing daughter would likely find her own match instead.

To emphasize parents' duty to give their daughters in marriage, some Bengalis invoke age-old Hindu traditions, such as codes for conduct set forth in the ancient Sanskrit text *Laws of Manu.*[30] One well-known prescription from the *Laws of Manu* stipulates that a father sins if he fails to marry his daughter off by the time she reaches puberty. One father explained that the text puts it this way: "If one drop of menstrual blood flows before his daughter is married, then the father has sinned." In the *Manu* text, this statement follows another well-known passage articulating the appropriate dependence of women on male kin: "Her father guards her in childhood, her husband guards her in youth, and her sons guard her in old age. A woman is not fit for independence. A father who does not give [his daughter] away at the proper time should be blamed" (*Manu* 1991: IX.2–4, 197). Giving a daughter in marriage at the appropriate time, according to the text as it goes on, is essential not only to ensure the purity of the daughter and her family line but also to foster reproduction. Just as it is reprehensible for a father not to arrange his daughter's marriage at the proper time, so "a husband who does not have sex with her at the proper time should be blamed" (*Manu* 1991: IX.4, 197). Further, "women were created to bear children, and men to carry on the [family] line; that is why the revealed canon prescribes a joint duty (for a man) together with his wife" (*Manu* 1991: IX.96, 209). Although some critique the patriarchal assumptions underlying such textual passages, the lines convey ideologies familiar to many in India.

Given the powerful expectation that marrying is proper, normal, and necessary, many have a hard time comprehending how some women remain unmarried. One Western anthropologist I met on a train returning to Kolkata from a rural fieldwork stint told me that she loved my project. She herself had never married and had tried for years to explain to her interlocutors in India that not marrying was a choice for her. They could not understand. Finally, she decided it was easier just to strike her forehead—the location of fate—and exclaim, "O, Bhagavan!" (Oh, God!), signifying that we cannot understand God's ways. This response, she said, goes over much better. When I reported the incident to Medha, she laughed hard.

SINGLES HOUSING, AND LIVING SOLO AS A UNIQUE FORM OF PERSONHOOD

Before closing this overview chapter on being single, I wish to probe a broader ideology of personhood and sociality at play—the fundamental matter of the suitability or unsuitability of any person living alone and/or apart from kin. An additional challenge to not marrying for women in India is that few housing options exist beyond the family. For most people in India, to live apart from kin, and especially to live alone, is not a familiar or accessible way of being. One of my Bengali research assistants, herself unmarried in her thirties while living in her north Kolkata natal home, reported by email her mother's reflections on the notion of living alone:

> If living by oneself was that easy and acceptable hereabouts, then other things that we take for granted—like the imperative on getting married, or on looking after one's parents when they're older—would fall apart quite soon. Voluntarily living by oneself outside one's family home when it's not required professionally indicates to my mother (and to me, now that I think about it) an adoption of a lifestyle quite different from what we think of as the Indian or Bengali way of life.

In contrast, recent research suggests that singles in North America and western Europe mostly prefer to live alone (e.g., Kislev 2019a: 174). National housing statistics reveal a lot. People who live alone make up 28 percent of all US households (Klinenberg 2012: 4–5), and the percentage of one-person households in several major European cities has exceeded 50 percent (Kislev 2019a: 4). In Japan, too, one-person households have recently become the most common type (Raymo 2015). In India, merely 3.7 percent of households are single person (Dommaraju 2015: 1246–1247). Although a few women in my study professed to enjoy living solo, one reason others were ambivalent about being single is the threat that they might have to live alone.

It may come as no surprise, then, that the most common living situation for unmarried women and men in India is to live with natal kin. Normally daughters are expected to be transient members of their natal homes in anticipation of moving to their husband's home upon marriage. Yet, 27 of my 54 key interlocutors lived with natal kin in their homes of birth, striving to legitimize the kinds of lifelong ties to natal kin and home that their brothers more commonly enjoy. Three more lived with sisters in other ways beyond the natal home—one on the floor of a hall in a married sister's home, and two more sisters with each other in a home purchased by the elder sister's former employer, for whom she had worked for thirty years as a live-in domestic helper (table 2).

Beyond the family, women in India still ordinarily have few housing choices. As I detail further in chapter 5, prospective urban landlords often refuse to rent to single women, finding them morally suspect. In rural areas, virtually no housing exists beyond family homes.

Yet, one transition making singlehood increasingly possible in India's metros is the expanding of independent living options, primarily for the middle and elite classes. These include

- the burgeoning of high-rise apartment complexes, featuring nuclear-family-style apartments appealing to some solo dwellers (although some housing complexes specifically forbid single women residents, or require that such a

TABLE 2. Living Situations of Single Women Participants

Living Situation	Participants (out of 54)
With natal kin in natal home	27
Alone in a single-person household	13
In a working women's hostel	7
In an old age home	3
With a sister (not in the natal home)	3
With friends	1

woman provide a letter from a father or sign a pledge that she will not drink alcohol, smoke, stay out late, or entertain men);

- the development of urban hostels for unmarried, divorced, and widowed working women, such as the Government of West Bengal Working Girls' Hostel in Kolkata, where I spent much time conducting participant observation fieldwork; and

- the emergence of a retirement home market, institutions often termed in English "old age homes" (although co-residence with adult children is still the norm in India).

Working women's hostels and old age homes provide two contemporary non-kin housing options for ten of the women in this study, seven in a working women's hostel and initially three in old age homes. Two more women subsequently moved into an old age home over the course of this research. The growing senior living market in India—ranging from modest informal apartments housing a handful of elders to upscale retirement villages—supports a broader social trend of independent living among especially the urban middle and upper classes, explored in chapter 4.[31]

To provide socially acceptable, safe, and inexpensive accommodations for working women needing to live away from their families due to professional commitments, the Government of India in 1972–1973 launched the working women's hostels scheme.[32] Some hostels are run by the housing departments of state governments, such as the Government of West Bengal Working Girls' Hostel in the Gariahat neighborhood of Kolkata, where I conducted fieldwork.

In establishing such hostels, the state assumes the role of paternalistic guardian of its city's working women living apart from families. The Government of West Bengal Working Girls' Hostel maintains strict rules, including restricted visiting hours from 7 to 9 a.m. and 6 to 7 p.m. (6 to 8 p.m. on Sundays and holidays), no male visitors (including no brothers or fathers) allowed indoors beyond the one public ground-floor visiting room where the door must be left open at all times, and a 10 p.m. curfew. Any woman who needs to stay out beyond 10 p.m. due to night duty must provide a written certificate from her employer to the hostel superintendent. This particular four-story hostel houses around three hundred women, two or three to a room, paying just 150 INR (around US$2) per month. (All the residents agree that this fee, which has not increased in years, is very inexpensive, especially in such a desirable neighborhood of Kolkata.) Most of the residents come from working- and middle-class families, and their ages range primarily from the twenties to sixties (although Sukhi-di, one of my key interlocutors, was in her seventies during the seven years of my research and had resided in the hostel for over thirty years).

Strikingly, only 1 of the 54 women in my core group lived with friends, revealing the dominance of kinship over friendship in ordinary housing arrangements. Moreover, this woman, Sana, expected her residence with friends to be temporary. Sana identified as a lesbian, but was not out about her identity to the friends with whom she lived. She owns her own apartment, which she had purchased and decorated while dreaming of making a life there with her longtime girlfriend. When her girlfriend ended up marrying a man, Sana found it too painful to stay in the apartment. I tell her story more fully in chapter 5.

Although Bengalis tend to regard living entirely alone as highly unusual and sometimes almost unthinkable, 13 of my 54 participants, or almost 25 percent, did live alone in single-person households. Each of these solo-living women lived in urban areas, and all but Nayani (the host from this chapter's opening vignette) had achieved education up to the bachelor's (2), master's (6), and PhD (4) levels and had established careers with stable incomes.

Medha was one of the thirteen who now lived completely alone, in an apartment she had purchased on her own. Sukhi-di, who resided with two roommates in the Government of West Bengal Working Girls' Hostel, exclaimed to Medha, "I can't believe you can live all alone! I would be so scared if I locked the door at night and no one else was inside! At least *one* person is necessary!"

Others would ask Medha in disbelief and pity, as we traveled together to various villages in search of other never-married women: "Who is in your home? Your parents are there? Your brothers? You don't have *anyone?*"—questions posed with a tone of rising alarm.

"I have no one," Medha would reply simply. "I live alone."

"You have *no one?!*"—incredulous, aghast, almost unable to fathom.

A never-married woman who had chosen to move into an old age home explained her decision, remarking simply: "Living cannot happen alone (*eka to thaka jae na*). No one at any age can live alone."[33]

Medha herself went through a period of hiring a woman to stay with her at night, on a mat on the floor next to Medha's bed, just so that another human presence would be there. Reluctantly coming for the income, the woman, who had been abandoned by her husband, would arrive quietly around 9 p.m. after depositing her two young children at her brother's house, and then slip out at dawn, tucking her mosquito net and mat under Medha's bed.[34]

Men also face deep-seated pressures to marry, as we have seen, and to not live alone. This is a problem that can be particularly critical for gay men. After twenty years of living singly in the United States, gay Bengali journalist Sandip Roy returned to India, a country where "the idea of a man living alone is baffling" (S. Roy 2015). Roy, trying to set up an independent apartment, made an appointment with a modular kitchen consultant, who beamingly asked Roy to return with madam to approve the final selections. "When it finally dawned on him that there was no madam at all," Roy writes, "he was aghast. I don't know what shocked him more—that a man might approve a kitchen design, or that I lived alone, or that a man who lived alone wanted a kitchen." Roy reflects, "I had not reckoned that what would be truly difficult was being an unmarried man," not necessarily being gay, "especially an unmarried man living part of the time on his own, away from family. That was what was regarded as profoundly abnormal."

Roy concludes: "It sometimes makes me wonder whether Indians can more intuitively grasp a right to marriage rather than a right to privacy or self-expression. . . . India might be a conservative country but if it understands anything, it understands marriage. That might just extend even to same-sex marriage one day. At least he married someone, thank goodness" (S. Roy 2015; see also S. Roy 2008).

A CLOSING TALE

I close this overview chapter on Indian singlehood by sharing a moving email I received while writing this book, from a woman who had read my first published article on being single in India (Lamb 2018). Her story powerfully illustrates many of this chapter's themes, surrounding both reasons for not marrying and the gendered marriage imperative. She gave me permission to repeat some of her email message here:

> I was raised by two parents of lower middle-class background in semi-urban Mumbai, and they were the earliest feminist influence on me. Me and my brother had exactly equal shares of food and privileges, and we were required to do an equal volume and scope of household activities. It was OK that my brother was more interested in household activities and would be with my mother in the kitchen and helping in cooking, while I was free to read books or follow my interests as long as I helped in the household in other ways.
>
> All this started to change after my father's death. I was 27. My feminist mother suddenly started pushing me to get married—those endless nudges to "settle down." It seems suddenly she became aware that without my father, it was solely her responsibility to get me married in a timely fashion. She almost turned it into a mission to get me married. I had my career dreams, and I simply could not relate to my mother as my own—it was too confusing to make sense of the mother I knew who had told me that there is nothing in this world that is beyond my reach just because I am a woman and that I could make my dreams come true if I worked hard for them,

with this new woman who started implying that my life is meaningless if I do not marry, and who would remind me of my ticking biological clock. We fought and argued endlessly.

I was working with [a large international organization] back then, and that income suddenly pushed us from the "lower" to the "middle" middle class. My mother started worrying that the society would think that she did not marry me because of the money I was earning. So she refused to accept my financial support to the family. Many of my male work colleagues also started telling me that I will not find a man for marriage because I am too independent and had too much income, which does not go well with most men, even educated ones. . . .

During that same time, a scholarship in 2009 helped me move to [Europe] to pursue a master's degree. . . . Meanwhile, a long-term male friend who was also being pestered by his family to marry asked whether we should marry. We were not in love but we understood each other well and thought this would be better than marrying some stranger. . . . [But] just before our planned wedding day, I called it off creating a huge social scandal. Though I was criticized for taking that step, it was my mother who paid the biggest price for it. She was now a double failure—she not only had failed to marry me off in time but she had also failed to raise me according to Indian values. She became suicidal and I had to start her on anti-depressants.

In this whole drama, my brother stood rock solid by my side, and made me aware that if I wanted to have a good life, I had to leave India. Society is not ready yet for women like me. I am in Europe since then. . . .

Reading your paper this morning brought back so many memories that I had to write to you. Thank you for studying and writing about us. Though now I am happily married, I still feel I belong to these women in your stories. We are the women making unconventional choices in my society, and in my class, middle class is really the worst affected where the pressure to confine to the norms is the highest. You rightly point out the price we pay for those choices.

This chapter has begun to make clear how singlehood can only be understood through the thickness of social-cultural specificity and attention to the intertwined phenomena of freedom and constraint in human life. The chapters to follow further uncover the intersecting conditions of social life making singlehood in India both increasingly possible yet incredibly challenging.

2

Education and Work

Medha was born into an impoverished family of the mid-ranking Mahishya caste of farmers and raised in a remote village, eight kilometers from the nearest paved road. She became the first girl in her village ever to graduate from secondary school. She went on to the university and received a PhD, becoming a professor of Bengali in a provincial college. After we had already known each other for several years, Medha invited me to her apartment for a delicious home-cooked meal and to record her life story.

"In the house where I was born, both of my parents were small farmers," Medha began, recalling a time about fifty-five years earlier. "We owned a tiny piece of land that they farmed, and they worked on other people's lands as laborers. They had a lot of children, but most all died, like from malnutrition, gynecological problems, and miscarriages. I'm the thirteenth child. Thirteenth! But only three of us survived.

"My mom was 'illiterate,' completely 'illiterate,'" Medha went on. "She couldn't write at all, not even to sign her name."

Medha told of how their family often went hungry and had trouble even buying rice. Her mother would sell vegetables on the footpath. Because of their lower-class status, they were forbidden to wear shoes when venturing near the home of the local zamindar (property owner), lest this demonstrate her family's insubordination.[1] Class status trumped any concerns over caste here, as both the zamindar's and Medha's family were of the same caste.

Despite their poverty, Medha's father had always admired education. He himself had had a few years of schooling as a boy, "at a lower-class school," and he encouraged his own children to study.

"I would study all the time," Medha recalled animatedly. "I didn't do work around the house or farm. I loved studying! My brother didn't love to study; he had good handwriting, but he wasn't good in studies." Medha's older sister was already married off by then. "I *was* good in my studies," she recalled proudly. "I always taught myself and studied by myself, and I always got good results.

"In that remote village, I had no access to country or world news," Medha recollected. "We didn't have money for newspapers or books. But when I was in class (or grade) one, I would go to someone's house in the next village over, and I would ask them to save their newspapers for me after they were done reading. . . . I would go once or twice per week, get the newspapers from them, read them, and then return them to the family. I would also read the shopping bags made from old newspapers. Back then, we didn't have plastic shopping bags; all the grocery bags were made from old newspapers. . . . In a different faraway village, there was a village library. I would go there after school, walking four or five kilometers to get books. My mother used to worry at night when I wasn't home yet. I would return at night carrying my books, walking through the open fields.

"I also listened to the radio whenever I could," Medha went on, describing her avid thirst for knowledge. "So, I learned about what London is, what America is. And all the places I learned about in books and on the radio, I wanted to see! I used to think that if I had two wings, I would just fly away from this place."

After higher secondary school, Medha would trudge eight kilometers, during the rainy season through knee-deep mud, to get to the paved road, where she could catch a bus to a provincial college, all the while struggling to pay the school fees and often going hungry.

As her life story unfolded, Medha conveyed several reasons for why she was not married, one being that she had become too well educated. She proclaimed, as shared also in chapter 1, "In Indian society, the groom must be superior to the bride in all ways, in *all* ways—except for looks!" In terms of looks, Medha describes herself as not attractive enough to be a sought-after pick on the marriage market—too "black" (*kalo*), short, and with larger teeth and higher cheekbones than considered ideal.[2]

When she was young, though, Medha did actively resist marriage. At one point after she had passed her grade ten exams, her family arranged a marriage match for her, but she protested, saying, "I won't marry—I will work." Medha went on, "Other girls wanted to get married, dreamed of having husbands, having guests over, wearing jewelry. I never thought this way. . . . So, that gentleman [her prospective bridegroom] said, 'I won't marry her. She doesn't really want to marry, so I won't marry her.' He said, 'This girl doesn't want to marry. Why are you all forcing her?'

"Other people in the village would say to my older brother in front of me, 'Why are you letting her study? What will she become? Why aren't you getting her married? What is she going to do—get a job?' After hearing all this, I would think, 'Yes, I *will* get a job.'"

Years later, when Medha finished her PhD and finally got work as a professor, she recalled, "I was 30-plus. I could have easily gotten married. In Indian society, professors are valued. . . . My brother would go around telling everyone, 'My sister is a professor.' It's like his 'identity.' If there is a professor in the family, they have more family status. But when people spoke to him of eligible men, my brother would be quiet and not say anything. . . . [My brother and his wife] didn't want me to get married because then they wouldn't have a way of getting money."

In conventional Bengali kinship systems, a woman after marriage is part of her husband's family and only tenuously related to her natal kin. In practice, many married daughters and sisters continue to visit and support natal kin in large and small ways, especially those who are earning and able to maintain some financial independence. However, the prevailing sentiment is that a married woman's income and labor belong centrally to her marital home, and it is difficult to predict ahead of time whether a husband and in-laws will allow their wife/daughter-in-law any financial independence.

Benefiting from her generous professor's salary, Medha's natal family has now replaced their crumbling mud hut with a two-story brick home with running water and electricity. Supported by Medha's income, Medha's brother's sons all became well educated, and now they have their own good jobs in the city—"Due to me! Due to me!" Medha asserted. "Now my family has money, education, status, jobs—because of me."

Medha recalled, "I finally advertised for my own marriage in the newspaper to see if I could get someone good, but I . . . just got a lot of weird and bad men. . . . They all came because of my job—that I would work and bring them money. My brother, sister-in-law, and these men all wanted me for the job. They all wanted my money. I am not valued as a person—only my money is valued."

Now living alone, Medha finds the condition highly unfamiliar, even unnerving. When I went to stay for two nights in her natal village home with her brother and sister-in-law, Medha put me in a separate room, laughing while explaining to her kin, "Americans like to sleep all alone with even the door closed!" She told me, "We prefer when relatives are visiting to have ten or twenty people piled into one room, lying on mats on the floor, all sleeping together!"

A few years earlier, after we had first met, Medha emailed me upon my return to the United States:

Do you mind if I share some personal matters with you? In Vishnupur, as a small town of West Bengal [where Medha teaches and rents an apartment, while owning an additional apartment in Kolkata], I have no opportunity to mix up with people from the same sphere of life. On the other side, the educated people of Kolkata are very snobbish about the small-town people. . . . Again, as an unmarried woman, I have to obey some rules of the Indian morality. [These "rules of the Indian morality" concern powerful ideas about respectability and sexuality, such as that solo women should not be out in public having fun or associating with men (chapters 5, 7).] The result is very depressive. I am cornered, cornered seriously. It affects my life as well as my career.

One thought I had had upon reading this email was that Medha might be alluding to being lesbian (in her comment, "I have no opportunity to mix up with people from the same sphere of life"). But when I got the courage to ask her over email, while suggesting a lesbian support group I knew of in Kolkata, Medha replied, "I am not lesbian, I am woman," and she later confessed how attracted she is to men, and how she would even love to have a (male) lover, if not a husband, if such could be possible. Her current "imaginary boyfriend," as she called him, was the handsome Pakistani actor Adnan Siddiqui.

Two salient themes in Medha's life narratives are, first, that of not belonging—of not receiving love from natal kin, community, neighbors, society—of feeling terribly isolated and excluded. We will see how this exclusion stems both from her unusual status as an unmarried woman and from her mismatched class. Medha combines in her one person both her impoverished rural background and the education, income, and profession of the cosmopolitan elite. For purposes of forging social ties—whether through marriage, friendships, or a wider community—Medha's class limbo excludes her. Medha articulated: "I have to fight with hostility in every step of my life due to my not being an ordinary person." I continue to explore these themes in the pages to come, as Medha's and other women's narratives illuminate the intersections of gender, class, sociality, and subjectivity in unmarried women's lives.

Second and more optimistically, Medha's narratives highlight how education and work have led to her empowerment and the vast opening up of opportunities. Her education and income did give Medha the two wings she aspired to as a young girl, the wings she needed to fly away. Medha has now traveled widely in India, Europe, and the Middle East, has crafted a meaningful career, and has established independent economic security. Over the following chapters, readers will continue to get to know Medha and the unfolding of her life obstacles and opportunities, forms of constraint and agency, and experiences of exclusion and belonging, oppression and pride.

This chapter focuses on the stories and experiences of the many women in my study who saw their aspirations to study and/or work as primary reasons for not marrying. Increasing recognition of the value of educating women and accepting women's desires to work are two backbones of a revolution taking place around the world regarding women delaying and foregoing marriage (Inhorn and Smith-Hefner 2021). In India, it is now near universal that parents wish to educate their daughters at least through grade eight and often much longer, a trend that has increased since the Indian Parliament passed the landmark Right to Education Act in 2009.[3] Further, most girls and women express a desire to work.[4] Indian media stories have publicized the growing trend of urban women over age 30 who are giving careers a priority over marriage (e.g., Ali 2017). At the same time, ambivalence persists in the wider society as to how much education and work are valuable for women; and recent studies report India with one of the lowest women's workforce participation rates in the world.[5] Why?

I suggest that one important answer is tied to the clash in many people's minds between work and marriage for women. The drive for education and/or work wasthe primary reason for not marrying for more than one-third of the women in my study. A good number of these women were not directly opposed to marriage per se, but they realized that marrying would interfere with their aspirations to study and work.[6] Girls and young women, and their mothers, widely report that continuing education and entry or reentry into the labor force after marriage is highly dependent on the uncertain support of a husband and in-laws. Considering global trends, Rebecca Traister suggests that if societies' institutions of marriage do not change to open up more space for married women to work, the result will be that more and more women will abstain from marrying (2016: 238–240).

This chapter explores what happens to Bengali women's gendered identities and life opportunities when they enter the labor market, giving work and/or education a higher priority than marriage, and eventually—due to deliberate choice, becoming "excessively" accomplished for their gender, and/or aging out—no longer finding marriage an option. I also explore the related problem of what I call gendered mismatches of class. If through education and employment a woman achieves a class status much higher than that of her natal family background, she becomes practically unmarriable. In an era of heightened middle-class aspirations, class change can seem achievable for a highly intelligent and industrious individual woman, but can make her marriage near impossible and steer her into a state of class and social limbo with uncertain belonging. Exploring women's aspirations to learn, work, and earn, we can see the overlapping and blurring together of constraint and freedom, exclusion and possibility, as single women build their lives.

EDUCATION AND ITS TRANSFORMATIVE POTENTIAL

Medha's life-story narratives shared with me over seven years reveal many themes, a central one being her drive for education. She described having an "immense thirst for knowledge" and an "extraordinary pull for outside things—first to leave this [natal] village; then to learn about the rest of the world." Her drive for education was the main reason, initially, for her not marrying. She insisted, to her parents when they were alive, and then to her brother, that she *must* continue studying. At one point when her family said it was finally time to stop studying, she screamed and shouted and refused to eat for three days until they relented.

The drive for education was also a salient theme in other single women's narratives, and for more than 20 percent a primary reason for not marrying. The majority in this group were from urban middle-class and elite families, and these unmarried women pursued studies up to the bachelor's, master's, and doctoral levels. Kalyani Majumdar, from a middle-class Kolkata background at age 73, told of how her marriage had been arranged when she was 14. The wedding was to take place the following day, when a member of the groom's family suddenly died. Some proposed postponing the wedding in the face of this inauspicious tragedy, while Kalyani's parents wished it to proceed. Kalyani herself made this unexpected turn of events into an opportunity to resist marrying. She said, "No, let me study more." So, the wedding was called off. Kalyani continued her education through the bachelor of science level, and forged a life and career as a single schoolteacher. Other women conveyed how schooling opened up their worlds, gave them visions of possible life paths, engrossed their inquisitive minds, brought them a sense of pride and confidence, and gave them skills they could use to support themselves economically and socially (see also Chaturvedi and Sahai 2019).

Not all women pursuing education over marriage were from the urban middle and elite classes. Manjuri Karmakar, born in 1952, grew up in a large, poor family in a small town, from a caste group recognized by the West Bengal Government as among the Other Backward Classes.[7] When I met her in her mid-sixties, Manjuri told of being devoted to studying ever since she was a young girl. We met one evening in the small city of Midnapore, several hours from Kolkata, introduced by two professors I knew from a local college who saw Manjuri as a paradigmatic example of a single woman by choice. Manjuri lives in a crowded household of twenty-one members, including three married brothers, her multiple nieces and nephews, and a few grandnieces and grandnephews. Manjuri took us to the small room where she does tutoring, its teal-colored walls lit softly by a kerosene lamp. She pulled out her diary, a ledger where she had recorded all of the schools she had attended, from childhood through to her MSc degree at age 54, and the various teaching jobs she had held, up to her present position at a college. She exuded pride and passion, while dressed simply in a white sari with red border—a traditional symbol for women who serve others in society.

Growing up, Manjuri was the only daughter among four brothers, and she demonstrated at a young age a much greater talent for studying than her brothers. The family was immensely poor. Recognizing her talents, her father took her from school to school to gain admission and a scholarship through the reservation system for Scheduled Castes and Other Backward Classes. Her schoolmasters recognized that she was "such a 'brilliant' girl" and helped her gain money for books. Manjuri would walk more than an hour each way to and from school.

In her life story, Manjuri seemed uninterested in the topic of marriage, never bringing it up on her own. When Medha, who was with us, asked why she had not married, Manjuri replied straightforwardly, "I loved studying too much, and I decided I only wanted to be a teacher, and to sweep in front of my own house," that is, to stay living forever with natal kin in the household of her birth.

She pulled out a paper published by the principal of the college where she now serves as a chemistry laboratory assistant and teacher, reading a passage aloud proudly in English:

> Coming from a poor and illiterate family of a very remote village of Midnapore [District], [Manjuri Karmakar] is a 54-year-old college teacher. Despite tremendous financial and circumstantial problems, she got her MSc degree at the age of 54. She is the only working person [with a regular, salaried job] in her family of 21 members. Her higher education made her able to look after her family and become a respectable person in her family as well as society.[8]

Manjuri added in Bengali, "God has been leading me for my whole life, my whole life."

Across India, expanding opportunities for girls' and women's education are giving many young women more agency over when, whom, and sometimes whether, to marry.[9] Recognizing the value of education for girls and women as the foundation of a strong, progressive society and economy, West Bengal's chief minister, Mamata Banerjee, instituted in 2013 a cash-incentive scheme to keep girls in school longer while delaying marriage. Mamata Banerjee, popularly known as "Didi" (elder sister), is herself known to be unmarried and the first woman to hold the office of chief minister of West Bengal, an office she has held since 2011.[10] Called Kanyashree Prakalpa, Mamata Banerjee's flagship girl-child empowerment scheme offers an annual scholarship of INR 1,000 to girls ages 13 to 18 from economically stressed families if they remain unmarried and in school. This scheme also offers a one-time grant of INR 25,000 (more than US$300, or around the cost of a high-end refrigerator in India) to any young woman from an economically disadvantaged family once she reaches the age of 18 if she has remained unmarried and enrolled in an institution of education or vocational training. The funds go directly into the girl beneficiary's bank account, of which she must be the sole proprietor.[11] As of July 2021, more than 7 million female students had participated in the program.[12] In 2017, the United Nations bestowed its highest award for public service to the West Bengal Government for the Kanyashree project.[13]

Public posters advertising the program are displayed across West Bengal in both English and Bengali, depicting smiling schoolgirls in uniform, often riding cycles, declaring: "I am a Kanyashree Girl. I am Progress," "I am Courage," "I am Determination," "I will read, write, and advance" (figure 1).[14]

Partly because of this scheme and the public dialogue surrounding it, Bengalis in both rural and urban areas are commenting that girls and women these days have more life-path and economic-security options than previously. They can choose marriage *or* education and work, pushing off marriage, at least for a period, while engrossed in their studies.

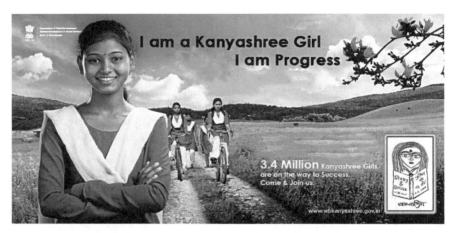

FIGURE 1. I am a Kanyashree Girl. I am Progress. Credit/source: Kanyashree Prakalpa.

"These days, girls are saying, 'I'm going to study. Then I'm going to work. I'm not going to get married now.'" I was chatting with a group of men and women from a mixed-class and -caste neighborhood of a Birbhum District village I had been visiting for thirty years. Learning of my current project on women who do not marry, they wanted to catch me up on the marriage and gender trends they are now witnessing.

"Our daughters are becoming much more aware. They all want to become independent," Chobi, my friend of thirty years, declared. "And these [educated] girls are saying, 'We don't want to marry just any kind of boy.' They are becoming very discriminating."

"Girls these days are going for studies and a career," a married female neighbor of about 50 added animatedly. "If the career doesn't work out, they will then look for another option—marriage. Moreover, after studying, they can get a better husband. So, either way, a girl will at least be able to eat." It was striking to me that this conversation presented marriage as a *second* option for a female life trajectory, and clearly articulated both marriage and education as paths toward economic security.

It is for these reasons that some people in Bengali villages have begun speaking of a perceived shortage of girls available for marriage. "We worry more now about marrying our sons than marrying our daughters!" Chobi exclaimed. "There's a huge 'crisis' in finding girls!" Alice Tilche and Edward Simpson (2018) report similar discourses in rural Gujarat, where women's increase in education has led to their ability to be more choosy about whom they marry, resulting in a marriage squeeze and threats to masculinity for men.

Becoming "Too Educated" for a Woman, and Other Visions of Education and Marriage at Odds with Education's transformative potential, is tied not only to the opening up of possible paths toward economic security and fulfillment, but also more implicitly to socially ambivalent impacts upon female gender itself. For one, not all women immersed in education tell of deliberately choosing never to marry. Instead, for many, "age happened" (*boyesh hoyeche*) gradually as they pursued their studies, or they became "too qualified" to find a suitable match. Aarini, the computer engineer in her forties from an elite Kolkata family, recalled, "I never thought that getting a PhD would mean I would not marry. But time passed, and then I was too old. . . . In the US, nobody would think that a woman past 35 years would be unmarried forever. But here the pressure to marry stops after that age because people think you are old."

In India, people widely say that some education makes a woman more valuable in the marriage market, but that too much education can be a problem in several ways. First, extensive education can lead to a woman becoming too old to marry— if while studying she passes the age (depending on the context) of 25, 28, 30, or 35 without tying the knot. In rural areas, even among families aspiring to reach the salaried, white-collar classes, parents and kin will become quite anxious about her advancing age if a daughter keeps pursuing more and more education without marrying by age 22 or 25. Among cosmopolitan families in Kolkata, the pressure to marry, and the ability to marry, dies down after around age 35, an age cutoff that implicitly connects a woman's marriageability to her reproductive potential.

Second, becoming highly educated can lead to a dearth of eligible grooms and an implicit sense that the woman is no longer conventionally feminine. Recall Medha's statement: "A man must be superior to his wife in all ways, in all ways, except for looks." Author Baichand Patel articulates: "To put it crudely, men generally, and Indian men especially, don't like to marry high achieving women. They become undesirable marriage partners" (2006: xii). Medha commented further: "Because I know so much, no men like me. Everyone thinks that the man should be above the woman. They respect a man for his knowledge, but not a woman."

A joke in China pertaining to "leftover women" unmarried past their twenties resonates with such perspectives: "There are three genders in China: men, women, and women with PhDs" (Fincher 2014: 43)—implying that education transforms femininity so much that PhD-holding women become like an alternative gender. Zachary Howlett further notes how, for women in China, "obtaining an advanced degree—particularly a PhD—can make it exceedingly difficult for them to find a husband. For this reason, people call 'female PhD's' (*nü boshi*) the 'third sex' (*disan xingbie*), a chauvinist label that testifies to the discrimination they face in the marriage market" (2021: 193).[15]

Indeed, it is common for women professors in Indian universities to be single. One distinguished professor in my study commented that at least half the women professors in her large English department were never married.

Some discourses about how a woman's education, professional drive, and age put marriage into jeopardy resonate also in the United States. A June 1986 *Newsweek* cover story, "The Marriage Crunch," opened with the headline, "Too Late for Prince Charming?" The cover was adorned with a graph depicting a precipitous drop in marriage chances for college-educated women after age 30, while the inside story announced that single women over 40 had a better chance of being killed by a terrorist than getting married (Garber 2016; McGinn 2006). Although that infamous line was later retracted as a joke "first hastily written as a funny aside in an internal reporting memo" (Barrett 2006), the piece's core message—"that single women have been, essentially, undermining their romantic goals by focusing on their professional ones"—still "feels true" to many people (Garber 2016).

One also frequently hears in India suggestions or explicit statements that too much education interferes with a woman's docility and adaptability, and her ability to perform household work, making her less attractive as a wife. Taking a morning walk around the lanes of a village I was visiting one bright day in January 2020, I came across a large household of women preparing for their new daughter-in-law to arrive and the major wedding festivities that would ensue. We chatted about the bride—she was reported to be very fair and attractive; she was 14 and had just completed class eight. I asked if she might still continue her education after marriage. The mother-in-law-to-be replied, "No, we don't expect so. Educated girls don't apply themselves to household life," or literally: "Girls who read and write [or study] (*lekha-pora meyera*) don't do household/family life (*shongshar kore na*)."

One evening in a crowded ladies' compartment on a train heading into Kolkata, several of us got to talking about when we would marry our daughters and how much education they are pursuing. My two unmarried daughters at the time were ages 23 and 26; I shared some photos. Another woman's daughters were still unmarried and studying, at ages 22 and 24. She reported that their (male) doctor, however, had recently cautioned that too much studying causes hormonal imbalance in girls. Girls and women are naturally soft and gentle (*norom*), the doctor had said, but too much education ruins that softness, making marriage difficult. When I reported the conversation to Aparna, a single Calcutta University professor, assuming she would agree with me that the doctor's theory was unfounded and sexist, Aparna commented that she had also heard similar cautions about too much studying leading to hormonal imbalance in young women. Aparna believed there to be some scientific basis to the theory.

I am afraid that I did not carefully pursue the underlying logic of this theory with either Aparna or my train companion, and these two women interlocutors seemed themselves a bit uncertain. Just what kind of hormonal imbalance was at stake? And how might marriage—or sex? or childbearing?—cure this imbalance? The theory seemed to resonate with other prevailing doxic ideas—that women naturally and automatically *must* get married—only in this case moving beyond social concerns to tie the marriage imperative directly to a woman's body and health.

Medha later described the history of women's education in West Bengal. In the early twentieth century, those developing British-influenced middle-class *bhadralok* (respectable, gentlemanly) lifestyles began to educate their women so they would make better wives and mothers for educated men and children.[16] "And now women have become *too* educated! There's nothing more to it!" She gave a scornful laugh.

There are also those who believe it inappropriate for daughters to move around too much "outside" (*baire*) to places like school, particularly after reaching puberty.[17] Such ideologies are conveyed in both explicit and implicit ways, and were revealed more in the narratives of older single women recalling attitudes in their youths, signifying some changes in social attitudes. Minu, a never-married woman in her seventies raised in a lower-middle-class family in a semi-urban town, told of how her father had failed to arrange her and her sister's marriages, being too ill and intoxicated. He also prevented Minu and her sister from going to school after they reached puberty, which could have given them an alternative path to economic security.

Minu recalled, "My father would say, 'Why will girls go outside?' Mother tried very hard to send us to school, but she didn't succeed—she could not win. A doctor who came to treat Father for a back tumor even asked, 'Why aren't the girls studying?' 'No, I don't like it,' Father replied. The doctor offered, 'I'll get them admission to a nursing school.' But Father said no." Minu worked as a live-in domestic housekeeper for more than thirty years. She later shared a home with her sister, purchased by her employer when she retired.

The award-winning 2018 documentary short film *Period. End of Sentence* contends with the topic of puberty and schooling for girls (Zehtabchi 2018). Coproducer Melissa Berton, upon winning the Academy Award for Best Documentary (Short Subject), declared in her acceptance speech, "A period should end a sentence—not a girl's education."[18] The film taps into the global tide of growing concern about menstrual equity, which in the United States includes promoting open conversations about menstruation and lobbying against sales taxes on tampons. In the developing world, menstrual equity includes dispelling shame and danger associated with menstruation and allowing menstruating girls and women to access basic menstrual products and go to school (e.g., Sommer et al. 2016). In 2019, I began to see graffiti around Kolkata demanding sanitary napkin vending machines in every school (figure 2).

Further, barriers to education for girls and women in India extend far beyond the practicalities of menstrual hygiene. Menstruation opens up fears about an unmarried daughter's vulnerability to pregnancy and signals in many minds her core domestic role as wife and mother. Despite the Kanyashree Prakalpa education scheme and the importance of education in many of the life-story narratives of the never-married single women in my project, around 40 percent of girls in West Bengal continue to be married before age 18, above even the high national average of 26.8 percent.[19]

National reports on girls and education also show a drop-off in the numbers of girls in school after grade eight,[20] and researchers wonder why. Some speculate

FIGURE 2. We demand sanitary napkin vending machines in every school. Photo by author.

that it is not menstrual hygiene but housework demands that keep girls above age 14 out of school (e.g., *Time* 2019). But I feel that both arguments miss the point of sexuality—the pervasiveness of social-cultural ideologies that girls and young women after puberty are sexually vulnerable to being assaulted, mixing inappropriately with boys out of wedlock, getting pregnant, and threatening their own and their family's respectability. Such attitudes are also evident in the "anti-Romeo" squads active since 2017 in the northern Indian state of Uttar Pradesh, ostensibly to protect women from sexual harassment in public spaces. Women's rights activists have criticized the squads, which involve both plainclothes and uniformed police officers and police-sanctioned vigilante groups, for their heavy-handed tactics and moral policing, as they target and publicly shame young couples in parks, colleges, and markets.

Of course, many girls and women across India continue their education through secondary school, college, and advanced degrees. However, through my years of fieldwork in West Bengal, I have found that especially in rural communities, attitudes about female sexuality are a powerful reason so many girls stop their education and marry before age 18.

Moreover, many women, both married and single, criticize Bengali society for continuing to emphasize the value of marriage over education for girls and young women. Chobi related, "When giving a daughter's marriage, the whole extended family will help out. They will all pitch in to offer money. They will say, 'Don't worry. We are here.'" We had just been discussing the tremendous costs of a daughter's wedding—including the wedding feast and all the required gifts and dowry items, such as gold jewelry, brass pots, stainless steel dishware, expensive saris, a bedframe and wardrobe, often a motor scooter or refrigerator or television, and sometimes cash.[21]

"But," Chobi exclaimed, "if a girl wants to *study*, no one will help! Studying requires plenty of expense, too, but no one will come forward to help!" Further, I gleaned through numerous conversations that for many parents, the primary value in educating daughters was to enhance their chances of marrying well rather than to achieve education for its own sake (see Chaturvedi and Sahai 2019: 81).

We see through these conversations and narratives both the persistent marriage imperative and education's ambivalent transformative potential. Education can open up worlds of information and possible lifeways that would have otherwise been out of reach. Advanced education can also transform gender in ways that make the highly educated woman at odds with conventional notions of femininity and wifehood. For women who reject such models of femininity for themselves, the value of education is clear; but some would prefer to pursue the world-expanding path of education without necessarily precluding marriage. Such stories of the gender of education highlight once again the overlapping nature of possibility and exclusion, exclusion and possibility.

EMPOWERMENT THROUGH WORK

Nine women in my study conveyed their commitment to work as a central reason for not marrying. Ena-di, from an urban elite family at age 92, declared, "If you get married, you have to be subservient to somebody, somebody's slave. I was in a job that involved frequent transfers—Delhi, Kolkata, Bangalore, then back to Delhi. I could not have held that kind of job as a married woman." She was born in 1923 to a well-established moneyed family in East Bengal, and she completed a social sciences master's degree at the London School of Economics before returning to India to work for the Government of India in the Ministry of Industry. Her father, a physics professor, reportedly did not mind that his daughter remained unmarried while pursuing her career; and it was Ena-di, not her brothers, who lived with and cared for her father in his last years.

Polly, also from an urban elite family, described herself as "single by choice" and recalled that her feminist-oriented parents never pressured her to marry but rather emphasized her career. "They always expected that I would have a brilliant career, and work very hard to achieve it."

In her mid-forties, Polly reflects in her life-story narrative: "I was never tied down by most gender stereotypes. . . . I had a grandmother who tried to teach me to cook and be domesticated, but my parents thought that a complete waste of time. My mother was supportive of my having a demanding career, but she was not one with a demanding career herself."

Earlier Polly had described her mother as "absolutely brilliant, but also very domesticated. Until this day, I'm amazed that she could be happy." Perhaps Polly's mother supported her daughter's career path in part as an outlet for her own ambitions.

Polly continued, "Initially, we lived with a joint family. Ma would call me, lock me in a room with her, and have me study. This would irritate my [paternal] grandmother. 'Do you think your daughter will be a judge? What will happen when she marries and doesn't know how to cook or do any housework?' But secretly Ma went on training me the way she wanted."

Then later, as her mother was expecting a second child and in order to give Polly the best chance to succeed, Polly was sent at around age 10 to England with one of her aunts. "So, from the very beginning, I had a very, very cosmopolitan upbringing," Polly recalled. She came back to India for college, then to the United States for a PhD, and then back to India, where she landed a highly competitive job as a professor at a leading university.

Polly continued: "At that time, for a little while, I did experience some pressure from my family to get married, especially from my grandmother. But then I got cancer when I was about 28, and after that, nobody cared anymore." In West Bengal, it is common for prospective brides with serious illness, infertility, or disability to be considered unsuitable for marriage, even if the affliction has healed (chapter 1; N. Ghosh 2016, 2018). In Polly's case, the cancer and its treatments did not impact her fertility, and she regained perfect health. However, she recalled that "Ma would say, 'My daughter will do exactly what she wants.' She had thought the cancer was psychosomatic, from the pressure my grandmother and others were putting on me to marry." So, the question of marriage was dropped. Polly reflected:

> Standing where I am standing now today, I'd say that I've had quite a good life. I am one of those lucky people who can do the things I like to do. I eat when I want to eat. I can write a paper until 3 a.m. in the morning, and then get up at 7 again to work on it some more. . . . I learned to really appreciate life after having cancer. . . . Every moment I try to be productive. . . . I have relationships with men sometimes, and lots of good friends—girlfriends from my youth and graduate school. I'm very sociable. I have parties, and I love to cook. . . . I can be alone, but very seldom feel lonely. . . . I take life as it is.

Polly's cosmopolitan milieu gave her social opportunities and sexual freedoms not available to most women.

Not all who choose a path of work over marriage, however, are from the well-educated classes, like Ena-di and Polly. Subhagi, a Scheduled Caste day laborer from the countryside in her mid-fifties, deliberately chose to work rather than marry, so that she could continue living with and supporting her natal kin through her labor and love. Subhagi's exuberant glowing manner makes it hard not to feel convinced that she is telling the truth that she purposefully chose not to marry. "*This* is my fulfillment—that we are all together and having enough to eat," Subhagi declared.

Subhagi was born into an impoverished family, members of the Lohar caste, one of West Bengal's officially designated Scheduled Caste groups of historically disadvantaged people formerly known by caste Hindus as "untouchable." She was born around 1960 in the middle of four sisters and one younger brother, and while the children were all still very young, both parents began to ail, her father with one hand paralyzed and her mother with cancer. They struggled to have enough to eat. Subhagi worked hard to support the family—through caring for the village school-master's young children, washing dishes and clothes in other people's homes, catching and selling fish, and working as a day laborer planting and cutting rice in the fields. "I was the one who worked so that they could eat," Subhagi recalled with pride.

Subhagi herself took the steps to arrange her sisters' marriages, with her uncle's help, having horoscopes made for each of them and for herself, too. "Everyone came to look!" she recalled. "And my sisters were very attractive and fair looking (*pariskar dekhte*). I would say, 'Whoever you like, you can choose and take away.'"

"And did some also like you?"

"Yes, they did!"

"It's not like no one liked you?"

"No, no, no, no!" Subhagi exclaimed, while laughing. "But if I were to go, then my sisters and brother would have to go from house to house begging. *I* was the one feeding them by working! If I were to go away, what would people say?"

"I would tell [the men]," Subhagi recalled, "Please forgive me, brother. Please forgive me," pressing her palms together in a prayer gesture. "For these children, there is no one else to look after them. . . . I would say, 'Even if you take me without dowry, I will not go. I will not go.'"

"So, men did want to marry me," Subhagi affirmed, "but if I went, who would look after my siblings and parents?"

Over her years while young and unmarried, Subhagi took care to not dress up at all, "so that people [i.e., men] would not do anything to me, 'touch' me or anything."

"Someone might have fallen for her!" women neighbors listening in exclaimed. "People might have looked at her, and something might have happened!"

"Still today, the whole village knows!" Subhagi laughed with pride. "Still today, the entire village knows what I did for my siblings.

"With all this, I am happy, I am very happy. *This* is where I was born!" Subhagi exclaimed, expressing the privilege that men have to remain belonging to just one family and place within conventional virilocal residence patterns. "Since I was young we were all together here, so I am so attached to this place. I have never left this place since I was young—from here I have not gone *anywhere* else at all!" she said proudly.

"And here there are grandchildren now," Subhagi added, hugging her brother's son's daughter to her chest as she spoke.

By this time, Subhagi's parents had died and her sisters married off to other villages. Subhagi lives in her natal home with her brother and his family—his wife, son, son's wife, and grandchildren. They all do what they can to contribute to the family's sustenance. Subhagi is proud to still work hard so they all can eat, describing serving her family as a moral-spiritual practice. She avowed, "Serving (*seva kora*) the people in this family, the happiness I receive is incomparable. Compared to serving a husband, and compared even to serving God, then serving one's family is the best!"

Each of these stories, from Ena-di, Polly, and Subhagi, reveal the ways work can serve as an important instrument for economic empowerment for women and offer a means of livelihood and fulfillment beyond marriage. Medha also often speaks of how much her job and its income mean to her. Her financial independence gives her an economic security that she still never fails to appreciate after growing up so poor, often without enough to eat. Her earnings also enable her to pursue pleasures and hobbies that she alone chooses, such as buying exotic organic foods, searching for lovely folk art to decorate her two flats (the rented one near her college and the one she owns in Kolkata), taking meditation-retreat vacations in the mountains, and even traveling abroad.

Subhagi's story also reveals the ways a woman's passion for work does not necessarily represent a shift in gender norms toward self-actualization and away from a primary focus on familial responsibility. Subhagi was proud of her work but narrated her central motive as working in order to serve (natal) kin, not to develop her own separate aspirations. Relatedly, many working women express feeling uncomfortable openly spending their earnings on themselves and their own pleasures, pressed by their social communities to direct their income toward kin, a theme explored further in chapters 3 and 7.

GENDERED MISMATCHES OF CLASS

Single women's narratives of education and work also illuminate how strongly social class is tied to forms of belonging, and how difficult it is to forge intimate social ties across class boundaries.[22] Leela Fernandes observes how, as dual-income couples become more common in urban settings, employed married women help propel aspiring marital families into the middle classes (2006: 162).[23] Little scholarship has been conducted, however, on what happens to her marriage prospects if an unmarried woman—through education and/or employment—achieves an individual class status very different from that of her natal kin.

Marriage takes place not only between individuals but between families. If through education or employment, a single woman achieves a class status much higher than that of her family background, she becomes practically unmarriable. I came to realize this fact most vividly through single women who had achieved dramatic class mobility as individuals, like Medha, who put it clearly: "I'm a professor now with a good salary—but I don't belong to that kind of family that another professor could marry me. . . . I also can't marry a village boy."

Such instances of upward class mobility are less problematic for men. Since a man (and his family) is meant to be ranked higher than a bride (and her family), a man who has climbed social classes can offer a hypergamous marriage to a woman from his natal class, helping then to raise her status through marriage, while together producing higher-class children. Technically, if someone like Medha could find a bridegroom with precisely the same class assemblage—a man from an impoverished village background who had achieved a PhD and a prestigious white-collar job—this could work as a match. But such a man is hard to find and would have as potential marriage partners any number of less-educated women from his village background who would be marrying up in a normal pattern. We see how to rise in socioeconomic status as a woman both outside of marriage and outside of the natal family propels a woman into class and family limbo, essentially foreclosing the possibility of marriage.

Nayani's Story of Class and Family Limbo

A vivacious woman in her mid-thirties getting to be past marriable age, Nayani was born into a village home struggling to feed its several daughters. In order to eat while earning money for her family, Nayani was given by her parents at age seven or eight to an elite Kolkata household to work as their live-in domestic servant. Recall that Nayani was our host at the Valentine's Day lunch described at the opening of chapter 1.

A few years after this lunch, Nayani invited me over to see her new one-bedroom flat. She was thrilled to have been able to purchase a home of her own, made possible by a generous gift from a never-married woman Nayani had befriended in an old age home—a home where Nayani's former employer, an elderly unmarried "aunt" (*pishi*), had also lived.

Nayani's three-by-three-meter bedroom-cum-sitting room was lovingly arranged with a single bed covered by a lavender cotton spread, a stuffed navy-blue armchair adorned with hand-stitched decorative pillows, a small lace-doily-covered table for eating, and a cabinet for clothing upon which sat a simple television. In the corner next to the armchair was a second small cabinet topped by three shelves upon which Nayani's toiletries and *puja* (worship) items were arranged, including framed photos of the Hindu deities Durga and Krishna with Radha, and a lime-green Buddha statue. Warm afternoon sun rays shone through the open door leading to a small verandah, decked out with flowering plants and overlooking the rooftops of neighboring flats hung with drying saris, in the densely populated working-class neighborhood of Ganguly Bagan in south Kolkata.

After we enjoyed generous cups of tea with homemade *papri chaat*, the popular street snack made of diced potatoes, chickpeas, crispy wheat chips, and tangy tamarind chutney, Nayani launched into her life story. My research assistant Anindita was also present, and the two hit it off, being of similar age and outgoing temperament. Anindita had also recently completed a PhD dissertation on the relationship between domestic workers and their employers (A. Chatterjee 2019). Nayani's life-story narrative unfolded as follows:

"I never imagined that I would not marry. But, you see, my family condition was not good, and so I thought I should do something for them." This was the first reason why Nayani had continued to work even after reaching marrying age, to be able to continue sending money to her family and help with the cost of her sisters' weddings.

"What happened to me was that I came to Kolkata at a very early age," Nayani explained. "I was studying in class three. I stood first in class three, in fact, and got promoted to class four. It was at that time that I came over [to Kolkata]."

Anindita interrupted, "Wow, it must be noted that you were very intelligent!"

"Well, that is something I now understand," Nayani replied. "I was good in my studies. I stood first in mathematics. But there was no one to guide me with my studies. I mean, what a shame, if I had the opportunity now. But at that time, I never realized the importance of education. I was a kid then, maybe just seven years old. I was living in a village, and in villages, people do not focus much on education. . . . Hence, I never realized the importance of education at all." She spoke as if she held herself responsible for having had to stop schooling as a young girl.

"It was right at that young age that my parents placed me in Kolkata in the care of my aunts [employers] and left." As is common in Bengali servant-employer relationships, Nayani used kinship terms to address the members of the family for whom she would work for the next twenty years. Nayani's experiences call to mind Ananya Roy's work on "distress migration" practiced by rural-to-urban women laborers in Kolkata. Roy writes of the "working daughters" of landless and destitute rural families "who are sent off to work as fulltime maids in Calcutta, rarely returning to the village during their years of wage-earning work" (2003: 40, 246). In Nayani's employer's large, three-story home in the affluent Ballygunge neighborhood of Kolkata, there was Pishi (literally, father's sister, an unmarried older woman), Pishi's younger brother Meshomoshay (mother's sister's husband) and his wife Boro Mashi (mother's elder sister), their only daughter, Didi (older sister), and two grandmothers, Thakurma (paternal grandmother) and Dida (maternal grandmother).

Nayani continued: "I later heard that during my childhood there, I would just sit on the verandah and cry. I mean, I had come away from my home at a very young age. What could I do?"

"To an unknown place," Anindita murmured.

"Oh, surely," I added.

Nayani continued: "There's another point you must understand. In our home [in the village], my father was such a type that he did not allow us to visit anyone else's house—I mean, not even relatives' houses. Once it so happened that I went to a relative's house. One of my older sisters was married already, and I visited her in-laws' house. Well, on that day, you see, since I had never visited them before, they did not give me any opportunity to return home." They insisted she spend the night. Nayani recalled:

> At that time, there was no telephone communication. So Baba [father] could not sleep the whole night. When I finally got home the next morning, Baba asked angrily, 'Were you kept chained there?' As a result, what happened was that during that whole childhood period, I had no habit of going anywhere at all. So, when I was brought and left there [in Kolkata], I could not understand what was happening. It seems that I would cry so hard that mucous would pour from my nose, sitting out there on the verandah.

Since she had so little connection with her own family after that point, Nayani gradually tried to believe that the members of her "aunt" and "uncle's" family were her own. She related:

> Not all people are able to accept an [unknown] person as their own. . . . When I began understanding things better, I did come to know them as my own. I did not have much attachment with my parents. There was practically no meeting with them. Hence, I came to look upon Meshomoshay [uncle] as like my father, you could say, and a friend, and Boro Mashi [senior aunt] as like my mother. . . . Gradually as I grew up, I became like their daughter. Even now, until today, their relatives give me that respect as the younger daughter of Meshomoshay.

Here Anindita interrupted: "But there is a distinction between 'like a daughter' (meyer moto) and 'daughter' (meye)." Despite frequent discourse in elite Bengali households that domestic servant and their employers are "like family" to one another, unequal power relations lie at the heart (A. Chatterjee 2019; Ray and Qayum 2009).

"True, there is a difference," Nayani agreed, laughing slightly. "I am getting to that."

Nayani described how close she became during the early years with her employer family's daughter, whom Nayani knew as Didi (older sister).

I was there for many, many years. I was so friendly with Didi that during the time of [Durga] Puja [the largest Bengali festival of the year], we would go out together. Didi held no job then, so she had no cash at hand, but whatever pocket money Mesho-moshay gave her, the two of us would share. On one such occasion during Puja, we went out together, and after putting together every last coin, we had just enough for one plate of mutton and two luchis [puffy fried breads]. And the mutton itself was just one piece.

So I said to Didi [using the intimate second person pronoun, *tui*, reserved for close childhood friends and young children], "You eat."

Didi said, "No," and the two of us enjoyed together in this manner, sharing from the same plate. It was like that. . . .

In addition, Didi was extremely stubborn and short-tempered. Whenever she had an impulse that she needed a particular thing, then she absolutely must have it and would not listen to any reason. If she did not get it, then it meant that she would stop eating for two days. It was my job to go to her. I had to feed her with my own hands, manage her. I had to do that. I mean, she was of that temperament. After all, she is the only daughter.

She being the only daughter, her father and mother wanted to pour everything on to her—including, they would have her learn painting, dancing, singing, playing the sitar—they did all that for her.

This was of course in stark contrast to how Didi's parents nurtured their domestic servant Nayani, whom they never sent to school, a fact that Meshomoshay only much later regretted, when he was an old man. Nayani continued,

However, whatever Didi no longer wished to study, she would absolutely refuse to go further. I mean, she did not complete any of these lessons. For instance, on one occasion, a teacher came to teach her singing, and on that day, Didi decided that she no longer wished to learn singing. So, she went inside the bathroom and locked herself in. She was like that.

Then her wedding took place, and she went away to Delhi. Even that wedding was an enormously huge affair. Her mother was not too happy, as Didi had chosen her own husband [rather than having an arranged marriage]. Anyway, she left for Delhi. . . .

Then, whenever Didi would quarrel with her husband, she would come back from Delhi to stay with us. Sometimes she would even leave her daughter with me and return to Delhi. Her daughter would stay only with me. My intimacy with Didi was so intense that whenever she would come from Delhi, she would always insist that she sleep in my room. There was just a single bed in my room. Well, it is under-standable that prior to one's wedding, we two slept together which is otherwise no problem. Now that she had a daughter, the three of us would still sleep together in the one single bed.

Around this time, Nayani also began providing a lot of care for the older members of the family. "Boro Mashi suffered for a long time from a bad kidney. She had to undergo dialysis, and all sorts of tests. The entire responsibility was on me. . . .

I used to get so involved with everyone. . . . When I first arrived, there were even more elderly people there—both Thakurma [paternal grandmother] and Dida [maternal grandmother]. Later they both died. But initially they all were there. What happened is that after my arrival [as a young girl], the responsibility for these two [grandmothers] also fell on me."

As Nayani reached marriageable age, she realized how much she could help both families if she continued to work and earn rather than marrying. Her natal family needed her income, with two sisters still waiting to marry. Nayani was also busy looking after the three old people remaining in her employer's house—Boro Mashi, Meshomoshay, and Pishi. "The responsibility for maintaining the entire household practically fell on me," Nayani recalled.

Anindita interrupted to ask, "While you were helping to arrange your sisters' marriages, you never thought about your own wedding?"

"No. No, I did not think about my own self then," Nayani responded. "I had responsibility for two families."

The yearlong dialysis expenses for Boro Mashi had depleted most of the money Meshomoshay and Mashi had saved for their old age. Didi also continued to spend her parents' money lavishly. Nayani recalled in a low-spirited voice, "During those days, the pension income was also quite little, and with even less savings, I had to maintain and manage the family accordingly," doing the household's marketing carefully and minding the household bills.

At the same time, the family's elder members were becoming more and more dependent on Nayani's care. "Meshomoshay would not let me go. When he was alive, I would look after him and take him to the doctor." It was around this time that Meshomoshay began to voice his regret that he had never sent Nayani to school or "really treated me as a true daughter." "He began to feel that he should have given me at least a little education," Nayani related.

Meshomoshay's unmarried sister, Pishi, also depended on Nayani:

With Pishi, she at first was very independent. She was unmarried and ate in her own room downstairs, and would go out with friends. In the early days, she would get a little mad at me, but then we began to get close. . . . Then when she grew older, she developed a huge fear—"If Nayani gets a different job, who will look after me?" . . . She became very dependent on me. I even tried to get her counseling. And if anyone would bring up the matter of my marriage, Pishi would get very angry with them.

This kind of co-opting of poor women's domestic-labor work to undertake the social reproduction of rich families is depressingly common, underwritten by ideologies of naturalized social class differences—ideologies and arrangements I will continue to highlight over the following chapters.

Gradually—she is not sure how it happened—Nayani began to hear talk that someone put into Didi's mind that Meshomoshay might hand over all his property in his will to Nayani and not Didi. "The reason was that there were constant conflicts between Meshomoshay and Didi. . . . As a result, someone must have put this idea into her mind. . . . Otherwise, you see, until then I never had any difference of opinion with her!" Suddenly Didi stopped talking to Nayani and began to harass her and try to spoil her reputation.

This is when Nayani made the painful decision that she must move out of the Ballygunge household where she had lived for twenty years and which she had come to think of as her own.

By that time, Nayani was also earning a very modest wage of 1,000 rupees, or about US$13.50 per month, working part time for the human rights organization, Sachetana, where Nayani met and learned from many eminent feminists, gained clerical office skills, learned to sew, and "experienced the joy of education." Nayani's job with Sachetana was to interview other female domestic workers about their working conditions and recruit them for education.

Nayani's elder brother was renting a small one-room shack in a slum in Kolkata, and Nayani joined him there. But the shack was not well built, and the neighborhood was unsafe. "It was very difficult to adjust living elsewhere," Nayani recalled. "I had grown up in one kind of environment, and I could not get used to this new environment—dirty, unhygienic, crowded. I felt great unease, and I began to feel sick. My appearance deteriorated. . . . It's OK if I eat or don't eat, but I want to live in a good environment."

While trying to manage on her own, Nayani was still often called back to the Ballygunge home to care for Meshomoshay and Pishi. Boro Mashi by then had passed away.

Nayani described the day Meshomoshay died: "I wasn't talking with Didi then—very little. The day that Meshomoshay died, I took him by rickshaw to the hospital. I can still recall how his face was swollen, and he could not speak properly. He lay on my shoulder, and he reported that since yesterday, he was not feeling well, 'but what did your Didi say, do you know?—That she did not have time.'

"She did not have time," Nayani repeated in a low, pained voice. "When we got to the hospital, I did not have the kind of money at hand that I could use to admit him. The doctors also did not even say to admit him. As we were returning home and going up the stairs, Meshomoshay collapsed. I cannot forget the scene. He could not go any further, and I was not able to carry him. I was calling and calling for Didi, but she was not coming to help. *Bas* [no more]. Right there was his end. This was a terrible experience for me.

"That was my last experience in that house," Nayani said.

Pishi, Meshomashay's unmarried sister, had become the only remaining member of the once-large household, along with Didi, who lived there on and off. Pishi continued to phone Nayani to ask her to visit. Nayani refused to enter the house again but would meet Pishi outside at a local tea stall. Pishi would tell of how so many things—necklaces and money—were being stolen from the house now that Nayani no longer worked there.

Nayani could see that Pishi was getting sick from not being looked after properly. So Nayani explored all the different old age homes springing up around Kolkata and settled on the one she liked best, arranging for Pishi to move in. Pishi's pension was enough to cover the fees. At first Pishi was angry, but she came to realize that at home she was not getting her meals at the right time or adequate care, so she agreed to move into the old age home. Nayani continued to visit her once or twice per week until Pishi also passed away a few years later.

Nayani recollected her feelings about the "Ballygunge matter." "I received immense pain, when all the tensions erupted and I decided to move out. I had felt that they were my own." Nayani paused. "But now I'm thinking that it is good that that all happened, and that I left that home. If I had stayed with them wrapped up in their lives, I would not have realized that they were not truly my own. Now I have established my own life and independence."

Upon coming down from the roof carrying her sun-dried laundry, Nayani added, "Another thing: After you get married, you can't do anything for your own family. That is another problem with marrying. . . . If I were to earn after marriage, the money would have to go to my in-laws' household (*shoshur bari*). If I don't marry, I have the freedom to work and earn for myself and my own family."

In Bengali kinship systems, as noted above, a woman after marriage is part of her husband's family and only tenuously related to her natal kin, a theme I explore much further in chapter 3. It is difficult to know in advance whether a husband and in-laws will allow their wife/daughter-in-law to continue working and control her own income.

Nayani's new friend at the old age home was able to give Nayani money to buy an apartment precisely because this friend herself had never married, while earning and controlling her own income through a steady career. With no children of her own to pass on wealth to, she felt very happy to help Nayani buy a place of her own.

Nayani urged us to have second cups of tea with biscuits, while reflecting on her situation. She enjoyed being able to work and earn for herself and her natal family, but added, "Still, since I am a single woman, people can say bad things. Whether in cities or villages, I have to face all those sorts of issues."

Nayani, like Medha, was also contending with a complicated social class assemblage within her one self. Living with the elite Ballygunge Kolkata family for twenty years, Nayani had learned to speak the most polished, eloquent Bengali, cook high-class Bengali cuisine, and live in a posh environment, with running water, polished floors, and Western-style furniture. Nayani described the first time she rode Kolkata public transportation after leaving the Ballygunge home, climbing onto a crowded train where her ears filled with so much screaming that she had to descend to recover and breathe for a few moments before re-alighting. She had always ridden in her employer's private cars. She felt extreme unease in her brother's "dirty, unhygienic, crowded" rented shack in an "unsafe neighborhood." She only feels comfortable living in a "good environment" (*bhalo poribesh*).

Nayani's habitus was of a high-class girl, yet her background in society's eyes was that of a poor villager and slum dweller. A concept developed and made famous by Pierre Bourdieu, with roots in earlier work by Marcel Mauss, habitus may be understood as culture and social class anchored in the body—the totality of learned and ingrained habits, beliefs, skills, dispositions, styles, and tastes, including aesthetic distinctions between the respectable and vulgar, "good" and "bad" environments.[24] These distinctions and habits are embedded in the body and sense of self through daily practice and upbringing, and are at the foundation of the ways persons classify themselves and others. A common sense of taste, Bourdieu writes, "unites all those who are the product of similar conditions while distinguishing them from all others" (1987: 56). With Nayani's incongruous habitus and mismatched class assemblage within her one person, she could marry into neither a village nor an elite city family.

Nayani's friend Nita had explained Nayani's situation of class mismatch at our Valentine's Day lunch: "There's a problem Nayani faces. The people in her village get married to others from the same village, but since she has lived in the city, Kolkata, most of her life, her ways of thinking are quite modern (*adhunik*). She cannot get along with the ways of life of the villagers. She cannot marry and live with a guy from a village." Likewise, no boy from an elite city family would find Nayani herself a suitable match.

Nayani's mismatched class assemblage not only impedes her marriage chances; it also pushes her into a state of family and kinship limbo. Nayani painfully came to realize that although she was "like" a daughter within Meshomoshay's household, she was never their "true daughter." The distinction between Nayani—a domestic servant who becomes like a daughter, and Didi, the pampered real daughter—is a focal theme in Nayani's life-story narrative. Didi received all of the money, education, and privileges, although Nayani was the one who gave the most love and care. We see poignantly how the rich are able to incorporate non-kin to supplement their own possibilities for social reproduction, and how gender, class, and marital status work together as vectors propelling an uneven distribution of care—themes explored further in chapter 3.

And, by residing in the elite Kolkata household for so many years, Nayani loses her relationship with her own blood family. She tells of almost never seeing her parents again after she is dropped off in Kolkata at the tender age of seven, and how she is called to the village of her birth now only when they need money. After Nita had explained Nayani's inability to marry a village boy due to her "modern" city upbringing, Nayani commented: "My only family and I also do not 'match.'"

Nayani related how she brought her mother once to Kolkata to see her newly purchased apartment, but that the "class factor" made her mother uncomfortable with the other people in the neighborhood, and her mother had no idea how to use household appliances like a gas stove. Even though Nayani showed her how to turn the gas flame on and off while going so far as to make guiding marks on the stove switch, Nayani came home once to find a strong gas odor in the kitchen. "Can't you smell that?" she scolded her mother. "How dangerous!"

"I have no real *bhab* [intimacy, like-mindedness, relationship] with Ma. I mean, I have never freely talked with my mother, ever. I have been here away from such a young age."

For those like Nayani and Medha—with a mismatched class status making marriage unfeasible and family relations tenuous—what about the possibility of forging ties with non-kin? The answer is that few extra-family options exist for intimate sociality and co-residence. Keen to find other women she might share a flat with in Kolkata, Medha eagerly accompanied me on research appointments to meet other single women who might become friends or housemates. But nothing worked out: some were happy living with their natal kin; most found the notion of sharing a private home with non-kin quite unfamiliar; and none had precisely the same class background—an obstacle, it turns out, to co-residence and intimate friendships as well as marriage.[25]

CONCLUSION

New possibilities for education and work are on many women's doorsteps. Each of the women featured in this chapter pursued work or education as a desired path toward economic security and a prideful sense of self-worth. Several of these women were delighted to have used education and work as a means to escape marrying. Yet, other narratives underscore the gender inequality built into conventional marriage systems, in which a woman who becomes "too" educated in society's eyes is taken out of marriageability, whether she chose to be unmarried or not. Further, the stories of Medha and Nayani highlight the ways naturalized hierarchies of gender and class interpenetrate, making marriage near impossible for a high-achieving individual woman who rises, unmarried, far above her natal class background, while fostering a shaky sense of social belonging. This harkens back to the idea of using queer studies as a lens because of how single women who work rather than marry are so unique in their positionality, as queered subjects in a queered situation vis-à-vis normative systems of gender, kinship, marriage, and social belonging.

We see how aspirations to learn and work can both expand and contract women's life-course possibilities in complicated and intertwined ways. This leaves some of my interlocutors arguing that what they want most now is a society that more fully and unambiguously recognizes the value of education and work for women, without propelling them into social limbo.

A Daughter's and Sister's Care

Medha and I sat on the broad steps of the Dakshinapan Shopping Center in south Kolkata, a faint evening breeze rustling our hair and scattering dust particles across my notebook. We were enjoying small plastic cups of lemon tea, reluctant to part ways after a day of fieldwork together. Set back from the bustling street, the shopping center's wide steps made a pleasant meeting place for other small groups of friends and young lovers.

"You know, I haven't hardly visited my natal village since we went there together last year," Medha commented. Dada, Medha's older brother, and Boudi, her brother's wife, were the only two who lived now in the place of her birth, her father's home. An unmarried Bengali girl or woman ordinarily speaks of her natal home as her "father's house" (*babar bari*). Once she is married, the name changes to *baper bari*—also translatable as "father's house," but with a modified meaning—a married woman's father's house, which is no longer the girl's or woman's "own." Since Medha had never married, she appropriately still called her natal home her father's home, *babar bari*.

"But they don't want to see me—they won't even feed me when I visit." Medha was hurt when the last time she did visit, she overheard her sister-in-law complaining to her husband, "Does she think this is a hotel?"—criticizing Medha for showing up and expecting someone to cook for her.

"I am absolutely a farmer's daughter," Medha declared. "My mother sold vegetables on the footpath. She was 'illiterate,' 'pure illiterate'! *Now* my family has money, education, status, jobs—due to me! Due to me!" As described in chapter 2, Medha's professor salary had helped fund the education of her three nephews and a lovely two-story home for the family, with electricity and indoor plumbing supplied by a large water tank on a spacious roof deck.

"This is another big reason I did not marry, you must know," Medha continued. "My parents, and even more so Dada and Boudi, wanted my salary. An Indian professor has a very good salary. If I married, the salary would go to my husband, his family, and our children. So, they did not try at all [to arrange my marriage]. They even opposed it and interfered."

Medha and I had made the trip to her natal village the year before, traveling by Medha's car, driven by a young man from her village whom she hired occasionally as her driver. I had sat with Dada, Boudi, and Medha on their front verandah as we talked about the past.

Medha's parents had given birth to thirteen children, but only three survived— the oldest sister, now married, then Dada (older brother), and finally Medha, who came much later, after ten miscarriages and infant deaths. "Before, all babies were delivered at home," Dada explained. "We didn't even have one rupee for medicine. Right at home! Sometimes babies died, and sometimes the mothers even died. We would put the babies on the ground surrounded by poison powder to keep the ants and bugs away."

"My oldest son was also born like that," Boudi added.

Boudi had married into the family when she was just 13 and Medha was 6. "How hard I worked to raise the kids and this sister-in-law (*nonod*) here," Boudi said, referring to Medha. "I had to raise the kids, do all the household work, and cook." Her mother-in-law had been too busy laboring in the fields to be able to take care of the household chores.

"Sometimes we couldn't even eat because we were so poor," Dada recalled. "We would eat puffed rice soaked with water."

Nonetheless, Medha and Dada had both been very engrossed with studying while growing up. Their father loved the idea of education. Dada was the first boy in the village from an "ordinary home, not a zamindari [landowning] house" to graduate from high school. Dada was so proud to have landed a job as a school-teacher with a salary and pension. Medha was the first girl in the whole village from any family to graduate from class ten.

Boudi recalled, "When our sons got a little older, Medha continued to do all her studying, and then she got a job. Because of Medha's job, she helped a lot raising and educating the children. First one son got a job, then the next son, and then the next. They all have jobs now, and so do two of our daughters-in-law."

Dada reflected, "In my kind of house, with my kind of background, the idea that my sons would get jobs [*chakri*, referring to a "real" job with a regular good salary, such as in a company or for the government]—that idea would never have entered my head! I could never have even imagined it!"

"Now we also own two *bighas* [one-half acre] of land. We grow rice and pea-nuts," Boudi added with pride.

"But back then," when Medha was little and Boudi was newly married, Boudi recalled, "I didn't even have a blouse or petticoat to wear under my sari, we were so poor." Ordinarily, saris are worn over a blouse and petticoat rather than tied over a bare body. The absence of these two essential items shows the direness of the family's economic situation. "I was only worried thinking about how we would manage to educate our sons."

"Before, the lower classes like us could not even walk with shoes on by the zamindar's house, or it would be a disrespect," Dada recalled.[1]

Medha turned to me and said in English, "Write that down! Before the lower classes couldn't even walk with *shoes* on before the zamindar!"

Dada turned to say softly and fondly to Boudi, tapping her shoulder, "How poor we were. What a transformation."

He pointed to the driver Medha had hired, who was now washing her car at the edge of their property, and said to me, "The boy who drove you—that driver boy's grandfather is the zamindar. My grandmother used to be their maid. We could not even wear sandals while walking in front of their house. And now he is driving our (*amader*) car!" He used the first-person plural possessive—ours—to refer to the car which Medha had purchased. "Imagine that!"

"We tried to get Medha married," Boudi stated (in an attempt, I felt, to uphold before me their reputation and sense of decency). "With one boy, but it turns out he wasn't good. Then she got a job." Boudi paused. The topics of marriage and class mobility were not unconnected here, as both income and marrying contribute to a respectable status. "Maybe it's just her fate," Boudi continued. "The older sister was married, and this one [Medha] is unmarried. *Jai hok* [so it goes]," Boudi uttered, reconciled.

We had a nice visit. I spent two nights, explored the village, enjoyed Boudi's cooking, and admired their beautiful, high-ceilinged home, adorned with wood doors and trim, ceiling fans, indoor plumbing, and a bathroom. The front verandah looks out to a pleasant hammock hanging between two trees and a pond where Dada fishes. The wooden shutters at the home's back open to expansive views of vibrant green rice fields.

Several months later, when Medha needed an emergency operation to have her uterus removed, however, no one came to help her. This deeply pained Medha and made her feel terribly insecure, cut off from affective kinship ties. She feels that Dada and Boudi, and now her nephews, want her only for her money.

"Other than taking my money, they don't want anything to do with me," Medha remarked. "After Baba [Father] died, I have no one who is my own (*aponjon*)."

This chapter explores the experiences of women who, as daughters and sisters, prioritize caring for their natal kin over marrying. That their parents and siblings needed their industrious labor, income, and care was the key reason for not marrying for a good many (10 of 24) of my interlocutors from poor and working-class families. Yet, prevailing Indian kinship systems deem women and girls to be only transient members of their natal families, expected to move on to join a husband's family in marriage. Srimati Basu writes of an Indian daughter, "Ties to the natal family are supposed to be severed, and she is to become an inseparable part of the affinal family" (1999: 129). Scholars and the public are well able to recognize these expected, familiar gendered kinship patterns for women who follow the normal path of marrying. While even married women aspire to keep the natal home an important affective space to continue to visit and receive love, it is only by marrying out and away—and by remaining in these marriages, even if troubled—that women ordinarily secure a place within kinship and all its hoped-for material, social, and emotional benefits (Basu 1999, 2015).

Partly because not marrying is still so comparatively rare for women in India, little public and scholarly attention has been paid to women's experiences of kinship when they do not marry. The ideology is that a husbandless sister and daughter should be supported by her natal kin both affectively and materially. But what happens in practice? This chapter highlights how poignantly precarious a woman's place in any family can be if she chooses to or is compelled to make a life path outside marriage, in a society where family and kinship are key to social and economic security. The chapter also spotlights how gender, social class, and marital status intersect to produce the unequal distribution of the labor and goods of care.

BECOMING THE BREADWINNER: A DAUGHTER'S AND SISTER'S CARE

That a natal family needed or wanted their income emerged as a key incentive to forego marriage for ten, or near one-fifth, of the women in my study, including Medha, Nayani, Manjuri, and Subhagi, among those we have already met. Further, even when women did not present supporting natal kin as one of their chief reasons for not marrying, the majority of my single women interlocutors spoke of caring for their own parents and often siblings as a central feature of their lives.

As we have begun to see, the convention in Bengali families is that sisters and daughters marry out and away from their natal homes. Their labor from that point on is expected to support their marital families, whether that labor takes place in the household—through cooking, cleaning, and caring for young children and old parents-in-law—and/or in the outer world through earning money. In contrast, a son conventionally works to support his own parents and natal family, while eventually bringing in a wife who can contribute to the labor. In this arrangement, a son's marriage supports his family of birth, while a daughter and sister's marriage takes her away and cuts her off, rendering her "other" (por).[2]

In practice, many married women continue to support their own parents and siblings in various ways, especially if earning their own income and if their husbands and in-laws allow them some autonomy over their own movements. Shalini Grover finds among the urban poor in Delhi, for instance, that married women regularly "visit their parents to assist them with chores, to look after them when they are sick, to attend to other siblings, or simply to drop in on the way home from work" (2009: 17). Yet, a traditional Bengali and wider Indian saying goes that parents should not accept even one sip of water in a married daughter's home. Further, women cannot be certain that their in-laws will continue to allow them to work after marriage. Gowri Vijayakumar observes how the young working women she studied in a small town outside of Bangalore "often insisted that life after marriage was out of their hands, impossible to predict. . . . Even if their parents currently allowed them to work outside of the home, as part of their new families, they would act in relation to their in-laws' preferences" (2013: 785).[3] As Nayani articulated when I was visiting her new flat, "Another thing: after you get married, you can't do anything for your own family. That is another problem with marrying. . . . If I were to earn after marriage, the money would have to go to my in-laws' household."

To be sure, sons also often move away from their parents, especially in the contemporary era of rural-to-urban and transnational labor mobility. Still, the expectation is that a son and daughter-in-law will provide some income and care labor to support the son's parents and any remaining unmarried siblings, even if they live away, while a married daughter's income, affections, and labor will end up being directed elsewhere. Such kinship and virilocal postmarital residence patterns lie behind some single women's decisions not to marry—so as to be able to go on supporting their families of birth.

Among the unmarried women who emphasized that they could not marry because their natal families were depending on their income and domestic labor, two main groups emerged. One consisted of women from very poor rural backgrounds (like Manjuri, Nayani, Subhagi, and Medha), and the other consisted of women from East Bengal refugee families. Following the Partition of India and Pakistan in 1947 upon independence from British rule, hundreds of thousands of Hindus flooded into Kolkata (then Calcutta) from the Muslim-majority districts of East Bengal claimed by Pakistan. Many of these refugee families had been middle class or higher in their homeland, and their women had not worked outside of the home. The massive displacement left once well-off families struggling to survive, propelling women out of the home to earn money (P. Chakraborty 2018: 2; Weber 1995: 207). They became teachers, office workers, tutors, tailors, and small shop managers. Josodhara Bagchi and Subhoranjan Dasgupta write of the refugee woman in West Bengal as "the tireless breadwinner, changing the digits of feminine aspiration of the Bengali *bhadramahila* [gentlewoman]" (2006: 6). Sometimes it was an older daughter or sister in a family who turned out to be the most industrious, intelligent, resourceful, and accomplished—managing to earn more or better than her brothers and parents. With little siblings and old parents relying on their earnings, many such women felt unable to marry.

The memoir "Becoming the Breadwinner" (B. Chakravarti 2006) is both an example and an exception. Bithi's suitor waited for her for many years while each supported their refugee families. Bithi's suitor had promised when first proposing marriage that money would be sent to her family, but Bithi refused. She recalls: "I wanted all my brothers and sisters to get properly settled before I could get married. I am grateful that he waited for me. We married only in 1967 [thirteen years after they "had developed a deep understanding"] when all my brothers and sisters had got jobs and our family started having a decent income" (154). "I am grateful that he waited for me" (154).

Other scholars have examined the ways employed married women are helping to propel the upward social mobility of their marital families, as an in-marrying wife's salary bolsters her conjugal family's ability to purchase status-rich consumer goods like refrigerators, microwaves, washing machines, color televisions, and cars (e.g., Fernandes 2006; Radhakrishnan 2009). Yet little attention has been paid to the breadwinning capacities and strategies of unmarried daughters and sisters. How may the earned income of an unmarried daughter contribute to her own natal kin's class mobility and security? We can see from this chapter's opening scenes how Medha's drive to become a professor lifted her natal family from desperate poverty to the comfortable middle classes. Then, what happens to a woman's own experiences of kinship belonging when she sacrifices her marriage prospects in order to devote herself to supporting her family of birth?

Some women who devoted their lives to serving natal kin rather than marrying felt proud and sustained by this life path. We saw how Subhagi of chapter 2—a Scheduled Caste day laborer who pushed away suitors in order to stay taking care of her little siblings and ailing parents—felt so proud and sustained by this decision. Even after her own parents died, she maintained a secure, vital place in her home of birth, with her brother, brother's wife, nephew, nephew's wife, and little grandnephews and grandnieces. Recall Subhagi exclaiming: "Serving the people in this family, the happiness I receive is incomparable. Compared to serving a husband, and compared even to serving God, then serving one's family is the best!"

Bhakti Chatterjee at age 68 also recalled proudly her years of supporting her natal kin. She was the oldest of eight siblings, born into a large, conservative, educated Kolkata family. Her father, a freedom fighter in the nationalist movement against the British, married late and had irregular income. Whatever little he had, he would spend on those in distress, while opening the doors of their home to other freedom fighters seeking food and lodging. Bhakti loved to study, and at age 15 when her parents and other senior kin began talking about arranging her marriage, Bhakti pleaded with her father to allow her to continue her studies instead. Against the objections of other relatives, her revolutionary-minded father agreed. By the time Bhakti completed her studies and took up a teaching job, she had become the family's primary breadwinner. Her father soon passed away, and Bhakti applied herself to educating her brothers and sisters, getting them married, and caring for her widowed mother. "Like a banyan tree, I gave shelter to my family for forty-one years," Bhakti related with pride.

Though Bhakti expresses no regrets—at least not to me, as we spoke in the old age home where she now lives—the trajectory of her life story conveys not only the pride, pleasure, and sense of belonging that can come from devoting oneself to natal kin, but also the ultimate tenuousness within prevailing kinship systems of women's connections to their natal homes. By focusing on single women's experiences, I came to realize how *the tenuousness of natal family belonging is true both if a woman marries and if she does not.* After Bhakti's mother died, she no longer felt comfortable living in what had now become the home of her brothers, their sons, and the sons' wives. On her own, she made the decision to move into an old age home after coming across an advertisement in a local paper. Her schoolteacher's pension pays for her modest expenses, while she continues to turn over the balance of her monthly pension to her nephews.

Time and again, never-married women tell of how after their parents die, they have no real kin to rely on or call their own. This is so even when they have been the family's key economic provider for years. As Medha expressed, "After Father died, I have no one who is my own (*apon*)."

The transience and displacement of the unmarried breadwinner daughter is powerfully portrayed in the classic 1960 Bengali film directed by Ritwik Ghatak, *Meghe Dhaka Tara*, often held up as one of the greatest Bengali films, and recommended to me as essential time after time by Bengalis learning of my interest in never-married single women. I reflect on this classic story at some length because of its powerful resonance with many of my fieldwork materials and the themes of this chapter.

"HOW DO I ENDURE YOUR LEAVING, MY DAUGHTER?" NITA'S SACRIFICE IN *MEGHE DHAKA TARA*

Meghe Dhaka Tara (The Cloud-Capped Star) features the tragic story of a beautiful daughter of an impoverished formerly middle-class family from East Pakistan struggling to get by.[4] Although the 1947 Partition of Bengal is never explicitly mentioned in *Meghe Dhaka Tara*, the film takes place in a refugee colony on the outskirts of Kolkata. The protagonist Nita sacrifices her own desires and life goals in order to support her natal family, and she ultimately meets a heartbreaking end. Although reviews and commentary highlight the film's portrayal of the plight of Partition refugees,[5] it is Nita's struggles as a paradigmatic unmarried daughter/sister that grabbed my attention and resonate powerfully with my data. We see Nita's tremendous sacrifice for her natal family, a cultural ideology of marriage as the only viable future for a daughter, resulting in tragedy if she fails to marry, and the poignant theme of a daughter's ultimately fleeting place in her natal home.

The film's narrative unfolds through Nita, the eldest daughter and sole breadwinner of the family, sacrificing her own goals for the sustenance of her parents and siblings. In the opening scenes, we see Nita with her thick black braid and plain white cotton sari walking home on the rough gravelly road of the refugee settlement. One of her sandals suddenly snaps; she looks down, sighs, removes her sandals, and continues on, barefoot. Signs of economic want are everywhere. Nita's father, a former school headmaster, talks with Ma about how responsible and intelligent Nita is—"doing not one but two private tutoring jobs, bringing home 40 rupees every month! And taking MA classes!" (Ghatak 1960: 5:55).[6]

The whole family is after Nita for her earnings. Nita's unemployed beloved older brother (*dada*), Shankar, who is devoted to classical singing, begs Nita for a few coins to pay for a shave. Ma is despondent and peeved when Nita does not hand over the full sum of her earnings for running and feeding the household. Everyone is excited on the first of the month, knowing that Nita will be paid. Over several pay periods, Nita gives money to her older brother for shaving and spending, to her younger brother Montu for new sports shoes, to her little sister Gita for a new sari, and to Ma for food shopping. Her highly educated father, who loves Yeats and Wordsworth, also asks his daughter for a little money, while entreating her not to tell Ma. Nita does not purchase new sandals for herself. Even her love interest, Sanat, asks Nita for money as he pursues his dreams of receiving a doctoral fellowship in science, while putting off getting a job.

Sanat is important to the narrative from the beginning. Shankar, Nita's older brother, comes upon Nita secretly reading a letter and pounces on her, teasing, "What, a love letter? So late in life?" (We presume Nita to be in about her early twenties.) Shankar grabs the letter from Nita and reads aloud, "At first, I did not recognize your worth. I thought you were ordinary. But now I see you amidst the clouds, perhaps a star, veiled by circumstances, your aura dimmed" (9:30). Sanat visits Nita and her family periodically, and Nita's father seems to find him an eligible suitor, pleased by his ambitions to pursue a PhD.

Woven through the unfolding plot, we encounter the cultural ideology that if circumstances are right, men, not women, and eventually sons, rather than their fathers, should be the primary breadwinners. Ma chastises her oldest son, Shankar, for not earning, while spending his time just singing and sitting at home: "Have you no shame? Dining off your father? And the little girl [Nita] works all day long just to foot your bills? While you spend your time in singing. . . . Does any young man just sit at home?" (22:00). Later Ma laments to Nita, "If Shankar had been a man, then you would not have had to take all the burden" (50:00).

As Shankar remains unemployed and Father gets older and frailer, it becomes clearer and clearer to Nita and her mother how much responsibility lies on Nita's shoulders. After Father seriously injures himself by tripping and falling on the train tracks, the doctor pulls Nita aside to say, "Such an injury in old age—it will take a long time to mend. Now the responsibility of running the household will be on you" (35:00). When Nita quits her MA studies to get a salaried clerical office job, she tells Sanat, her suitor, "What else can I do? So many at home are depending on me" (39:00).

Under these circumstances, Ma becomes increasingly afraid that Nita will depart in marriage. When Sanat visits Nita, Ma looks on with fear and a

scheming face. She allows Nita's younger sister Gita to flirt with Sanat by bringing him tea and strolling with him by the ponds and fields as Nita is out doing
her tutoring.

One evening, Sanat and Nita are sitting on a bench in the train station before
Nita's commute home. Sanat tells Nita that it is unbearable that she has quit her
studies to work. He promises that he will get a job, saying that he could easily get a
job, allowing her to return to her studies.

"Then, our wedding?" Sanat asks softly (42:30).

Nita replies, "It cannot happen now."

"Why not?"

"How could it happen? If I leave the household today, then my old father, my
little little brother and sister—"

Sanat responds dejectedly, "That means, until then, for all those days—"

"We will have to wait," Nita interrupts.

"Why should we wait?" Sanat utters sharply.

"Don't be silly." Nita gets up to leave for home. Sanat tells her that he will come
visit in a few days.

Meanwhile, back in the colony, the local grocer scolds Shankar, "The lot of you
is eating off the labors of one sister, destroying her future. Aren't you ashamed? . . .
Aren't *you* the elder brother?" (44:30).

Returning home, Nita devotedly checks in on her dozing father, and then sits
with Ma, their shack dimly lit by the light of a kerosene lantern. Ma is mend-
ing; Nita is reading. Ma tells Nita that she believes Father will never get better or
earn again.

"Don't worry, Ma. I am here," Nita consoles her.

Ma protests, "I do worry. After all, you too may have your own hopes. . . . The
truth is, you are my sole support." Ma sobs, "But even you scare me. . . . What if
you too go away?" (50:50).

Later that evening, Shankar tells Nita how badly he feels that he and the rest of
the family are exploiting her. "Your whole future. Your marriage," Shankar worries,
equating the promise of a future for his sister with marriage (and not, for instance,
with Nita's passion for education), recognizing that Nita's self-sacrifice for her family is preventing her from pursuing that married future (53:37).

Nita declares, smiling dreamily, "If someone loves me, if he really loves me,
then he will surely wait for me. It doesn't worry me. I absolutely won't marry right
now." Yet when Nita soon discovers that her suitor Sanat is romancing her younger
sister, Nita's anguish is acute.

Shortly after, carrying in dried laundry to where Father is reading, Ma asks her
husband whether he has thought of getting their younger daughter Gita married.
Father replies, "Only after Nita. One should think serially" (1:09).

Ma protests, "But *you* educated Nita. That is why she can run the household."

Father states, "Finding a groom for a working girl is less difficult."

Ma responds sarcastically, "OK, get her married fast, and you'll have time to suck your big fat toe. . . . If Nita marries, what will happen to this household?" (1:09:57). Ma stomps out.

Father calls after her, uttering with pain in his voice, "But to exploit this innocent daughter all her life—"

Ma, from the next room, scolds, "Without her, what will you eat?" (1:10:10).

Gita soon announces to Nita that she is getting married. "To whom?" Nita asks. "Does Ma know?"

"To Sanat," Gita replies sweetly. The camera holds on Nita's devastated face as she fights back tears.

Shortly before Gita's wedding, Father grasps Nita's hands and looks penetratingly into her eyes. "At one time, they married off their daughters to dying men," he says, recalling the former practice of Kulin Brahmin polygamy, where young daughters were nominally married to elderly men of the very highest Brahmin caste, who could have dozens of wives.[7] "And now we're supposed to be educated, 'civilized'!" Father's tone rises in vehemence. "We educate our girl, wring her dry, and destroy her future!"

Nita is taken aback. Her voice breaks as she gasps, "Oh, Father. It's time for your tea—I'll go get your tea" (1:13:46).

Nita rushes out and picks up a little girl in the courtyard who is visiting for the wedding. "Would you like some sweets? You haven't had sweets yet?" Nita asks, drying her eyes on the edge of her sari.

Meanwhile, Shankar leaves home to try to earn a living as a singer in Bombay, and younger brother Montu is injured in an accident at the factory where he had taken up a job. As Nita tends to Montu in the hospital, her nighttime fevers and coughing fits worry a nurse, who advises Nita to get an X-ray. Nita refuses. "What if I am really ill? I'm the only earning member" (1:27).

As Nita becomes increasingly sick—coughing blood into a damp towel and splashing water on her face during feverish nights, hiding her illness from her family—a melancholy, haunting song plays in the background. Sung by many female voices and repeated throughout the film's closing scenes, the wailing lament is a wedding song, usually sung at the moment of a young bride's departure from the home of her childhood:

> Come my daughter Uma to me. . . .
> Let me bid you farewell now, my daughter!
> How can I endure your leaving, my daughter?
> Let me bid you farewell now, my daughter.
> You are leaving my home desolate, for your husband's place.
> How do I endure your leaving, my daughter? (1:30)

Shortly thereafter, Nita meets up with her former love, Sanat, who is now her brother-in-law. Sanat still shows feelings for Nita, and Nita confesses that she now understands that she herself is to blame for much of her own suffering—"because I have never protested against any injustice. That is my sin (*pap*)" (1:34:30). Paulomi Chakraborty notes how Nita's confession makes clear that "the film does not preach or even morally sanction the kind of gendered violence to which Nita allows herself to be subjected" (2018: 197). Yet, viewers cannot help but feel that Nita's sacrifice is valorized, even as we deplore the injustice.

Finally, during the film's culminating scenes, Nita's family discovers that Nita has a serious case of tuberculosis. Elder brother Shankar is now a famous singer; sister Gita is pregnant; younger brother Montu has recovered from the factory accident while earning a solid financial compensation; and Ma hopes that their refugee shack will soon be replaced by a concrete two-story home. As Nita is lying feverish, hallucinating about happy childhood memories, her helpless and agonized father comes in, at first seeming to comfort Nita affectionately, stroking her forehead (1:50:09). Torrential rain is pouring outside.

Then, Father hands Nita a small cloth bundle, and tells her, "I've packed your clothes." While weeping, Father says to his daughter, "You go away. You go away," making a shooing away gesture with his hand. "They are dreaming of a two-story house! You have been 'successful'! You have put them on their feet, dear. It matters little now if you are no longer here. They pity you now. You were not made for carrying the burden, but you had to carry the burden."

Father's weeping increases, as his voice takes on a loud and sermonizing tone. "Now you are the burden yourself! There is poison in your breath. This room is now for the newborn" (1:51:35). Father weeps, "Go away, dear. Go away. Go away." Father walks out of the room, turning his back on his daughter, into the dark rainy night (1:51:59). Nita stares, huddled with her small sack of clothing, dressed in a simple white cotton sari, hair loose. At once the most cherished and least cherished, the most important and least important, Nita is now expendable.

As Nita opens the door and steps out into the stormy night, the melancholy song plays again: "Come, my daughter Uma, to me. Let me garland you with flowers. . . . Let me bid you farewell now, my daughter. You are leaving my home desolate, for your husband's place. How do I endure your leaving, my daughter?" (1:52:40).

In the end, Shankar brings Nita to a tuberculosis sanatorium in the hills. He visits her some time later, bringing news of home. His income has indeed built the family a two-story house. Gita and Sanat's toddler son gets such a thrill running up and down the stairs, "giving Father hell," so full of life and laughter.

Nita begs, her desperate cries resounding across the hills, "Brother, but I really, really wanted to live! Brother, I love life! Brother, please just say once that I will live! I will live! I will live!" (1:58:45).

"But the mountains remain indifferent and unyielding," Paulomi Chakraborty writes. "Nita's cry meets only emptiness" (2018: 189).

The melancholy song plays again as the film closes, lingering even after the screen has gone dark: "Let me bid you farewell now, my daughter. You are leaving my home desolate for your husband's place. How can I endure your departure, my daughter?" (2:00:30).

DAUGHTERS AND SONS, SISTERS AND BROTHERS, LABOR AND LOSS, FUTURES

What is striking about this remarkable emotional film for my purposes is how much it resonates with central themes in many never-married Bengali women's life stories. I will shortly introduce Sukhi-di, an older East Bengal refugee woman whose life circumstances overlap with Nita's.[8] We also see how refugee status and economic exigencies can push women out of the home to earn a living, although here due more to necessity and circumstance rather than a drive for emancipation from conventional gender roles. Relatedly, we see how the Uma lament—"How can I endure your departure, my daughter?"—takes on a double meaning: it comes to signify not only the poignant emotional pain of losing a beloved daughter in marriage, recognizable to all Bengalis, but also the matter of economic dependence on a daughter's labor. Nita's mother explicitly articulates their family's dependence on Nita, arguing with Nita's father: "If Nita marries, what will happen to this household? . . . Without her, what will you eat?" (Ghatak 1960: 1:10). But such economic dependence on a daughter and sister's labor is at the same time not normal in Bengali kinship systems and can be viewed and experienced as exploitation, especially if not reciprocated with future material and emotional support.

Although not the expected norm, being an essential breadwinner as daughter and sister is a familiar theme among never-married single women from poor and refugee families. One impoverished rural widowed mother with no sons and two unmarried daughters in their thirties at first explained that the family lacked money for dowries. She then commented, "If my daughters get married, then I will have to live and cook alone. Who will look after an other Mother (*porer Ma*)?"—conveying the sense that a married daughter's husband's kin become her "own" (*apon*) and her natal kin "other" (*por*). This widowed mother explained that a married daughter will look after her ma "maybe for two or three days. Then the people from the in-laws' house (*shoshur barir lok*) will say, 'Just stay there for a few days, then come back home.'"

This widow's older daughter, Nabami, had landed a job as an aide in a nursing home, commuting by cycle, and the younger daughter worked as a day laborer in the rice fields and in a brick factory. When I asked the daughters if they were disappointed not to be married, Nabami replied matter-of-factly, "Whether we marry or don't marry, either way, we will have to work to eat." She paused. "But if marriage does not happen, then of course there will be sadness."

Recall how day laborer Subhagi begged visiting potential grooms not to choose her for marrying, underscoring in her life-story narrative, "I was the one who worked so that they [my parents and siblings] could eat." Sukhi-di, the second-oldest daughter in a large refugee family from East Bengal, also told of how she could not get married "because I had to take care of all the siblings." Now 75 and residing in the Government of West Bengal Working Girls' Hostel in the Gariahat neighborhood of Kolkata, Sukhi-di recounted how her father died when the youngest of her twelve siblings was just one month old and Sukhi herself around 19 or 20. Sukhi and her oldest brother became the family's primary breadwinners, her brother in the coal yards and Sukhi balancing several jobs, including as a schoolteacher and telephone operator.

Like Nita of *Meghe Dhaka Tara*, Sukhi did have a suitor whom she loved. She recalled pushing away her suitor, knowing that her mother and siblings depended on her: "I told him that if you want to marry me, then you'll have to wait for another ten to fifteen years. By then we will be an old man and old woman! What will be the use then?" She persuaded him to move away from Kolkata and find someone else.

"Finally, later, he did marry," she recalled, still with a sense of love in her tone. "Why wouldn't he? All people should get married." Sukhi-di had excluded her own self from "all people" here, though.[9]

An unmarried daughter's and sister's economic labor is often intertwined with her daily household and emotional-care labor. Bengalis commonly tell of how daughters are more "loving" than sons, even though daughters are supposed to be merely transient members in their natal homes. A group of elderly widowed mothers in a village replied to my questions about daughters versus sons: "When you give birth to a daughter, yes, sadness happens," one woman mentioned quietly, expressing their society's patrilineal ideals.[10] "But we realize now that girls love their parents more. We are sad when they are born, but we realize now that daughters love their parents more."

Indeed, many of the single women in my study told of how they cared for their aged parents, especially mothers, cooking for them, nursing them through illnesses, loving them, and supporting them in all sorts of daily ways—much more so, they reported, than did their brothers and sisters-in-law. Nayani also described all the daily household and emotional care she provided in her role as "like a daughter" (*meyer moto*) for her employer Pishi. This led to a situation, as Nayani describes, where "if anyone raised the topic of my marriage, Pishi would get very angry with them" (chapter 2).

Despite the vital economic and emotional support daughters and sisters often provide for their parents and siblings, their place in their natal homes tends to be quite precarious. This is another central theme in *Meghe Dhaka Tara*—the transient and insecure place of daughters and sisters in their natal families. Paulomi Chakraborty's compelling analysis of *Meghe Dhaka Tara* emphasizes this theme, as she reflects on the film's melancholy refrain: "Let me bid you farewell, my daughter. You leave my home desolate [for your husband's place]. How can I endure your departure?" (2018: 183). This wailing lament is a wedding song, sung by women as a young bride departs the home of her childhood to relocate "to the unknown, often unfriendly and hostile, house of her in-laws" (P. Chakraborty 2018: 183). The song is addressed to Uma, identified in Bengal especially with the goddess Durga as daughter when she arrives on her once-yearly visit to her natal home during the autumnal Durga Puja festivities. (Durga Puja is the largest Hindu Bengali holiday, akin in some ways to Christmas in Western countries, when schools are closed for several weeks, families gather together, and gift-giving is practiced.) The song echoes the sadness of the goddess Durga's departure each year after the four-day-long sacred festivities.[11] As Chakraborty writes, the imagination that anthropo-morphizes the departure of the goddess "also echoes the heart-breaking but banal displacement daughters of Bengali households suffer" (184). In this way, the film's lament "provides an associative sense of loss and violence that exceeds Nita's death and includes the violence of the paternal giving away of daughters that marks gen-dered everyday life. It reminds us that within patrilineal marital arrangements in Bengal, as elsewhere in South Asia . . ., women are the 'original displaced persons' (Bagchi and Dasgupta 2003: 3–4)" (P. Chakraborty 2018: 185).[12] Chakraborty's analysis highlights the everyday violence of the giving away of daughters in mar-riage as they are displaced from childhood homes.

Chakraborty seems to have trouble making sense of Nita's never-married sta-tus, however, explaining it as an "anomaly, as a sign of a world turned ruthlessly exploitative, an out-of-the-ordinary event caused by the Partition" (2018: 185). I have also not been able to find any other analyses or reviews of the film that con-tend with Nita's never-married status. Yet to me, the never-married status of Nita is hugely significant, as it is also in the eyes of many Bengalis—some never-married women themselves—who have recommended the film as crucial for my project. In the Bengali patrilineal kinship system, women regularly experience displacement from their natal homes both if they do marry *and if they do not.*

More than half of the participants in my study—30 out of 54—resided in one fashion or another with natal kin as their primary living arrangement, but many experienced these arrangements to be highly insecure.[13] In Bengali kinship, the relationship between brothers and sisters is regarded as ordinarily easy and warm. However, "if an [adult] sister goes to live with her brother, their love is seen to be hierarchical and difficult" (Inden and Nicholas 1977: 25). For instance, two single women slept only on mats in the corner of halls or storage rooms in their fathers' and now brothers' homes, clinging to maintain their rights to even these small spaces, as their brothers' wives would prefer to expel them.

Unmarried Nita in *Meghe Dhaka Tara* is driven out from her family home, ultimately to face an abandoned death. Her father tells her, "You have put them on their feet, dear. It matters little now if you are no longer here" (Ghatak 1960: 1:51). Such a statement would never be made to a son. My research assistant Hena, also never-married, commented to me via email regarding stories like Nayani's of chapter 2 that she was helping transcribe: "Girl children and young women get displaced from their own families and are never accepted back, although their earned money is welcomed." Medha told Hena the incident of how she had overheard her brother's wife complain that she has been cooking for Medha since she married at age 13 and is tired of it, complaining to her husband when Medha visited her natal home, "Does she think this is a hotel?" Hena exclaimed, indignant, "Why don't you just cook for yourself, then? No one should ever relinquish their place in their father's home." But the reality is that, once adult—even if their income and labors have been used to establish and sustain the family—both married and unmarried women are no longer regarded as normal, regular members of their father's and brothers' patrilineal households.

Aarini, the never-married computer engineer in her forties who had worked in Silicon Valley before returning to her ancestral home in Kolkata, was adamant about her right to be in the family home, but she still felt insecure about her future there. She had refurbished the whole three-story house with furnishings sent by ship from America, moving into the top story above her parents. Her brother and wife, with their children, were currently living separately, although everyone knew they could and might at any time wish to return to the lovely ancestral home in a posh Kolkata neighborhood. Relatives reportedly criticized Aarini's decorating efforts, insinuating that this was all part of her strategy to inappropriately lay claim to the home.

People would ask, "Oh, you've moved back in with your parents?"

Aarini would reply, "No, it's my *ancestral* home, *my* family home. It's *my* home, too."

Friends would respond, "I mean, it's great if you think that way, but—"

Aarini told of how before she left to pursue a PhD in the United States, when her parents were trying to arrange her brother's marriage, no one would give a bride to a son with an unmarried older sister. Prospective brides' parents would ask, "Is the property to be divided between the two siblings?"

"I felt that my parents wanted me to get out of the way," Aarini recalled. "So, the minute I announced I was leaving for the US to get a PhD, everything fell into place, and my brother married."

Later Aarini commented, "Bengali parents will say, 'I love my daughter so much, but *still* she wants her share in the assets?'" Aarini told of how her own ties and birthrights to the house are deeper and more emotional than her mother's, who only married into the family; but no one else sees it that way.

After we had been dining out and chatting one evening, Aarini sent me a follow-up email: "Hi Sarah, One more insight—the same attitude which enables men to get paid more for the same job, relative to their women colleagues, helps sons get more credit just for being the son, even if the family owes more to the daughter."

Sanjaya, who runs an NGO for disabled women, commented similarly, "Regardless of the laws, Bengalis believe homes rightfully belong to sons and wives. If parents die and there are brothers, the unmarried sister is a soft target. For some time now, the law has stipulated that daughters and sons are to get an equal share of their parents' property. But in reality, brothers throw away their sister or get her to sign away her portion."

In terms of laws, the Hindu Succession Act, passed in 1956 in India and amended in 2005 and 2020, theoretically gives daughters an equal birthright to inherit joint Hindu family property, and this law has been hailed as a major moment for gender equality (Agarwal 1994; Basu 1999; *Hindu* 2020). Yet, in her examination of the contemporary workings of property law in India, Srimati Basu details how few women in practice lay claim to natal family assets. Drawing from interviews in middle-class and poor neighborhoods of Delhi, Basu explores how people across genders and generations very often do not believe that an adult woman should receive either property or maintenance from her natal kin. Such views are tied to common "rationales based on the idea of women's separation from the natal family at marriage" (1999: 123). Negotiating such rationales, married women are often reluctant to claim parental inheritance out of fear they will be regarded as uncaring and greedy, and to keep natal family relations harmonious and support-ive (1999: 117–143).

Basu's research highlights "the idea of marriedness as the prime form of women's property" (1999: 224).[14] For women who are not married, claims to material support and affective belonging through kinship are fragile. As I also often found, Basu observes how "husbandless daughters," both single and divorced women, "were at best grudgingly given small portions of family prop-erty and more often expected to make their own way and support themselves through wages" (224).

The insecurity of a daughter and sister in her natal household means, to many, that it is only through marriage that a woman can achieve a secure future. This is another cultural principle portrayed in *Meghe Dhaka Tara*. The film equates "the future" (*bhabisyat*) and marriage for Nita at several explicit moments, such as when brother Shankar tells Nita how badly he feels that the whole family is exploiting her: "Your whole future. Your marriage" (Ghatak 1960: 53:37). The local grocer scolds Shankar: "The lot of you is eating off the labors of one sister, destroy-ing her future. Aren't you ashamed?" (44:30). When Nita's father is pressured into giving his younger daughter's marriage rather than Nita's, he bemoans, "We edu-cate our girl, wring her dry, and destroy her future!" (1:13). It is at the very moment when Nita realizes that her marriage to Sanat will not happen, as she descends the stairs from his flat in anguish, that the poisonous rattle of tuberculosis is first heard emanating from her throat. The film's two married women, Ma and little sister Gita, do have a future and security—through their husbands and sons. Unmarried Nita is sacrificed, with no secure place in the kinship system after she labors to establish her natal family.

SUKHI-DI'S STORY OF WORK, LOVE, AND SACRIFICE

I close this chapter with a portrait of Sukhi-di, briefly introduced above, whose life story resonates with many of this chapter's themes regarding a daughter's and sister's care, including her labor and loss, love deferred, and insecure future. Sukhi-di, in her seventies over the seven years of my fieldwork and friendship with her, was born in 1942 in Barisal, East Bengal, five years before the region was transferred to East Pakistan. Along with hundreds of thousands of other Hindu refugees, Sukhi's family migrated to Kolkata, where Sukhi became the third-oldest sibling of twelve. "I was the one to look after all my brothers and sisters," Sukhi-di pronounced, presenting her responsibility to support her parents and siblings as the central reason she never married. Her life-story narratives also resonate with themes in chapter 2, as Sukhi found pride in her working life and the independence it gave her.

A bright and industrious young woman, Sukhi pursued her education up to the BA level before her father died, and then quickly found ways to earn money to support her family and contribute to the marriage dowries of her many younger sisters. Her father, a film director, died when her youngest sister was a tiny infant and Sukhi about 19 or 20. Sukhi and her oldest brother became the family's primary breadwinners. Neither married. Sukhi was like a second mother to all the little ones.

Sukhi-di proudly recollects how she juggled several jobs, including as a successful schoolteacher even with no formal training, and next as a telephone operator, coming first out of two hundred in the telephone operator class. Sukhi then moved on to work as a field researcher for UNICEF and the Asiatic Society. She would travel around rural Bengal as the only woman with a team of researchers. Some of her male colleagues were shy about dressing and sleeping together in the same barracks, but Sukhi would matter-of-factly stretch a sari across the room as a barrier, and manage herself just fine. To one male coworker she declared, "You're just like my little brother—and such a big bed, what will happen?" She invited him to share the single bed with her. "I got into bed and slept just fine!" Sukhi recalled, laughing. "But he stayed in a chair all night long."

Sukhi-di loved her work and independence. "I lived in places all by myself," she recalled. "I was really brave and never scared! You constantly have to have precautions. When I lived alone, for safety, I always kept a knife under my pillow!" she exclaimed proudly.

One evening during the 6 to 7 p.m. visiting hours at the Government of West Bengal Working Girls' Hostel, where she now lives, Sukhi-di pulled out a framed photograph taken when she was around 16 and her parents were considering arranging her marriage. Sukhi looks beautiful in the black-and-white frame, with long black hair and a subtle Mona Lisa smile. My research assistant Anindita asked, "When your brothers and sisters got married, and you made all the arrangements for their marriages, did you not ever think about your own marriage?"

Sukhi-di replied vigorously, "That a female person (*meye manus*) would not think about marriage? That would never happen! A girl will *definitely* think about it!"

Sukhi-di continued passionately, this conversation taking place after I had already known her well for five years. "That I wouldn't be aroused by 'sex'?" She used the English term. "'Sex' will of course be aroused!"

"Look," Sukhi-di went on, "within every person's life, whether beautiful or not, that person faces a moment when she stands in front of the mirror and says, 'Well, today I'm looking quite attractive! This is a *rule*. . . . Therefore, that my own 'sex' [sense of sexual desire] was not aroused, that is not the case! That no sexual arousal took place, and that I did not love anyone—I cannot say that. *I* also fell in love! But, I did not bind him to me."

"Hmm," I commented softly, "You had other commitments," thinking of the deep responsibility she had felt for all her siblings.

"Yes, I had other obligations," Sukhi-di agreed. "I was the one to look after my brothers and sisters. How could I discard so many little brothers and sisters and leave?"

Sukhi recalled, as partially reported above: "I told him, 'If you want to marry me, then you'll have to wait for another ten to fifteen years. By then we will be an old man and old woman! What will be the use [she implies, of having sex and of reproducing] then?' At that time, it was *his* ripe age to get married. But he was saying, 'No, I will not marry if not to you!' Then I said, 'If you wait so long, then you won't be able to be fulfilled, and neither will I be fulfilled.'" She used the term *bhog* (to enjoy), in this context connoting sexual enjoyment. "'Neither of us will be happy! How is that necessary? I will be fine,'" she had insisted.

"So, reluctantly, perforce, he ran away from Kolkata, taking a job and moving to another place. Finally, later, he married. Why wouldn't he? All people should get married! I personally think so. If not, why would have God created us that way, with different reproductive systems? Creation and re-creation will not happen if there is no marriage."

Anindita and I sensed the enduring feelings of love and memory in her voice.

After Sukhi-di helped to establish all her younger siblings in life, as they married and moved on to create families of their own, she needed a place to stay. She was then in her forties.

"I could not think of entering into marriage then at an age when, according to our society, it is not acceptable to marry. I had to live somewhere," Sukhi-di recalled. "My father had passed away and my brothers were all living somewhere else. I would have to live with my married sisters," not a normal Bengali kinship option. "I did not have enough money to buy an apartment."

Some friends and a former professor told her about working women's hostels, so she began to investigate. The one she liked—run by the Government of West Bengal, very affordable and in the desirable bustling Gariahat neighborhood of south Kolkata—had a hundred-person waiting list. "But I said to them, 'Why can't you give me a room? I'm living in someone else's house and I need a place to live. I don't have any relatives here.' I also implored, 'I'll just live on a balcony!' After fifteen days, they said I could live here! That was in 1989." Sukhi-di was 47 at the time, and thirty years later at this writing, she still lived in the same three-person room on the third floor of the hostel.

Sukhi-di never gave much thought when she was young to how she would care for herself in old age, but her situation had now become quite precarious. She stopped working at around age 70, has no pension, and depleted her savings by paying for knee replacement surgery when she was 72. Her eight surviving siblings occasionally drop off a bit of money or a new sari. Sukhi keeps a doll above her bed, dressing him fondly in warm clothes in the winter, grinning as she calls him "my son." She climbs up and down three flights of stairs to and from her room for her daily marketing, and she prides herself on staying fit and thin. From March to November, she walks at dawn to exercise daily in a nearby pool, the only woman near her age to partake.

One evening Anindita asked Sukhi-di while we three were together, "Do you ever feel—?"

"Loneliness?" Sukhi-di completed the question. (I was uncertain whether loneliness had been the intended topic.) "Yes! I feel lonely *very* often! This is the reason I say to everyone now that everyone needs one person. If you do not have a person beside you, it does not work. It is for that reason that marriage is necessary. You would be living with each other. Not that it always happens well, but at times it does happen that you really like a person, isn't that so?" she queried enthusiastically. "Then even if he would have died after forty years of marriage, some memories would be there that one could live with. And his children would be there, and then the grandchildren. I could live with them all, and my days would pass nicely. But now, I am completely alone. If I look all around, it is like a desert. I am *completely* alone. No one at all!

"These kinds of hopes and memories," Sukhi-di reflected, "these days they come to me a little more often, now because I am old."

Like Nita of *Meghe Dhaka Tara*, Sukhi-di sacrificed her own opportunity for romantic love, marriage, children, and a secure future, while fulfilling her breadwinner role as daughter and sister to her East Bengal refugee family. Although Sukhi-di often presents herself as an optimistic and resilient person who is proud of her successful working life and who continues to receive love from siblings and a few girlfriends from her youth, she, like Nita, finds herself in the end to be ultimately alone. She compares her desolate situation to living in a desert.

Sukhi-di worries about where she will go next if she can no longer manage shopping and cooking for herself or climbing up and down the three flights of stairs at the Working Girls' Hostel. And what if the management expels her for being no longer a "working girl"?

"Maybe I would go to an old age home. It would have to be cheap, though. If it's in my fate. Or maybe I would go to one of my sisters. But all my sisters live in their in-laws' houses, not their own households. If they are both unmarried, sisters can live together; but that has not happened. Each of my sisters is in her *shoshur ghor* [in-laws' home]. I would put them into trouble. If I go to someone else's house like that, it would be *very* inconvenient. Strained . . . but whatever is in my fate, that will happen. This is my life. Wherever I go next, God will take me. It's not in my hands."

One evening some days later, Sukhi-di commented softly with regret, "My life did not happen" (*amar jibon to holo na*).

CONCLUSION

In closing this chapter, I invoke Marshall Sahlins's definition of kinship as "mutuality of being": "people who are intrinsic to one another's existence" (2011: 2), "persons who belong to one another, who are members of one another, who are co-present in each other, whose lives are joined and interdependent" (11). Kinship is vital to most Bengalis' senses of self, well-being, and life. Listening to their stories, I came to well understand why single women would work so hard to maintain ties with their natal kin, even amidst obstacles, because for a woman outside of marriage, the natal family is the only family she has.

Some women in my study did succeed in upholding wonderful, secure, mutually sustaining relationships with natal kin, including Subhagi and Manjuri of chapter 2, and all three never-married single moms featured in chapter 6. In the next chapter, I also tell of how Sukhi-di's siblings stepped in later, during her time of crucial need amidst the COVID-19 pandemic, to offer support. Kinship is not an inflexible institution.

Yet, narratives like *Meghe Dhaka Tara* and those of other unmarried daughters and sisters highlight the ways normative Indian patrilineal kinship systems are not set up for non-marrying women—and how kinship can involve not only "mutuality of being" but also inequalities and exclusion. Even when women choose not to marry so that they can support their natal kin, their brothers often feel no obligation to reciprocate that support. Unmarried daughters and sisters are routinely called on to care for natal families—from cooking, to child and elder care, to financial provisioning—yet they feel unentitled to receive reciprocity of care in return ("Does she think this is a hotel?"). In these ways, we see how marriage unevenly distributes labor and care within families, not just between men and women, or among women by age cohort (such as mothers-in-law and daughters-in-law), but among women according to marital status.[15]

The narratives in this and earlier chapters also bring into sharp relief the ways social class connects with gender and kinship to generate the uneven distribution of the labor and goods of social reproduction and care. It is only women from financially struggling families—like Sukhi-di, Nayani, Srabani, Nabami, and

Nita of *Meghe Dhaka Tara*—whose care labor is required by their natal kin in ways that end up precluding marriage. We saw further in chapter 2 how Nayani's employers—who treated her "like a daughter"—so relied on her care that Nayani's unmarried "aunt," Pishi, threw a fit each time the possibility of Nayani's marriage was raised. Yet, after the wealthy family's care needs were exhausted, they released Nayani nearly kinless into the city. As I relate in chapter 1, Medha herself was able to hire an impoverished woman to sleep at her house, contributing to Medha's support as a successful independent professional and dispelling her loneliness, but also taking the woman away from her own children. In such ways, well-off single women are able to incorporate non-kin to enhance their possibilities for care and social reproduction, while the impoverished are left with no recourse beyond kin, in a system where kinship for women without marriage is very fragile.

4

Who Will Care for Me?

Single women across social statuses face a perpetual question, from parents, extended kin, friends, and coworkers: "Who will care for you?" The question serves both to convey a real concern and also to criticize and goad. When addressed toward a younger woman, it aims to convince her to be sensible and marry, part of a broader process of gender socialization, sensitizing girls to feel that marriage will bring them patriarchal protection and security. If chapter 3 spotlights single women's labors of caring for others, this chapter focuses on the related question of how to be cared *for*.

Despite becoming annoyed at the question, my single women interlocutors also directed the question personally toward themselves: "Who will care for me?" "What will I do when I get old?" This was a matter of real concern and a recurring theme in my fieldnotes. In a society where taken-for-granted, doxic visions see old age as a time for naturally needing, deserving, and enjoying care from kin, single women with tenuous kin connections and no children can feel particularly precarious.

Never mind that even those with children can also feel anxious about where and how they will receive care. The prevailing sense in India today is that families are changing, and people can no longer count on secure old age care from their children.[1] In her introduction to *Single by Choice: Happily Unmarried Women!*—an anthology of narratives by thirteen single women in India—Kalpana Sharma argues that the question of what you will do when you get old, directed at so many single women, "is a question that applies to everyone, married or single" (2019: 5). Sharma suggests that the never-married may even be advantaged, as "they may actually make plans, because they cannot assume that someone will be there to look after them" (2019: 5).

In their everyday conversations and life narratives, my interlocutors spoke of both plans and insecurities about future care. Medha regularly remarked to me and others, "I have no one, so of course I'll have to go live in an old age home or something." She would also convey to me her yearning for some care *now*, even before she reached her "old and ailing age"—such as when she had to have her uterus removed, and when the pandemic lockdown struck and she felt herself coming down with a fever, with no one to offer even one cup of tea. Others would also worry: my sisters are all married, my brothers and their wives don't want me, an old age home is financially out of reach. Where can I go? Where will I live? What if, even now, before I'm old, I get sick and need some care? Who will care for me?

Sanjaya, the polio survivor who had founded the single women's support group I attended, commented, "Aging and singleness are connected. . . . At this age, when single and I still have physical strength, I can go around to the market. If I am sick, I can get to the doctor. If I want to eat, I can cook for myself. But what about later?"

Nabami, the older of the two rural unmarried sisters living with their impoverished widowed mother, remarked, "Marriage is necessary. It is crucial. Look, I am looking after Ma. Won't *I* also get old? Then who will look after me?"

This chapter explores visions, dilemmas, and strategies of securing care in older singlehood. Eric Klinenberg, in *Going Solo*, documents the striking demographic rise in the numbers of people aging alone in nations around the world, from the United States to Europe, Japan, China, South Korea, and India (2012: 157–158). Some gerontologists have resurrected the phrase "elder orphan" to refer to older people who do not have a spouse or children they can depend on, currently about 22 percent of US adults age 65 and older.[2] How to meet the challenges of later life alone is a key theme in singles studies scholarship.[3]

In India, singlehood has not received much attention in the broader public discourse on new ways of aging beyond the family. Yet singlehood is highly relevant. For one, solo single women with economic resources are especially well situated to take part in new ways of non-kin-centered aging. India's metros are witnessing a rise in market-based senior housing and a self-focused ethos suggesting that "the responsibility to 'age well' rests with the individual" (Samanta 2018: 94). These trends, concentrated among the cosmopolitan elite, are motivated by social-cultural changes such as the national and transnational dispersal of family for work, and evolving ideals of modern nuclear-family-style living and individualism (Lamb 2009, 2020). Still, approximately 80 percent of older Indians in both rural and urban areas continue to live with adult children in multigenerational households, and much public, state, and everyday discourse still articulates that family-based old age care is normal and best.[4] For single women in India who live apart from kin (about half those in my study), to plan for and experience growing old solo becomes another way that their lives diverge from normative visions of the life course.

I turn first to examine the old age home as both a conventional site of abjection and a modern site of aspiration and care particularly appealing to single women. I then explore some women's strategies for cultivating independent forms of sustaining self-care. I highlight how both these non-family forms of care are greatly facilitated by access to social and economic capital. I view care as simultaneously a resource and a relational practice (Buch 2015), unequally distributed and achieved. As such, care is a critical site for illuminating the ways gender, kinship, marital status, age, and social class come together within local understandings of well-being and singlehood over the life course.

THE OLD AGE HOME AS MODERN SITE
OF ASPIRATION AND CARE

In September of 2020, almost seven years after we first met and seven months into the COVID-19 pandemic raging across our two nations, Medha sent me a momentous WhatsApp message:

> I have taken an important decision of my life. I have booked a room in the Loving Respect Senior Citizens residence (*briddhashram*) in Shantiniketan.[5] I can stay there any time. Actually I was very much anxious about my old and ailing age. Nobody is around me anymore. The members of the [senior citizens'] house are friendly and supportive. So I took the decision. . . . I have to give them a handsome amount of money. I agreed. . . . Good night my dear!"

This message was followed by a second one with a heart emoji, and then a third: "You are my strength."

I quickly replied: "Dear Medha, Your plan for your old age sounds very good and practical. I think you made a good decision. It will be great to have the help from the people at the Loving Respect home. I remember visiting [that home] with you last year, right?! . . . I will be excited to visit you there!" Then I followed with a second message: "You yourself are strength!"

Medha had only just turned 60 and was in excellent health. She dedicatedly walked at least five kilometers per day, practiced yoga and meditation to sustain her mental and physical health, and was still at the peak of her career as a university professor. But throughout the years we had known each other, Medha had been worried about how to secure care in old age. She saw herself as having "absolutely no one"—meaning no one whom she could rely upon for care in times of current need or during an envisioned period of frailty and natural dependence in old age. Recall that Medha's parents had both died, her one older sister had long ago married and gone to a different family, and Medha still felt quite estranged from her brother and his wife. The Loving Respect home provided some answers for Medha. After having stayed there for a few days, she sent me another upbeat WhatsApp message: "I am in my new home. 'Loving Respect.' Almost good management.[6] Caring. The young owner of this Ashram is very helpful. They have taken almost all responsibilities. The room is good. Plenty of natural beauty."

In societies like India with prevailing models of familial old age care, the concept of senior living is relatively new.[7] It was not until around the turn of the twenty-first century that senior residential accommodations began to proliferate in India, often labeled "old age homes" in English to signal their alien origins. In the early days of their emergence, senior living institutions were often regarded by the news media and wider public as sites of abjection for families "throwing away" their elders and going against Indian values. "Old Age Homes against Our Culture," read one representative newspaper headline (*Hindu* 2004). In my own research on old age homes in their early days in Kolkata, one resident who had chosen to move into a posh home for the aged remarked in 2005: "'Old age homes' are not a concept of *our* country. These days, we are throwing away our 'culture.' . . . 'Old age homes' are not our way of life. My parents died right with us" (Lamb 2009: 1).

Still now, some decades later, many continue to think of the old age home as a site of abjection, to which those without sons are especially vulnerable. This is because in majority patrilineal India, it is sons and daughters-in-law who are the primary ones expected to provide care for their parents in later life, as married daughters move out to support their marital families. Utpal Sandesara was struck to find in his research on sex-selective abortion in western India how prominently the specter of ending up in an old age home figured in his interview data. His interlocutors intensely longed for a son both to carry on the family patriline and to avoid the calamity of being thrown into an old age home, or "home for geezers," as they put it in Gujarati, in later life.[8]

Similarly, some public media and literary discourse continues to represent the old age home as an unethical institution for the forsaken. Such is the case in Sunanda Bhattacharya's short story "Naxaler Didi Ebong Iswariccha" (Elder Sister of a Naxalite and God's Wish), published in a collection of Naxalite movement stories sent to me by one of my single women interlocutors (Bhattacharya 2017).[9] The story centers on an elder sister from an East Bengal refugee family who, like those featured in chapter 3, sacrifices her own marriage prospects while devotedly caring for her natal kin, only to be abandoned ultimately in an old age home for the destitute. The protagonist, Bordi (eldest sister), labors away for her widowed mother and brothers—cooking, cleaning, scrubbing clothes, serving endless cups of coffee and tea to her brother's political-activist Naxalite comrades, and maintaining both vegetarian and non-vegetarian kitchens to meet the family members' differing needs—all the while saving only scraps of food for herself. By the time Bordi's mother passes away, her three brothers have successfully established themselves in lucrative professions, one well settled in America, another living in a big fancy house in the affluent Alipore neighborhood of Kolkata. Gradually the brothers lose all touch with their once-beloved, self-sacrificing sister. Neighbors place her in a government old age home for the destitute. When Bordi finally dies, a sole family friend joins the other old age home residents at her final cremation rites.

The residents look at the visitor with intense rebuke. "All of you together deserted this human being, eh?" The residents describe Bordi's loving, generous spirit and how her God-gifted singing had sustained them all in the home. "It would make our hearts burn," as she sang the lyrics: "This world does not know how to love" (Bhattacharya 2017: 930).[10]

Yet, residential senior living is gradually becoming a much more positive and aspirational idea in the Indian public imaginary, as more and more people find the option an attractive one for those with no children, or whose children live and work far away, or who desire to embrace a perceived modern system of generational independence (Lamb 2013). The *Silver Talkies* online magazine and social engagement platform for the 55+ in India published in 2019 an inspirational essay, "Retirement Communities in India: An Idea Whose Time Has Come."[11]

In my fieldwork, positive views of the old age home were especially common among never-married women with no children—by far the majority among my fifty-four key interlocutors, only three of whom, the three featured in chapter 6, had borne or adopted children. In fact, I had first become interested in the topic of single women after studying old age homes in West Bengal in the early 2000s and finding so many never-married, childless residents.[12] Most of these "unmarried" women and "bachelor" men, as they were frequently called using the English terminology, were highly appreciative of finding care in a novel nonfamily setting, as if the retirement home had emerged as an Answer to the Dilemmas of Old Age Singlehood. Lawrence Cohen, who visited in the 1990s one of Kolkata's earliest old age homes, named Nava Nir (New Nest), found the majority of residents to be old women without sons, and commented that "the rise of homes like Nava Nir suggests less a sloughing off of parents than the emergence of a different response to old people with weak claims upon family support" (1998: 119).

One major problem, however, is that senior residential living in India is restricted largely to the economically privileged, like those with amassed wealth or, at a minimum, a secure retirement pension from a government or corporate job. Few state-run or charitable elder-care institutions exist for the working classes or poor. Malobika Ganguly, who worked as a clerk in a household goods store and had managed to secure a spot in the inexpensive Government of West Bengal Working Girls' Hostel after her widowed mother died, often worried about her old age. As she reached her mid-fifties, she worried, "*What* will happen to me when I get old? Who will look after me? . . . Old age homes are so expensive! *Who* would take me there? I have absolutely no one."

She tied her old age insecurity to her lack of both money and children, remarking to me: "You have children. So, you have nothing to worry about. But me? I won't be able to do anything about it! I have neither children nor money." She emphasized a bit later: "The main thing is that you need money. Without money, you cannot do anything."

Recall that Sukhi-di in chapter 3 also wondered aspirationally if an old age home could be an answer for her future, but remarked skeptically, "It would have to be cheap, though." As she reached her late seventies, she entreated me to search out an inexpensive old age home that could answer her gaping question of how to secure care in old age.

For those who can afford senior residential living and choose to move in, many describe being delighted by the experience. A mixed group of both never-married and widowed women living in Kolkata's Rabindra Niketan Retirement Home exclaimed, "We're all happy here!" "We're doing tremendously well!" "We have come here willingly!" "There is a long waiting list to get a 'seat'!" They told of appreciating the security, companionship, stress-free provision of meals and tea, and the family-like atmosphere that at the same time allows for some independence, such as coming and going. One woman joked that the care was almost too good—like how someone comes daily to clean their rooms and wash their clothes—so that it is easy to quickly become too "inactive."[13]

In exploring singlehood and elder-home living, I also began to see how, in the context of the old age home, the status of being "unmarried" seems to carry some respect and transparency. For the first time in their lives, the unmarried ones in a retirement home are not the ones faced with the puzzling, unanswerable question. The question "Why are you here?" posed to those in old age homes who have children becomes the equivalent of the question "Why didn't you marry?" posed to unmarried women outside the homes. Each question challenges those whose lives fail to match prevailing kinship and gender norms. The "Why are you here?" query implies a parallel critique, "What's *wrong* with you that you are here, instead of with your children?" (Lamb 2009: 93ff.). But for unmarried women and bachelor men, the reason for choosing an old age home is clear, transparent, simple.

The relative status of being unmarried in a senior living setting seemed apparent when Medha gave me a video tour of her new retirement residence during the Durga Puja festivities of 2020. A few days after Medha moved into the Loving Respect home—where she planned to stay only off and on until she became very old and in need of care—I video-called her to see how things were going. She was dressed in a bright red-and-yellow silk sari, with a pandemic mask hanging loosely around her chin and neck, excited to be joining the home's Durga Puja festivities a bit later that evening. As she toured the residence, showing me her freshly decorated room, hallways hung with celebratory holiday lights, lofty Goddess Durga image installed in the main function hall, kitchen bustling with food preparations, and outdoor gardens with walking paths, Medha introduced me to fellow boarders. "This *didi* [older sister] is 'unmarried,'" Medha smiled as she greeted one woman making her way down the stairs in a lovely green sari. "Oh, and this *didi* is also 'unmarried'! Oh, and this *didi* is 'unmarried,' too!" Medha exclaimed, smiling broadly. I noticed Medha's positive tone—she seemed to pronounce "unmarried" in English in her otherwise Bengali dialogue with a sense of mutual pride and almost delight.

Just the winter before, Medha and I had visited together a different old age home in Kolkata, and I recollected how all the never-married women residents proudly introduced themselves according to their former careers—as retired schoolteachers (the most common), a university professor, an engineer, a lawyer. The women residents who had married and were now widows mostly described themselves instead as having been "just a housewife."

Medha and I ended our video tour in time for her to join the holiday performance commencing at the Loving Respect home. Later, during Medha's next morning and my evening, I sent Medha a WhatsApp message to try out my ideas: "Good morning! I was thinking, in a briddhabas [old age home] to be unmarried is the best status! Because no one wonders why you are there. If someone was married, people always wonder—why are you in a briddhabas? Why aren't you with your children? What happened?"

Medha only partly agreed. She replied, "Yes. But in India, especially the Bengalee people always wonder. First day, one male friend of the owner asked me, 'Don't you have any family member? Brother, sister, or nephew? Don't you have good relations with them?'" This gentleman's questions pointed to the hegemonic sense that everyone is supposed to be part of and live with a family.

I replied to Medha's message, "I see," and added a thumbs up emoji. But I didn't want to relinquish this train of interpretation altogether.

I persisted: "But do you think it still might be better to be an unmarried woman than a person in an old age home who has children?? I was thinking, because you introduced me to three unmarried didis with such a big smile, and they were smiling also. And then I remembered all the old age homes I used to go to, and my sense is that the unmarried women there had a little more status. Especially if they had been working women with professions before, like schoolteacher?"

Medha replied: "It's true. I will write you elaborately when I get time."

I responded: "Don't worry about writing me elaborately. I know you are so busy with your own work! I was just thinking. Enjoy the day."

It has also seemed to me, over my years of conducting fieldwork in Bengali old age homes, that never-married female residents achieve some implicit respect from having finally achieved (people presume) an entire life of celibate sexual propriety. Crossing age 70 or 80, an unmarried woman is finally no longer deemed sexually dangerous. Further, in the Hindu Indian tradition, asceticism generates spiritual power and prestige, especially for male deities and persons, but with some room for women also to pursue spiritual asceticism while renouncing ordinary domestic and sexual life (Khandelwal 2004). On several occasions, it was my research assistant, Hena, herself never-married and in her sixties, who openly admired the never-married women we met in retirement homes who had rejected marriage while dedicating their lives not only to careers but also to spiritual asceticism.

Finally, some women in old age homes find the never-married to be advantaged emotionally in this setting because of their relative freedom from ties to ordinary family and domestic life (*shongshar*). A group of five never-married and several widowed women residing in Kolkata's Rabindra Niketan Retirement Home discussed this distinction with me in early 2020. One never-married woman, Tapati, remarked, "I'm well off. I never have to look back." Arati, also never-married, concurred: "I have no regrets—that I left my home. I haven't looked back. Everyone who *has* a home (*bari*) looks back and feels a lot of *maya*." The core Bengali concept of maya entails attachment, love, affection, bodily and emotional ties to people, places, and things (Lamb 1997, 2000). The women all began to debate at once, affectionately, about who among them has more or less maya—"She still has maya!" "Yes, she has maya!"—pointing to one another while concurring that it's best to have less maya in later life and that those who never married are in this way better off. One widowed woman with children commented: "At this age, one *should* reduce maya, but I am seeing that it is increasing. I still miss my old home a lot." Another widowed woman with children remarked: "I am also very much 'missing' my home—everything there! The people. The food. I was there for forty years, no? Over that time, I developed a deep attachment, and then when I came away—I miss a lot."

These fieldwork materials help us see how the retirement home can become not only a site for receiving care, but also a place of fit and belonging for single women, where being unmarried finally makes good social sense. What I have been glossing as old age "care" is conveyed in Bengali with the terms *dekha*, "to look (after)," and more formally *seva*, "respectful care and service," which can be offered to old people, deities, and the public, such as through charitable work. As in English, these terms connote both affective concern (caring about) and practical action (caring for) (Buch 2015: 279)—that is, practical acts of care (like preparing and serving food, calling the doctor) carried out with caring feelings of love, affection, respect, and concern.

Contrary to the United States, where people imagine and hope (often unrealistically) that they will not really need so much care in old age or become dependent, in India, people widely take for granted that they *will* need and even desire old age care, and that this need for care is part of being human.[14] The life course entails phases of both caregiving and care receiving, and the intertwined experiences of dependence, independence, and interdependence (Lamb 2014). So, to need and receive care in old age is natural and expected, even (when it all works out well) enjoyable. The old age home as a relatively novel institution in India expands the forms that this care can take, offering sources of care beyond the family.

Sukhi-di, whose story I told in chapter 3, was struck with the novel coronavirus in the fall of 2020, while still living at the Government of West Bengal Working Girls' Hostel, which she had called home for more than thirty years. At age 78, she was expelled from the hostel and sent to a state quarantine center. The time had arrived that she had long dreaded, when she no longer had a stable place to live. Wonderfully, Sukhi-di recovered, and her surviving siblings came through to set her up in an inexpensive, modest, yet reputable and loving old age home for ladies, Abode of Hope.[15] I spoke with Sukhi-di by phone two weeks after she had moved in. Our connection was poor, but her voice sounded cheerful. She seemed delighted to be no longer climbing up and down the three flights of stairs on injured knees to do all her own daily food shopping and cooking, on tiny savings. She fills her time reading books, sewing, and conversing and watching TV with the other residents and staff. To live in an old age home had been an aspiration of Sukhi-di's for many years.

STRATEGIES FOR SELF-CARE

One evening, Medha, Bipasha, and I were talking over hot tea at a pleasant coffee shop in the Gariahat neighborhood of Kolkata. Bipasha was one of Medha's few other single friends, a journalist in her thirties who was still open to marrying. We ordered a second round of hot drinks and some more snacks to share, a veg sandwich and fish fry, laughing at and enjoying our indulgence. Bipasha commented, "Single women don't usually care well for themselves. They don't think they deserve good food." Medha agreed, "This is true of all women. Women are brought up to think that they should serve others—be it her husband, her elders, her children, or her household members. Not herself. Women are trained not to care for themselves."[16] However, I gradually came to see the ways many single women purposefully worked against the social grain to develop vital strategies for self-care.

A google search for "self-care and singlehood" results in a plethora of upbeat essays offering tips for taking care of oneself even while single, including "One Isn't the Loneliest Number: Self-Care for Singles," "4 Self-Care Tips for Single Women," and "10 Ways to Take Better Care of Yourself While You're Single."[17] Related stories from the *Times of India*, drawing on globally circulating themes, include "Self-Care is the New Empowerment, "5 Ways to Practice Self-Care in 2020 (without spending a lot)," and "Happily Self-Partnered."[18]

A few among the more elite women in my study were in tune with such public self-help discourse, striving to implement it in their lives. Others described ways of developing their own strategies of self-care quite independently, perforce. Since taken-for-granted ideas are strong that everyone needs care—not only in old age, but also in sickness and in daily life, to feel both valued and secure—many single women worked hard to cultivate ways of caring for themselves. This was especially true, I felt, for those who lived separately from kin, almost half of the women in my study.[19] I began to see care for the self as a feminist and ethical project, involving both resistance against implicit and powerful social norms—that

women should care for others and not themselves—and a journey of self-transformation: I deserve care. I am valuable. I am strong. I can learn to rely on and
care for myself.

Sanjaya, the polio survivor first introduced in chapter 1, was one who had very
purposefully developed techniques for her and other single women to cultivate
self-reliance and self-care. Sanjaya and two of her friends, the lesbian couple Ajay
and Anindita, had founded a support group for both lesbian and heterosexual
single women in Kolkata. Sanjaya described the development of her ideas around
the need to promote self-care for single women, speaking here mostly in English:

> A widow gets some government protections, and if her husband was employed, she
> may receive a pension. But the government provides nothing secure for an unwed
> daughter or sister.[20] If her father dies, she won't inherit while her mother is still living.
> Then once her mother dies, if there are brothers, the unmarried sister is a soft tar-
> get.[21] . . . Motherhood is so glorified in our society; if you don't give birth to a child,
> you are nobody, and you have nobody to care for you. So, if an unmarried woman is
> dependent on her family, this is very difficult for her, almost impossible. . . . The gov-
> ernment should offer some security, but the government doesn't bother. . . . There's
> also the mental and emotional problem of feeling lonely. This has to be addressed in
> a different way. You can't ask the government to give emotional support.

These concerns about care and precarity were what motivated Sanjaya and her
friends Ajay and Anindita, whom she had met while agitating against violence
against women, to found their single women's support group.

"We are all trying to create a bond, sharing thoughts and ideas," Sanjaya articulated. She told of how they had each been caring for their ailing widowed mothers
when they first met. "'But who will take care of me?' we wondered. We three said
that we need to create our own support."

Sanjaya went on: "We are each her own independent woman. We all have earnings. So, now we also need to learn how to support ourselves in other ways."

They recruited more members, and one of their first projects was to acquire
driver's licenses. "Because in the middle of the night, if an emergency comes up,
whom do you call?" Sanjaya asked. Still relatively few women in West Bengal know
how to drive, although car sales to women are on the rise in India.[22] Ajay quickly
attained a license to drive a motorcycle. "I persevered for a few years to learn to
drive a car," Sanjaya reported, "and, finally, I got my driver's license last year! We
are all working on this. We must be independent." None in Sanjaya's group yet
owned a car, but a few were thinking of going in together for one. They also felt
that having a driver's license opened up possibilities for borrowing a car from a
neighbor or family member in a time of need.

Sanjaya further discussed the value of having close friendships as a form of support for those living apart from kin: "Four or five of us are very close. When my
mother was sick, Ajay and Anindita were always with me. . . . And at the end of the
day, you just want to talk to someone. So, I look for friends."

Hanvi, too, was very deliberate about cultivating an ethic of self-care and independence. At one point, after meeting Medha through me, Hanvi chided Medha for thinking about family all the time and about how she has no one: "Once you know you are not going to get married and will be alone, you should accept that, come to terms with it, and focus on other things." Hanvi lived and cooked alone, in her family's large, crumbling ancestral home in north Kolkata, pursued meaningful work with the blind, maintained friendly relationships with the local vegetable vendors, shopkeepers, and rickshaw drivers, lived frugally, and carefully saved for what she envisioned to be her own self-sustaining and independent old age. She was not wealthy, but was still privileged enough to enjoy sufficient financial security and the wider social-cultural resources provided by her advanced education (MA degree).

Then, when breast cancer struck Hanvi when she turned 65, she carried her independent ethic of self-care to new, deliberate heights. Various kin, such as aunts and uncles, offered to pay for her medical care at a private hospital, but Hanvi resisted. "My relatives said, 'You should go to a fancy hospital. We'll collect money to pay for it.' My aunt insisted. She asked, 'Why not? We are here.' But if I don't have to," Hanvi explained, "I don't want to depend on anyone. I've been strong and independent (*svadhin*) my whole life. I don't want to change now."

So Hanvi chose to go to a free government hospital for her cancer surgery and chemotherapy treatments. There, one pays just 2 rupees (about 25 US cents) per visit. Hanvi would purchase and carry to the hospital her own plastic bedsheet, IV needles, and chemotherapy bag for each chemotherapy session, both to ensure the quality of the supplies and to save the free medicines for those who were even more needy. She told of how the nurses and doctors began to see her as very strong. "Your mind/heart (*mon*) has tremendous strength," they would say. She related: "Doctors don't like to talk directly with the patient. 'Where are your household/family members?' they would ask. I would reply, 'There are no household/family members. *I* am the household people (*barir lok*). You must explain to *me*.' After that, they offered me much respect."

When I met up with her several months after her final chemotherapy treatment, as her short gray hair was slowly growing back, Hanvi looked robust, healthy, and cheerful. She was pleased to report that all the tiredness and weakness was now gone. After completing her cancer treatments, Hanvi had quickly returned to her work at the institute for the blind, commuting to and from by crowded bus, buoyed to be with her colleagues doing meaningful work together for an important cause. Hanvi also now made extra effort to carefully prepare nutritious meals for herself, including plenty of fruits and vegetables, and chicken and fish for protein (which she previously didn't eat much), as well as vitamins and other supplements.

She reflected, "To be frank, I learned a lot from the cancer experiences. I learned that one's 'mind-set' is the real thing. At age 65 now, I want to live an active life, a good life, and then, when it is my time to go, when God calls, I will go—with no attachments. Until then, I want to be happy, to work, and be independent, and not depend on anyone."

Daily exercise is another popular means of self-care among several of my interlocutors. About two years after we first met, Medha began industriously exercising to promote both physical and mental health. She began walking five kilometers per day, while hiring an exercise coach to train her in yoga and calisthenics. She became so strong and skilled that her coach encouraged her to enter a local exercise contest, where she was proud to receive first place in the age group for ladies in their fifties. Sukhi-di had long been devoted to keeping her body fit, through swimming, calisthenics, and walking. When she had to get her knees replaced at age 72, she worked assiduously at the difficult physical therapy exercises to foster recovery, and she was soon walking, climbing stairs, and swimming again.

"I don't want to die, mind you!" Sukhi-di exclaimed whole-heartedly. "I *love* life! This vibrant life, I love it. All the beauteous things—the sky, trees, stars, flowers, birds. I love all the beautiful things in this life!" She continued: "And so I need to keep this one body fit. It's the only body I have in this life. And I don't want to become bedridden! I need to keep fit, so I can continue to care for myself."

Medha and several others also purposefully practiced self-care through preparing for themselves highly nutritious foods. Shortly after we first met, Medha began conducting online research on organic foods and nutrition. She switched over to almost all organics, purchased expensive organic black rice instead of white rice, and concentrated her daily diet on vegetables and *daal*. Each morning, she would awake to first drink a liter of plain water, and then prepare a smoothie of raw carrots, beets, cucumber, tomato, roasted cumin, lime, and wheat grass juice. I loved staying with Medha and eating her nutritious foods, not only because they tasted good and felt nourishing, but also because of the pleasures of companionship and commensality focused on self-nurture and good health. In the mornings after her smoothie, Medha would prepare for us a wholesome delicious breakfast of boiled cabbage and plantains, garnished with a homemade pesto of roasted organic nuts and raw sprouts.

Despite such successes in cultivating sustaining forms of self-care, I witnessed how caring for the self can feel very unfamiliar and unnatural, for Bengalis raised in a cultural milieu where living singly is not a normal, unremarked part of habitus for most people. An interaction with Aarini brought this perspective home to me—a sense of the unfamiliarity and challenges of self-care.

One evening in Kolkata, Aarini and I went out to dinner with a never-married single Bengali man in his fifties, Suvabrata, around ten years Aarini's senior. Aarini kept turning our conversation toward the topic of care. Suvabrata lived entirely alone; his parents had both passed away, and Aarini was very curious to learn how Suvabrata managed on his own. She had told me before the dinner that she was keen to find out how being single is different for a man and a woman in Bengali society.

"What happens if you get sick?" Aarini asked Suvabrata with some intensity. "Who will look after you or call the doctor? Must you do this on your own? Would your aunt and uncle do it? Do you have any friends who would do it?"

Suvabrata answered simply, "You have to look after yourself." I wondered how much his simple response might be influenced by his gender. Is it because women are so trained to care for others that some feel so uncomfortable caring for themselves?

"So that's it," Aarini probed, unsatisfied with the simplicity of Suvabrata's response. "You have chosen just to be very independent and look after yourself?"

"Not by choice, but by necessity."

I asked Aarini, "Would your parents look after you if you were sick?" Aarini's parents were still alive, living on the two floors below Aarini in their three-story ancestral home.

Aarini paused. "That's the issue." She seemed uncertain and disquieted.

Later, as she and I were heading home in a taxi, Aarini confessed that her parents often do not look after her adequately when she is sick, giving the example of how her mother had recently refused to call the doctor for Aarini. Aarini feels that her mother's reluctance to care is tied to her profound disappointment in Aarini's failure to marry and her discomfort with the notion that her adult daughter would still be living unmarried in her natal home. I wrote in my fieldnotes that night upon reaching my place: "In the US, I would just call the doctor for myself, although in A's case there might be some concerns about funds, too. But A in long conversations on this topic seems to focus not on who would be paying, but on the matter of care, affection, love—shown through tangible acts of both practical and affective caregiving."

Aarini longed for care from others both as a practical resource (summoning a doctor, paying for the doctor's visit) and even more as an affective practice (demonstrating love and concern, effecting kinship intimacy and human connection). Yet, Aarini also strategically cultivated her own capacities to care for herself. Shortly after our dinner out with Suvabrata, Aarini set off on a solo pilgrimage to the Himalayas. One of her aims, she disclosed, was to cultivate her own independent sense of strength in being alone, planning for a future without even her parents.

MEDHA'S JOURNEY OF SELF-TRANSFORMATION AND CARE

I close this chapter on finding and creating care as a single woman with a portrait of Medha's self-transformation as she aspired to security and well-being as a person "who has no one" living entirely alone. Over the seven years of my fieldwork for this project, I had grown to know Medha as my closest interlocutor, consultant, and friend. Over this period, I also witnessed Medha's purposeful journey as a person feeling tremendous precarity as a woman alone, to one who had found unconventional ways to forge meaningful relationships beyond the family, while learning to care for and value her own self.

I arrived in Kolkata in January 2020 after almost a year's gap and was greeted effusively by Medha. "I have huge important news for you!" she declared with an ebullient smile. "I'm so happy! I've had an absolute transformation! I'm tremendously happy! All the times I cried with you before—now what a transformation. I'm having fun (*moja*)! And I'm really happy!"

We walked over to Kolkata's Rabindra Sarobar Lake Park, to find a sunny bench where we could talk and "loiter" together.[23] Medha had been striving to cultivate projects of well-being and self-transformation since we first met, and she felt that many of these endeavors had finally come to fruition.

First, she told about how she has some good friends now. She is on good terms, as friends, with the man who had been her partner for a year or two, whom we will meet in chapter 5. She described how they now have a "very normal and comfortable relationship," and that they support each other a lot, mainly by talking by phone and sharing meals when she comes from her university town to stay periodically at her Kolkata flat. She had also developed a close friendship with Nayani, the one single woman she had met through my fieldwork with whom she was able to develop a real friendship—mainly, I believe, because of how they each shared a similar incongruous or mismatched class background (chapter 2). They would sometimes spend the night at each other's homes, cook and share feasts together, and talk on the phone—sharing the details of their days and offering support and advice.

Second, Medha had invested in herself by going on a monthlong meditation, yoga, and naturopathy retreat for women. There she had practiced yoga and meditation throughout the day, listened to lectures, and eaten nourishing foods. She described the retreat as a profoundly transformative experience.

"Why I had been so unhappy earlier—" Medha remarked, "I came to the realization that the sadness was mine [i.e., self-generated]. I came to realize that I myself have everything I need. . . . And I only have so many years left to live. I should live well!

"I came to realize that people can't disrespect me if I don't disrespect myself," Medha continued. "And if I don't respect myself, how can others respect me?"

She was pleased to report, "I don't really maintain relations with my *barir lok* [household people, i.e., kin] anymore. All they want from me is money. But I don't spend energy being angry at them either." She had earlier continuously felt yearning for family and profoundly hurt and often angry that no one among her kin really seemed to care for her. "That's the best thing," she shared. "From all this self-care, I'm no longer angry with anyone like I used to be."

All the healthy eating and exercise routines Medha had developed over the past several years had also led to what she described as "a huge change in my body and mind." From dedicatedly eating organic and nutritious foods, concentrating on a plant-based diet, and practicing daily exercise, Medha had lost weight and felt great. "At our age, so many people have cholesterol, 'sugar' [diabetes], and other problems. I have nothing like that!" she exclaimed. "How terrific I feel!

"I am also realizing now that I am so privileged," Medha divulged. "I got a salary raise. I receive so much salary!" This is someone who was born into a family of poverty, foundational experiences Medha never forgets. "I only need to spend about 10 percent of it!" Medha seemed quite astonished at her level of financial security, while she has also learned to enjoy spending some of her salary on pleasures for herself, including the yoga retreat, lovely locally produced items to decorate her home, pricey organic foods, and occasional treats to stylish clothing.

"I published an editorial in *Anandabazar Patrika* [the leading Bengali daily newspaper]," Medha continued, "and people are praising it a lot! From that, I receive so much pride." Medha realized that she is both a talented teacher, dedicated to inspiring students to succeed, especially those from underprivileged backgrounds; and that she has much to offer the wider society through her public essays.

Medha continued, describing her past year of self-transformation: "I say to God each day, 'Good morning, God! Whatever good day you give to me, today I will spend it well.' I say this!" She laughed.

Then Medha made a pronouncement really significant for my own and readers' thinking regarding this larger project about single women: "I finally realize now that compared to other Bengali women, I have so much privilege. I have a salary, education, a meaningful job, respect, and freedom. I say to myself each day inside: 'I am a happy soul. I am a peaceful soul.' And gradually I start to believe it. For these reasons, I am very happy and grateful."

By bringing to light the many hardships unmarried Bengali single women face, one can lose sight of the myriad hardships that can also come with marrying, and from the forms of structural violence tied to gender, sexuality, social class, and caste experienced by women and men across society.

I recalled how when I first met Medha, she felt so insecure and abnormal about living alone that she had hired the impoverished single mother deserted by her husband to come sleep at night, next to Medha's bed on a mat on the floor. Medha would tell me over and over how it is "absolutely terrifying" (*bhoyankar*) to be and live alone, especially as one looks ahead to old age. Medha no longer felt the need to hire an overnight companion.

Medha was now claiming her own sense of self-worth and self-strength, while strategically taking the next steps in her pursuit of care and security, by establishing her place in a retirement home—convinced that no one can count on being fully able to care alone for one's own self while old. At the same time, as I write now in 2021, Medha is pursuing the next project in her journey to give and receive care, and to support the self in community with others. She is working to establish a charitable organization in a village adjacent to her retirement home, where she and other like-minded senior citizens will offer educational tutoring and career training to local underprivileged girls.

CONCLUSION

Probing the ever-present questions—"Who will care for you?" and "Who will care for me?"—posed to and by single women in India helps us recognize the local workings of care as "a form of moral, intersubjective practice and a circulating and potentially scarce social resource" (Buch 2015: 279), shaped by structural conditions of social class, gender, age, kinship, and marital status. To care and be cared for is central to security, sociality, and being human. To imagine a future of growing old alone, apart from kin, can feel highly precarious.

We have seen how this precarity can be magnified intensely among working-class and poor single women who lack the economic resources to fund forms of care beyond the family. Recall how Nayani's elite employer Pishi, who herself had never married, became angry each time the topic of Nayani's marriage was raised, and how Pishi later successfully purchased care in a comfortable retirement home. Medha, who had achieved remarkable professional success after being raised in poverty, first had plentiful economic resources to hire an overnight sleeping companion and then to reserve a room in the Loving Respect home in her quest to craft a sense of security. Medha's economic and social capital, which included her tremendous access to knowledge and the internet, also allowed her to actively participate in both virtual and in-person communities of like-minded people seeking self-actualization and personal growth, through projects such as yoga retreats, self-help discourse, and organic foods. Tannistha Samanta explores similarly the "cultural possibility of internet spaces as surrogate 'places' for later life non-kin sociality" among middle-class and elite professional seniors in India (2020: 114).

Recall in contrast Malobika of the West Bengal Government Working Girls' Hostel, who exclaimed: "*What* will happen to me when I get old? Who will look after me? . . . Old age homes are so expensive! *Who* would take me there? I have absolutely no one. . . . You have children. So, you have nothing to worry about. But me? I won't be able to do anything about it! I have neither children nor money. . . . The main thing is that you need money. Without money, you cannot do anything." As the COVID-19 pandemic raged across India and much of the nation went into lockdown, I came to learn that Malobika had lost her job as a home goods store sales clerk. I reached her by phone, and she was in great distress, with only a few months' savings in the bank. I and one of my research assistants, who had become very fond of Malobika, wired her some money. At the same time, Malobika's brother came down with COVID and requested Malobika to come nurse him—another example of the ways the care labor of unmarried sisters is routinely called upon with no secure sense that reciprocal care will be extended in return.

This chapter has also highlighted how living singly and caring alone for oneself can be a highly unfamiliar way of being in the world for women in India, even for those with sufficient resources to manage fairly well. Such a sensibility forms an important counterpoint to the current popularity and familiarity of solo living in places like North America and Europe.[24] For many of my Bengali interlocutors, to live and care alone is too individualist, independent, and precarious for comfort.

Yet, the chapter also showcases single women who push against the comfortable and familiar—reconfiguring possibilities for non-kin-based care, respect, and social belonging beyond marriage. In these ways, older single women may be viewed as vanguards in a broader societal reckoning of expanding ways to live meaningfully and achieve security in old age.

5

Sexuality and Love

It was on February 14, Valentine's Day, when I returned to Boston from a fruitful fieldwork trip to India in 2019. The following day, settling back into my home routines, I happened to have National Public Radio switched on, playing a segment on Singles Awareness Day. Who knew that the day following Valentine's Day was Singles Awareness Day, with the unfortunate acronym of SAD? NPR host Steve Inskeep began: "This next one goes out to all the single people out there. It is Singles Awareness Day. Couples have Valentine's Day, but single people have SAD."[1]

I learned from this NPR segment that restaurants and bars around the country offer perks to single people on this day, like discounts on cocktails. Phoenix tiki bar owner Dana Mule announced: "We even have a fire pit on our patios. We allow people to bring a picture of their ex to burn in the fire pit." Co-host Rachel Martin added, "A picture of your ex will also get you discounts at the Knoxville Tennessee School of Beauty."

My mouth opened in amazement. I entered one of those post-fieldwork moments, when during the first few days upon arriving home, one can see one's own society more sharply, lending it an estranged sensibility.[2] The story encapsulated some of the striking ways singlehood is experienced and understood in the United States so differently than in India. In the United States, no one would imagine that a "single" person had never had an "ex," whose photo they could conjure up to throw into a bonfire. Single in the US context signifies not currently coupled. But not never coupled. Single also might signify not currently sexually active. But not never sexually active, not even with oneself. Some research also suggests that single people in the United States are having sex more often than married people are (DePaulo 2017a).[3]

Just a few days earlier, Medha and I had been interviewing together Rinku Sen, a 64-year-old never-married woman from an upper-class family who had recently retired as a schoolteacher from an elite girls' high school in Kolkata, and who now lives alone in her family's grand old home in the small university town of

Shantiniketan, the favorite nature getaway for well-off Kolkata Bengalis. Rinku's only brother, technically sharing half inheritance rights to the home, lives abroad as a surgeon in Malaysia, and Rinku's parents had both passed away. Rinku had been narrating her life story in English, when Medha suddenly interrupted to ask intently in Bengali, "Not having any sexual relations your whole life, how difficult was it to control your 'urges'?"[4]

"Hugely difficult (*bhishon kothin*)!" Rinku replied vehemently.

"Me, too!" Medha rejoined.

Rinku reverted to English to continue discussing topics too taboo for her to discuss easily in Bengali: "The older I grew, I became more conscious. I gradually began to feel a loneliness. Then I gradually realized this to be a sexual loneliness. To recognize this as a physical urge comes a little later. First, there is an inchoate desire; you don't *know* your desire. . . . This is something that tormented me when I was younger—tormented me like hell. Sex, society, social attitudes about sex, and taboos about sex—all used to torment me. Now my knowledge is more whole."

Later that evening when Medha and I returned to the two-bedroom cottage we had rented in central Shantiniketan for our fieldwork trip and pleasurable getaway, Medha brought up Rinku's conversation about sexuality. Medha and I had traveled to Shantiniketan to pursue some local single women contacts and enjoy the rural town's peaceful surroundings. We were sitting drinking green tea on the verandah of our Airbnb cottage encircled by vibrant green mango trees and a lovely kitchen garden.

As I was writing up some of the day's notes in the dimming evening light and Medha was browsing the internet on her phone, Medha turned to me to pronounce, "'Sexuality' must be a huge 'pillar' in your book. It has to be. People in this society are obsessed with controlling women's 'sexuality'! *This* is why there is such pressure to get them married, and why we cannot accept it if a woman is single! And 'society' even exerts a huge pressure on single women to control *all* their sexual urges—to not even 'masturbate'! This is a huge problem for single women! Remember how Rinku-di said that this was a huge problem for her? Right! I said it was for me, too!"

I told Medha that I had noted to myself during that conversation that I wanted to ask her about this very topic—whether masturbation or pleasuring oneself was an option for single people.

"No, not in this society!" Medha replied emphatically. "It is considered an offense (*aparadh*) and a sin (*pap*)! People do it; they do do it sometimes; but then they feel like they did something filthy (*nongra*)."

She asked me about the English terminology I had just used, "to pleasure oneself," finding the phrase rather more accepting than other Bengali terms she had encountered. She then commented: "But one thing in this society you have been seeing—women are not supposed to pleasure themselves! Not for sex, or anything! You are supposed to focus on your *family*! Sexual pleasure is for producing *children*—and especially a son!"[5]

Rinku's and Medha's comments highlight the ways Indian society has long treated female sexuality as profoundly dangerous and as best contained within marriage, controlled by a man to whom a woman is legally married (see Mitra 2020). Such ideologies are inflected by class, and some of the most elite women in my study conveyed that they had no problem pleasuring themselves or taking lovers, participating in what Ira Trivedi describes as a broad sexual revolution sweeping through urban India and especially among the urban youthful middle classes (2014). Novels such as *Almost Single* (Kala 2009) and *Losing My Virginity and Other Dumb Ideas* (M. Banerjee 2011) offer up portrayals of single, solo-living, cosmopolitan Indian women approaching or just reaching their thirties who boldly embrace their sexuality, pursuing erotic encounters with various men (before ultimately marrying). The award-winning *Lipstick under My Burkha* unapologetically gives platform to women's sexuality, featuring self-assured female characters such as the unmarried Leela (although soon to enter into an arranged marriage), who resolutely enacts her sexual desires with another man, willfully defiant of sexual-moral social imperatives (Shrivastava 2016).

Nonetheless, Deepa Narayan found through more than six hundred interviews with well-educated middle- and upper-class women in India's major metros that most women felt uncomfortable about their own sexuality. Although they might articulate intellectual ideas about gender equality and a woman's right to sexual pleasure, in practice, they had been taught from a young age that women's sexual parts were dangerous and shameful. When Narayan casually asked women what word they used for girls' genitals in their native tongue, "most women either giggled or looked uncomfortable. Some did not answer. Some said they had forgotten. Some suddenly looked very serious. Some averted their eyes. Some said don't ask technical questions and get into scientific matters. It turns out the most frequently used word for women's genitals by women in Delhi is '*susu*,' the same word as urine" (2018a: 135). In reading this passage, one of my research assistants commented further how *susu* is also taught to children as the word for "private parts" for all genders, functioning as a noun for both private parts and urine, and as a verb for urinating, adding: "The shocking thing isn't the definition but the fact that adults are still using it as the primary way to name their genitals." Ira Trivedi further tells of how "like most Indian kids who came of age in the '90s, I thought sex was bad, something so awful that it must never be talked about" (2014: 34).

The single women of this study—all who had grown up in the 1990s or decades earlier—tended mostly to feel much like Medha and Rinku, that their single status left little opportunity for an active sexual or love life. More exceptions came among the elite, some of whom were successful in creating satisfying romantic and sexual relationships outside marriage, facilitated by participation in a cosmopolitan public culture emphasizing perceived "modern" or "Western" notions of sexual freedom, as well as their privileged access to private spaces such as independent apartments and cars. In certain respects, lesbian women also experienced more possibilities than heterosexual women for having relationships, since lesbian love was invisible to much of the society, excluded from social and cultural recognition and interpreted instead as homosocial friendship.[6] Medha developed a relationship in her fifties, toward the end of my fieldwork for this project. But many among my interlocutors never had had—or did not feel that they could reveal to me—any life experiences involving the actualization of romantic love or sexual desire. Further, single women across social classes and sexualities must contend in all sorts of irritating and constraining ways with powerful public sentiments about the dangers of a single woman's sexuality when uncontained by the sanctioned framework of marriage.

This chapter takes sexuality as the focal lens, probing why so many view a woman's sexuality outside marriage as so threatening, along with single women's penetrating critiques. In addition, the chapter explores women's narratives of past and present sexual and romantic experiences and desires, revealing the transgressive paths some women succeed in taking to form partnerships outside marriage. We see the ways agency for single women involves the intertwined processes of problematizing resilient norms to invent new gendered and sexual possibilities while also strategically conforming to hegemonic demands of gendered and sexual respectability.

VIOLENCE, STIGMA, EXCLUSION: THE LIABILITIES OF UNATTACHED SEXUALITY

As Medha articulated, and as I have begun to explore in previous chapters, the marriage imperative for women rests strongly on ideologies of the impropriety and dangers of an unattached woman's sexuality. Families and the wider society exert a tremendous pressure upon girls and women to contain their sexuality within compulsory heterosexual marriage, or, if single, to vigilantly guard their sexual purity. Such expectations are changing to some degree, especially among the youthful urban middle and elite classes, such as on college campuses and in hip, upscale metro neighborhoods like Bandra in Mumbai. But the single women I came to know who came of age in the 1990s or earlier recalled very little sexual freedom. Further, Trivedi found that young urban Indian women who had become sexually active worried that their prospects for marriage would be jeopardized if potential grooms and their families learned of any premarital sexual activity. As a result, sexually active young women in India's metros are increasingly seeking "re-virginization" surgeries to tighten the labia and repair the hymen in hopes that this will make them appear physically virginal on their wedding nights, while urban medical doctors report that abortions among young people are also on the rise (2014: 41–42).[7]

Why? Social control over female sexuality, including the vigorous guarding of female chastity and desire, is a common feature of gender and sexuality systems cross-culturally. In her classic "The Traffic in Women," Gayle Rubin writes of how the smooth function of kinship systems involving the exchange of women in marriage requires constraining female sexuality (1975). Rubin elaborates: "It would be in the interests of the smooth and continuous operation of such a [kinship and sex/gender] system if the woman in question did not have too many ideas of her own about whom she might want to sleep with. From the standpoint of the system, the preferred female sexuality would be one which responded to the desire of others, rather than one which actively desired and sought a response" (1975: 182). To Rubin, of course, societies shape and constrain the sexualities and desires of persons of all genders, including men (1975, 2011a, 2011b); but "the asymmetry of gender—the difference between exchanger and exchanged"—tends to entail a much greater control over female sexuality (1975: 183).

What is important for my purposes here is the question of how and why single Bengali women experience such immense constraints over their sexuality when living outside the dictates of heterosexual marriage. Like Gayle Rubin, I am concerned with how configurations of gender and sexuality "are located in specific times, places, and cultural contexts" (2011a: 2). What explicit ideologies and tacit sets of assumptions underlie the sexuality systems of contemporary West Bengal, with which the single women in my study must contend?

In everyday conversations and interviews, Bengalis across social classes and rural-urban contexts conveyed remarkable consistency when explaining societal ideologies as to why marriage is so important and an unattached woman's sexuality so dangerous. The most elite were often exceptions in their own lives, participating in a cosmopolitan culture in which dating, taking lovers, and accepting a woman's right to sexual pleasure were possible. However, even cosmopolitan women were able to articulate their society's prevailing sexual ideologies. These interrelated ideologies include the following:

- Single women are sexually vulnerable, especially if living apart from natal families, not protected by male kin.
- Single women are sexually unfulfilled, and therefore easily available and unusually susceptible to temptation (therefore also posing a threat to properly married men and their wives).
- Single women are at risk of becoming pregnant outside of marriage—endangering the reputation of not only the girl or woman herself, but also her entire (natal) family.
- Single women are at risk of rape and other forms of sexual violence, for to be unattached and "loose" can invite violation.[8]

An implicit and sometimes explicit assumption running through these ideologies is that a single woman is at risk of becoming, or is in some ways already like, a sex worker or prostitute—the paradigmatic example of the morally threatening sexually active woman outside marriage.[9]

Strictures surrounding female sexuality are also connected to concerns over caste and class endogamy, the practice of marrying within a prescribed group. Often in the name of "safety," families and communities curtail their unmarried daughters' movements in public spaces in order to keep their daughters from forming relationships with "undesirable" men—seeking to uphold (upper) caste purity and class status.[10] The *Hindustan Times* reports that 57 percent of people surveyed in India's metros declared that neither they nor their children would marry into castes considered lower than their own (Wadhwa 2007). In her work on Brahmanical patriarchy in early India, Uma Chakravarti (1993) examines how women were regarded as "gateways" of a caste, which needed to be guarded in order to protect the caste's purity. As Shalini Grover finds, "Caste-endogamous arranged marriages continue to ensure a family's prestige and status and to preserve the normative kinship order" (2018: 32).[11]

Ideals of caste endogamy, however, do not explain all dimensions of the social control of unmarried female sexuality, such as why communities deem it unacceptable for a young unmarried woman to be sexually involved even with a partner of the same caste and social class (that is, someone who could make an eligible groom, although the possibility of swiftly arranging a marriage can be a reputation-saving remedy in such a case). In questioning the idea that women's sexuality is controlled primarily in order to preserve the purity of the caste, Janaki Abraham argues that we must look beyond caste alone to examine the complex ways in which "patriarchy and caste meet-and-mesh to protect male privilege and power" (2015: 183). To Abraham, caste endogamy "is reproduced less as a value in itself and more of an ideal critically tied to power and [various, intersecting] forms of social status" (2015: 183).

As family life in India "requires that women serve as the social barometers of family honor," the behavior of an individual woman reflects on the entire kin group (Dewey 2009: 132). The danger and dishonor of an unmarried woman's sexual impropriety implicitly spreads (one could say, is socially contagious)—traveling from the individual woman to her sisters and the rest of her family, to her neighborhood and the wider community. One of my Bengali research assistants commented over email: "Internalizing the danger of having sex since childhood, becoming socialized with the correct sexual-gender norms to be followed—these are all a part of our gender awareness program within our households while being raised. If one transgresses the normative order, she disrupts the system, hence she is out of the system altogether [can be ostracized and expelled], since she will be spreading a different meaning of sexual life and a different gender awareness."

Many single women, like my research assistant, explained their society's sexual rules and assumptions in order to criticize them. Sanjaya—who ran the NGO for disabled women's rights and had founded the single women's support group introduced in chapter 4—strongly critiqued her society's attitudes about women, sexuality, and marriage. After describing a particularly atrocious case of rape that had taken place in rural West Bengal in 2013, when five men had brutally assaulted a menstruating rural schoolgirl returning home after an evening tutoring session, Sanjaya told of how within a few months, most of the postpubertal girls in that village had been withdrawn from school by their families. Sanjaya's single women's support group had gone to talk with some of the village girls who had organized a small movement to protest the rape.

As Sanjaya recounted: "The families married off their girls. 'We don't want to take that risk,' they said. 'Menstruation has started; let's get her married.'"

Sanjaya explained that it is less stigmatizing for the girl's family if she gets raped *after* she is married. "Otherwise, people will say, 'A girl got raped in your house. You have a bad girl who got raped.' As if she wanted to get raped! 'You sent your daughter in the evening to have tutoring. She talked to boys. She was dressed like that. So it is natural that she got raped. It's your fault. Our girls don't do like that.'" Her voice betrayed her antipathy and rage.

Much of the everyday talk about the urgency of girls' marriages accentuates not only the broader goal that female sexuality be contained safely within a sanctioned marital union, but also the narrower yet urgent goal that a girl not become pregnant out of wedlock. Recall that Mrs. Chatterjee in chapter 1 spoke of the natural "biological difference" between boys and girls, and the related risk of pregnancy, as the central reason people worry if a girl or young woman remains unmarried for too long. Retired schoolteacher Rinku from this chapter's opening declared, in part to explain why she had never dated or had an affair, "If a girl gets pregnant without getting married, the collective guilt of the whole society is put upon her." Bengalis in the early twentieth century used the term *arakshaniya* to refer to an unmarried daughter after puberty who could no longer be safely kept or protected (*raksha*) in her natal home (Majumdar 2004: 448).

Asha, a married woman from a high-caste but poor rural family whom I have known since her girlhood, first introduced in chapter 1, had a daughter who at age 15 began flirting with a boy from a Scheduled Caste community in the adjoining neighborhood of their village. Upon finding out about the situation, the daughter's family quickly arranged the girl's marriage to a suitable groom from their own Brahman caste, despite the fact that current Indian law prohibits the marriage of girls below age 18.

In the conversations that ensued when I visited with Asha and her two grown married sisters a month after the young girl's wedding, the sisters' talk emphasized how none of them had wanted Asha's daughter to fall into the same predicament faced by Asha's sister Mithu thirty years earlier. At that time, I had been living in the sisters' village neighborhood as a dissertation researcher.[12] As an unmarried girl of 16, Mithu had become pregnant, violated by two men, a father and son, known to her from her same neighborhood. The pregnancy caused immense trauma to Mithu and her family, and when the matter became public (despite the family's success in terminating the advanced pregnancy with the help of a local midwife), the news jeopardized Mithu's and her three younger sisters' chances for marriage. Finally, after several years had passed and the lack of marriage situation was growing quite dire, village people ended up saying, "Let a girl's marriage happen," and they refrained from gossiping about Mithu's pregnancy when a prospective groom came to visit. Mithu at last was able to marry, and she bore two children: a son and a daughter. When her daughter turned 13, Mithu swiftly arranged the girl's marriage.

It is important to note that it can be possible for people to find ways to overlook the fact of a *married* woman's sexual assault or liaison outside marriage—even a pregnancy from someone other than her husband—because her marital status gives her and her kin a kind of plausible deniability. In one case in a village I had been visiting for years, a young woman who had stayed in her marital home for only one week following her wedding returned to her natal home, where she gave birth to two children several years later. In her natal village, she continued wearing the signs of a married woman—vermilion in the part of the hair and red-and-white marriage bangles. She never visited her husband again, and several pointed out to me how the facial features of her son and daughter, two years apart in age, resembled those of a married man in her village neighborhood. But people could look the other way because the mother was technically married.

Many of the experiences single women face—such as feeling sexually vulnerable and compelled to modify daily behaviors to guard their reputations and safety—are also faced by women more broadly. A 2018 Thomson Reuters Foundation survey, "The World's Most Dangerous Countries for Women," listed India as the most dangerous country.[13] This finding dismayed many in India, who challenged the survey's methodology.[14] However, social scientist Deepa Narayan, author of *Chup: Breaking the Silence about India's Women* (2018a), argues that India must face the reality of sexual violence. Narayan's own research, based on interviews with six hundred women and some men across India's cities, found that "a majority of [India's] women do not feel safe alone on the streets, at work, in markets, or at home, even though they have learned how to cope with this existential anxiety" (2018b). The minority of women in Narayan's study who reported that they *did* feel safe had learned to modify their behaviors in order to feel safe: "They don't go out alone unnecessarily; come home at night before dark; get permission to go out; are always careful and alert; and censor their speech, their clothes, and their body posture" (Narayan 2018b).

The sense of an accepted informal curfew for women after dark—"Of course, bad things could happen to women after dark!"—and other everyday cautions that women take to feel safe naturalize what Sharon Marcus terms a "rape script" that women internalize—that it is "natural" for women to be vulnerable to assaults (1992: 390–393, 398; Dewey 2009: 129). US readers should take note that the United States also figured in the Reuters report as the world's tenth

FIGURE 3. Priya's Shakti: "Loose girl! No one will stop us!" Credit/source: Priya's Shakti, https://www.priyashakti.com/priyas_shakti/, p. 6, accessed July 18, 2019.

most dangerous country (see note 13), and US women practice many of these same measures to stay safe.

The popular Indian comic book "Priya's Shakti" tackles such ideologies underlying sexual violence.[15] In the wake of a brutal gang rape on a Delhi bus in 2012, "Priya's Shakti" was created to raise consciousness among young people and the wider public. The storyline features Priya, a woman who has herself experienced a brutal rape and the ensuing social stigma and isolation. The goddess Parvati is horrified to learn about the sexual violence women on earth face on a daily basis. Inspired by the goddess, Priya breaks her silence, inspiring thousands to take action against sexual violence around the world. "Priya's Shakti" captures the ideologies single women and their married peers encounter daily—the harmful notion that solo means "loose" and inviting sexual assault (figure 3). Medha commented, while narrating her life story: "In India, there isn't a girl who has not been 'sexually harassed.' I have also been harassed. . . . There isn't a single girl in India who has not been sexually harassed in her life."

It is because single women are viewed as sexually loose, vulnerable, and dangerous that many landlords will not rent to them. Some Kolkata apartment complexes even have explicit written rules forbidding single women tenants. Others require that the parents of a prospective single woman tenant sign an agreement that their daughter will not come home after 9 p.m., drink alcohol, smoke cigarettes, or have male visitors (S. Ghosh 2013). The fear is that single women might bring in lovers, be secretly a prostitute, tempt the upstanding married men in the environs, or be subject to sexual assault. Then the reputation of everyone else in the building also suffers in a form of social contagion, especially any families with unmarried daughters.

Aarini, the computer engineer who had returned to Kolkata after receiving her PhD and working in the United States, told of how religious ashrams across India also often prohibit single (Indian) women visitors (although solo Western women travelers seem to be acceptable). Aarini loves to travel and has a spiritual sensibility. She finds ashrams safe, desirable, and affordable places to stay. She gets around the no-single-women rule by booking a double room in advance and communicating that she will be traveling with her aunt. "Then when I show up, I inform them that my aunt got ill and could not accompany me. If I told them it was my *mother* traveling with me—this wouldn't work, because a good daughter should stay home to care for her ill mother! But if I tell them it's my aunt, there's no problem!" Aarini laughed. But she resented having to engage in such ploys, which also prevent her from visiting the same ashram twice.

Returning from an autumn trip to the Himalayas, Aarini described how one ashram made her wait outside with her luggage for four hours after her "aunt" did not show up. Aarini had talked briefly with two European women solo travelers who had smoothly entered the ashram. She pleaded her case to the ashram's monks, telling them that she herself had resided in the United States for many years.

"Why should that make a difference?" I asked.

"Oh, they think Western women can take care of themselves and are very independent," Aarini surmised. As Aarini's next lines elucidate, monks may also perceive Western women as already "loose" as well as alien, and thus not in need of their paternal protection.

"What's their concern about single women, anyway?" I was keen to hear Aarini's understanding.

"For one, they are worried that the monks will be tempted," Aarini replied. "For two, they are worried that I might bring in a lover. For three, if something were to happen and they wanted to kick me out, they could not just kick a single Indian woman out into the streets. They could kick a man out, or a Western woman, but they would feel that they needed to protect the Indian woman and not expel her. So they don't want to take the responsibility."

Eventually, the informal curfew of dusk setting in changed the situation enough to require the ashram to assume responsibility for Aarini. The monks let her in as the evening grew dark. "This is what we have to deal with every day," Aarini protested.

Malobika Ganguly, the store clerk in her fifties who lived in the Government of West Bengal Working Girls' Hostel, described how terribly trying it had been for her to find a place to stay as a single woman. She at first dismissively gave her reason for not marrying as, "Maybe no one liked me!" Later she told me how she feels some repulsion toward men (implying in particular repulsion regarding the thought of engaging in impure sexual relations with men). Things had been going basically fine until Malobika's mother, with whom Malobika had always lived, died when Malobika was 46. They were a working-class family and did not own a home. Malobika's income as a store clerk was sufficient to pay for her food and a modest rent; but she needed to find a place to live. I realize now that I never learned why she could not continue to live in the rental apartment she had shared with her mother.

"I thought I had found a place," Malobika recollected. "But then the landlord asked, 'Who will live here?' 'I will live alone,' I replied. And so he no longer wanted to give it to me!

"I was *very* distraught!" Malobika recalled. "*Where* would I live? A girl cannot live alone on the streets! I was weeping and weeping, and I was so mad at Gopal." Gopal is the deity Krishna in his baby form, whom Malobika worships and cares for daily, keeping a shrine in her room. Malobika speaks to Gopal, a very dear guardian figure for her, using the intimate second-person pronoun, *tui*, generally reserved for close childhood friends and children.

"I was walking and walking and walking here and there searching. I'm a female person, right? I can't just live alone on a footpath!"

Finally, someone told Malobika about the working girls' hostel. She filled out all the forms and pleaded with them to let her in. "Not today, tomorrow," they would say. She struggled for nine months like that, most of the time living in her sister's marital home (*shoshur bari*, literally "father-in-law's home"), not a socially acceptable or comfortable situation.

Malobika continued, "Then finally I said to Gopal, 'Today, if you don't make arrangements for me—.' And I received a room!" That was in 2011, five years before she and I first met and eight years before this conversation.

Mindful of prevailing stereotypes, many single women also foreground stories of carefully maintaining sexual propriety throughout life. Recall how Subhagi of chapter 2, the Scheduled Caste day laborer proud to have supported her natal family her whole life, described how she always took care to avoid dressing up, so that "people [i.e., men] would not do anything to me, 'touch' me or anything." "Someone might have fallen for her!" women neighbors listening in exclaimed. "People might have looked at her, and something might have happened!"

Sukhi-di also highlighted her strategies for guarding her sexual propriety when describing her work traveling around rural Bengal as the only woman with a team of UNICEF researchers. As first reported in chapter 3, Sukhi-di's male colleagues were shy about dressing and sleeping together in the same barracks, but Sukhi would treat her colleagues like brothers and comfortably sleep in the same room, matter-of-factly stretching a sari across the room as a barrier. She smiled proudly when describing how she would keep a knife under her pillow for protection at night whenever traveling or living alone.

The imperative to guard their sexual propriety leads to all kinds of daily exclusions for many women. Single women professors tell of how their married colleagues do not like to invite them to social events, out of fear that married male
colleagues—or the male husbands of married female colleagues—will be tempted
to start up an affair with the single women. The two unmarried sisters in their
thirties, Nabami and Srabani, from a rural Scheduled Caste community who lived
with their widowed mother, described the restrictiveness of their daily lives. They
had not married due to their family's poverty after their father died when
they were seven or eight; they had to support their mother. A few of their kin and
neighbors also commented that prospective grooms had not liked them for being
"too black."[16] Often, as I note in chapter 1, a higher dowry can compensate for perceived bodily imperfections, such as dark skin color; but Nabami's and Srabani's
kin lacked the resources for even a small dowry.

Nabami, the older sister, described the cloistered life of unmarried girls as her
younger sister Srabani listened: "If we go out and mix with anyone, people will
criticize us. They will slander us, saying, 'She is vulgar!' [conveying people's perceptions that any social mixing outside their household involves immoral, indecent sexual behavior]. So, we don't mix with anyone at all. At least I have my sister
here; together we can talk a little."

Nabami then went on to tell of being excluded even from family events where
men will be present. "We can't go to anyone's house where there will be boys or
men, either married or unmarried. Even if it's a family event, like a festival or a
wedding! We face this kind of problem. We can't really mix with anyone at all."

Sanjaya, who lives alone in a working-middle-class neighborhood near the
NGO for disabled women that she directs, told of how she would be very happy
to find a male partner, if such an occurrence could be possible. But she added: "If
I were to live with a man, or bring a man home, the whole neighborhood would
immediately talk! 'What a girl!' They would start beating me; their perceptions
would absolutely change. They would start saying very bad things about me,
behind my back, and to my face as well. 'Our children will be ruined!'"

One afternoon after interviewing Bukun, a never-married rural woman in her
forties from a working-class family, Medha and I invited her to come enjoy a cup
of tea with us out at the public tea stall on the main road. Bukun hesitated, at first
declining. She said she had barely ventured out of her natal family home for years,
after it had come to pass that she would not marry. She spent her days cooking,
sewing, and caring for her brother's children. Medha and I worked to persuade her
to join us. Finally, we succeeded by telling her that single women in my country
go out all the time, and that Medha herself, a Bengali never-married woman, loves
to travel and dine in public. We three walked to the roadside tea stall and together
enjoyed hot milky tea with freshly fried samosas while sitting on long wooden
benches out in the open air of the spring afternoon. Bukun spoke softly with us
and kept her gaze down, as the local men in the tea stall smiled and made casual

teasing remarks about our unusual outing with their village's normally cloistered unmarried woman.

Pratima Nag, in her early sixties and recently retired as a schoolteacher, lived alone in a rented Kolkata flat in the middle-class neighborhood of Salt Lake, Kolkata. She narrated, describing her life as an unmarried woman who lived alone:

> I was always careful to lead a highly restricted life. I absolutely went straight from school to home. If I returned a little later in the evening, people would talk. I never allowed any male visitors. . . .
>
> It was difficult to find places to live. The landlords would want to know, "Why are you leaving home to come live here? If you're not married, then why aren't you living with your parents? If your parents aren't there, then why not with your brother?"
>
> I would explain, "I have no mother, no father. My brother lives in Shantiniketan [three or four hours by train from Kolkata], and this is where my job is."
>
> "You should go live with your brother," the landlords would say.
>
> "But if I have no job there? I don't want to simply depend on my brother as his big sister. . . ."
>
> People, still now [that I am retired and older], are watching my every move. That you came this evening, maybe you did not notice, but the neighborhood people surely noticed you! Tomorrow, everyone will talk to try to figure it out. The servant girls will all talk among themselves and then gossip with their employers. . . .
>
> I can't mix at all. I don't like it. . . . Our society is not yet ready for a single woman to live alone. . . . I tell my students now, "You should think very carefully before you decide not to marry. To live alone [as a woman] is a very restricted, difficult life."

One evening after Medha and I had listened to Manjuri Karmakar of chapter 2 tell her life story, focused on education and supporting her economically struggling natal family of twenty-one, without ever bringing up marriage, love, or sexual yearnings, Medha exclaimed to me, feeling almost angry: "It's not natural or even possible to have no sexual feelings! *Everyone* has sexual feelings, no? She *says* that she is happy and that she never thought of love, but—"

I interrupted to ask, "Do you believe she *says* she's happy, but that she's really not?"

"No, not that. She's not lying. But she *killed* herself (*nijeke mere pheleche*) to be where she is now. She killed herself!" Medha went on, "Manjuri has no desires for herself! But *I* can't be like that! I will never be like that!" Medha uttered with force, anger, protest, and pride. Not directing any desire toward oneself is at once humanly impossible, she felt, yet socially imperative—a terrible quandary to endure.

My thoughts turned to Nita of *Meghe Dhaka Tara*, who felt compelled to quash all her individual desires to serve her family of birth, ultimately leading to a tragic death. I was spending a few days in Medha's flat near the provincial college where she teaches. The next morning as Medha was preparing for us a healthy breakfast of steamed cabbage and boiled peanuts,[17] she commented, "'Sexuality' in Bengali society is hugely important for your study! Did you know that Kulin Brahmans used to marry fifty wives and have sex with all of them, but the wives usually could never have a real sexual life at all?[18] Men also have affairs all the time. This is 'patriarchy.' Men have so much sex, yet they so control the 'sexuality' of women!"

Dominant ideologies about the need to control women's sexuality help explain material from previous chapters, too. Bengalis may not articulate the problem of single women so bluntly, but the implicit ideology is that the risk of sexual impropriety from the unmarried woman spreads—from the individual woman to her sisters and the rest of her family, to the people in her building (apartment house, ashram), to the whole neighborhood. People quarantine the source of contagion (cloister her away from other men) or expel it—get her married off, refuse to rent her a room, keep her from settling down in the family home, separate her from others.

Durba Mitra's (2020) intellectual history of modern Indian social thought surrounding sexuality exposes powerful historical foundations of such present-day ideologies. Focusing on the period from the mid-1800s to the mid-1900s in colonial Bengal, Mitra examines how British officials and Indian intellectuals utilized a common language linking the control of female sexuality to the evolutionary progress of Indian society. Marriage became regarded as essential to discouraging sexual promiscuity, with chastity "the sole imperative of the modern Hindu woman" (2020: 67). Administrators, doctors, sociologists, and social critics wrote of the "need to safely transfer a woman from the protection of the father to the protection of the husband" (184) and were "contemptuous of all women outside marriage" (190). Social analysts argued that "it was the perpetual surveillance in the institution of heterosexual monogamous marriage that would save women from their otherwise inevitable fall" (202). *Indian Sex Life* in these ways "tells a history of social strictures that have organized, disciplined, violated, and left a void in the place of women's desires" (Mitra 2020: 1). Ideologies change and evolve over time, of course, yet Mitra's intellectual history of modern social thought reveals roots of powerful logics about sexuality that continue to hold sway in present-day India.

Contending with such powerful ideologies constraining women's sexuality, some single women nonetheless negotiate opportunities for love and desire, as I get to shortly. Elite women especially often have more room to maneuver. First, I look at how the push for self-chosen "love" marriages among today's elite proves a barrier to those who see themselves caught in a cultural limbo between conventional and modern systems of love and marriage.

"ARRANGED" AND "LOVE" MARRIAGE
IN CULTURAL LIMBO

Although the majority of marriages in India are still arranged by parents and extended kin—while usually now also including opportunities for the prospective bride and groom to meet one another and express preferences—so-called love marriages are becoming increasingly popular across social classes and rural-urban contexts, and especially within India's metros.[19] Love marriage is often interpreted as a marker of modernity, and several elite women in my study felt that their parents and others in their cosmopolitan circles rather expected them to find their own match, as part of their participation in modern culture. At the same time, several felt that they had not received any cultural training in how to date or find a partner on their own. This experience of feeling caught between two worlds—of arranged marriages and love marriages, of convention and modernity, of "East" and "West"—became a central reason for not marrying.

Aarini, who booked travel to ashrams with her "aunt," described contradictions in elite families like hers in the way girls are raised. On the one hand, daughters are taught to uphold Indian gendered conventions as "good girls" by not dating or having boyfriends. These strictures are changing now among the urban elite, where parents may allow or even encourage their daughters to date and socialize in mixed-gender circles as long as they do not have sex or get pregnant; but for the women in my study, all over age 35, most had not participated in more permissive singles dating cultures. At the same time, those in well-educated elite circles are beginning to find arranged marriages unfashionable.

Aarini recalled, "When Ma came to visit me in the US, she asked, 'Where is your boyfriend? Where are you hiding him?' I told her, 'If I had a boyfriend, you would see him! I'm not hiding anything. And you *told* me not to get one!' 'Yes, that's true,' Ma said, 'but I didn't expect you to listen to me.'"

Aarini's parents arranged a few meetings with potential grooms. Aarini tells of meeting one or two for very awkward encounters: "I had no way of evaluating them, whether they were good or not, a good match for me or not, never having really mixed much with men, never having dated, and having gone [when young] to an all-girls school. It was very awkward. I couldn't choose any of them for marriage. And that was that."

Aarini, now 45, remarked, "Previously, girls like me would be married through arranged marriages by age 20, and we would simply accept what came our way."

"Would that have been better for you at all?" I asked.

"Absolutely not!" Aarini replied. "But yet—" She described a catch-22 situation of negotiating a liminal space between the old and new: "Girls growing up these days of my class are told both that we should not mix with any boys, *and* that we should go ahead and choose our own husband! Our parents say, 'That's fine—you can choose your own—you decide whom to marry.' But we are given absolutely no training in how to select a husband! I have absolutely no way of knowing who will be good to marry, and who not!"

Rinku, age 64, from this chapter's opening, told a similar story. When Medha forthrightly asked Rinku why she had not married, shortly after we had been introduced by a mutual acquaintance, Rinku replied, "I can tell you that, but I will need to do it in my long, roundabout way." She thus began her two-hour narrative, speaking loudly and articulately in English with almost no interruptions, a good storyteller. We were seated on plush chairs in the sitting room of her old family home. At one point, a domestic staff brought us tea and biscuits as Rinku spoke. Rinku highlighted a theme she labeled "cultural difference."

"My father was a surgeon," Rinku began. "His boss was very impressed by my father and sent him to England for further medical studies. I was about two years old then, and my little brother age one. . . . My mother was also very well educated. She looked for and got a job in London with the Indian High Commission—quite an exclusive job. . . .

"So, the first five years of my schooling took place in England, from ages 5 to 10. After that, my father had the option to stay on in England, but my mother was especially keen to come home—she was very homesick. And although my father had gone abroad to get more training and work, he was committed to coming back to serve his country."

Before heading home to India, Rinku's parents decided to tour Europe together, and they sent their two children, ages 10 and 9, back to India with their grandfather. Rinku continued: "So, my first encounter with India was without my parents! Yes! And India was even more different back then than it is now! I couldn't even speak Bengali. All this before I was 10 years old! The real shocking part of it— that I would be coming away from England *forever and ever*—grew on me gradually. That I will have to stay here in this country forever, whether I like it or not.

"I'm sorry for all these details," she interrupted her narrative, "but if you want to understand, I need to explain all this.

"While my father was trying to find a suitable job in India near a good English medium school, my mother educated us at home. She also taught us about the very different Indian educational and social systems. . . . Being a girl, this all was not so easy for me—adjusting to the new systems."

Eventually, Rinku graduated from an elite English medium high school, and went to college to study English. Her brother followed in his father's footsteps to become a doctor. Rinku continued to miss England.

"About the marriage question, I have to say," she continued, "I had friends who were boys when I was very young; but I did not come across any boys whom I could admire. I had comparatively such a high intellectual background. And I was constantly comparing the culture of the West with the culture of the East. The cultural difference was so sharp! . . .

"In India, I found there was a lot of male chauvinism. I was of an age that girls were not only getting married but also looking forward to it." She jiggled her shoulders, imitating the girls' eager anticipation and flirtatious ways. "I was not feeling that way. I did meet some boys, but I did not feel a strong attraction— they seemed more like brothers. . . . And I had a very strong anti-chauvinist feeling. . . .

"So, my first reason for not marrying was that anti-chauvinism in me is very strong! I have this in my personality. My second reason has to do with cultural difference—the way in which one approaches marriage in their country [England] and in ours. . . .

"I finally went to England again after many years. . . . Father came to realize how much he had tormented me, his daughter, by pulling her out of that culture. Father said, 'You didn't marry; I didn't pay for a trousseau.' A dowry was out of the question for our family [that is, they were too modern to participate in dowry exchanges]. 'So, if I can instead pay for you to go back there to England, I can give your personality back to you.' I was in my mid-thirties then."

Rinku completed an MA degree in English and resided in England for a few years before returning to India to work as a schoolteacher in an elite English medium girls' high school in Kolkata until she retired.

"It was my luck in life that neither my father nor my mother pushed me to marry," Rinku went on. "Father said, 'You have your right to have your own opinion.' . . . My mother did worry a little. Both parents would say, 'If you like someone, then let us know. If you find someone, tell us, rather than eloping. Or let us know if or when you want us to arrange.' . . .

"I could see that here [in India], what would be normal would be an arranged marriage. . . . But, I felt when I was growing up," Rinku continued, "that I was very against arranged marriage—that someone else would choose for me. Of course, with good intentions. But if I say yes just to please them, and then later if I am in a swamp, they won't be able to lift me out. That is, the parents and kin take the responsibility only to *choose* the person—but after that, you're on your own! If the marriage fails, *I* am the one to have to face the consequences—not you who arranged it! . . . And because of all the cultural differences and my strong anti-chauvinist feelings, I could not find any boys or men I admired enough to choose to marry on my own."

Rinku said that she remained single and avoided all sexual relations throughout her life.

LOVE, DATING, ROMANCE, AND DESIRE

Given prevailing social expectations that single women should be vigilantly asexual, it is not surprising that many women in my study did not emphasize or even bring up, when narrating their life stories to me, any experiences with love, dating, romance, or desire. In addition, no woman in my study ever brought up having once fallen in love with an unrequitable love partner as a reason for never marrying, although this is a story I have heard from unmarried Bengali men.[20] Moreover, some women might have identified as asexual if the category as an articulated sexual identity—that of neither wanting nor needing sexual contact with another person to feel fulfilled—had been more familiar to them.[21]

Experiences with love and desire did figure importantly, however, in some women's life-story narratives and daily conversations. Some of these stories emphasized love that was not, or could not be, consummated. Recall Sukhi-di disclosing in her life story, "That no sexual arousal took place, and that I did not love anyone—I cannot say that. *I* also fell in love!" (chapter 3).

Rachana Sen, a history professor in her fifties from an upper-middle-class family, told of how she had had a strong emotional and physical attraction to someone when she was younger, and how he had wanted to marry her and take her to America with him, where he had been offered a good job. But Rachana had declined. It had been a very difficult and painful decision at the time, but Rachana had not wanted to leave Kolkata or her budding academic career. Moreover, she was repelled by the superficial social life of dressing up, gold jewelry, saris, and parties that she envisioned went along with marriage. "I think I would have been trapped," Rachana reflected. "I was uncertain at the time, but now I think it was the right decision to say no." Other men had approached her from time to time since then, but Rachana asserted, "I cannot allow myself to be involved with a married man."

About one-fifth of the women in my study did share stories of pushing against norms to pursue sexual relationships that were sometimes very meaningful for them. Of these women, only one had been living in a rural area at the time of her relationship. I tell her difficult story, "Navigating Being an Unwed Village Mother: Suravi's Story," in chapter 6. The other nine women all hailed from the urban professional or elite classes, at least at the time of their relationships—a class positioning that carries with it some opportunities for privacy and sexual freedom.

Shoumi, a geologist with the Geological Survey of India who also does some work as an independent consultant and researcher, has maintained a years-long relationship with one male partner. Now in her early fifties, Shoumi spends months each year living together with her partner, but she describes herself as too independent and too devoted to her career to wish to get married. She travels in highly elite circles, both in India and abroad. Her wealthy surgeon father, now a widower, supports his daughter's independence. Shoumi moves between the family's large Kolkata home, where she created her own flat above her father, and the family's beautiful summer place in Kalimpong, in the Himalayan foothills of West Bengal. Shoumi finds her love life to be happy and satisfying; but she warned Medha, as the three of us talked over green tea one evening on the verandah of Shoumi's home, that Medha should absolutely not take her as a role model. Medha had just divulged to us that Shoumi inspired her. Shoumi reminded Medha that although both women hold PhDs and earn salaries, Shoumi's elite social class gives her freedoms, opportunities, social and economic security, and forms of privacy that would be very difficult for Medha to achieve.

Yet, love also figured importantly in Medha's own life story. In college, she had had a big crush on one boy. The boy, Medha's best girlfriend, and Medha used to spend a lot of time together, talking, studying, and sharing tea and coffee at student cafés. Medha had thought the boy liked her, too, but then her best friend and the boy announced their plans to marry. Medha felt heartbroken.

Medha spoke of how love and romance play such a huge role in movies and literature. "Imagine!" she said. "I was in my forties and still a 'virgin.' I had never experienced something that everyone deems so important in human life!" Medha then described:

> In my forties, I was into a bad guy. . . . He told me a lot of heartwarming things. He saw that I was single, and he thought he could 'use' me and get a lot of money from me, and he really did take a lot of money from me. Since I was so completely alone, I fell prey to his sweet, sweet words, and he took about 5 lakh rupees [about $7,000] from me over four to five years. . . . He said sweet things to me, and I thought, "No one in this world thinks of me. . . . This is the only person who calls me and thinks of me." He acted like he loved me. I knew it was an act, but I was just 'helpless.' This was a mistake. I was 44 years old at that time, and I continued that relationship for four to five years before I really realized that he was using me and that I had to stop.

Then, a few years after sharing this difficult story, Medha sent me a WhatsApp message with unexpected news: she was excited to have started up a relationship with an older divorced man, and she felt that she might be falling in love.

Even before this point, Medha had confessed that she falls in love easily—mainly previously through having crushes on public figures, such as a distinguished Indian journalist she took me to see lecture, and the handsome Pakistani actor Adnan Siddiqui, whom she eagerly watched on television. She had met her new "boyfriend" (using the English term), Safal, while on a European tour for Bengalis. She described how they had gradually gotten to know each other on the two-week tour. He would wait for her in the mornings so they could eat breakfast together at a table for two. They began to sit with each other on the tour bus. He respected her intelligence and education as a professor. He also found her innocence as a never-married woman alluring. He made her feel attractive and valuable. (The other Bengalis on the tour apparently disapproved of the budding relationship, and cautioned Medha not to spend so much time with Safal.)

After they returned to their homes in West Bengal, Medha and Safal would speak on the phone every evening, sometimes for hours. When he came to visit her in the college town where she works, he respected her by booking a room in a hotel rather than staying at her place. When she was sick once, Safal brought Medha food, washed her clothes, and sent them out for ironing—tending to her as a family member (*barir lok*) would in a way she had not experienced since childhood. Eventually, the two did sometimes discretely spend the night at each other's places, and they took a few trips together, posing as husband and wife, to the ocean and the mountains. She was 58 when they met, and he was in his late sixties.

FIGURE 4. Why should not single elderly people fall in love? Credit/source: Pixbay.

One evening when I was in town, Medha, Safal, and I gathered at Safal's apart-ment in an upscale high-rise complex in south Kolkata. Medha had found a Kolkata-based organization on Facebook, Thikana Shimla, which offers not only residential accommodations for senior citizens but also social gatherings focused on matchmaking for elderly singles, including widowed, divorced, and never-married persons. Medha read animatedly to us from a Bengali essay on the Thikana Shimla Facebook site, accompanied by an image of an older man and woman sit-ting affectionately together on a park bench (figure 4): "We invite elderly men and women to dispel their loneliness and fall in love (*prem korun*). . . . Why should not single (*ekaki*) old people fall in love? Old people's marriage or 'live in' is nothing especially new. Abroad, these things have been current for quite a long time. A lot of 'dating sites' have even been established for old people abroad. . . . Just keep in mind, you are not committing any offense or sin. You are just wanting to live in joy for another few days [until life's approaching end]."[22]

Over the following months, Medha would exclaim: "Who could have ever thought that at this old age, I could find this kind of love?" She spoke to me by phone when I returned to the United States: "I would never have believed it! . . . To have a person. Just talking with someone—this little is so much. That one person is there. . . . I had been so lonely—dreadfully alone."

Gradually, after the first honeymoon-type months passed, Medha found Safal to be not feminist or intellectual or politically liberal enough to seem a perfect match. After about two years (at this current writing), Medha prefers to see Safal as a close friend rather than a boyfriend. During the COVID-19 pandemic lockdown period in India, they talked with each other by phone most every day.

Sukhi-di and several others also spoke of the importance and naturalness of love and sexual attraction, even if they had not been able to fully participate in such experiences. When describing how she had fallen in love in her girlhood years but had then pushed her suitor away, Sukhi-di reflected, as I shared in chapter 3: "All people should get married! I personally think so. If not, why would have God created us that way, with different reproductive systems? Creation and re-creation will not happen if there is no marriage." Then, when telling me and my research assistant Anindita of how sexual desire will naturally be awakened in everyone, whether or not they can act on it, she recited lines from a poem to illustrate her point: "Whether the flower blossoms or it does not, the spring will definitely come." When first hearing of Medha's boyfriend, Sukhi-di had exclaimed in delight, "I wish I could rush over to meet him right now and see them together!"

Sanjaya also commented thoughtfully, speaking mostly in English: "Sex is an important part of an individual's life. It cannot be undermined in any way. But that should not undermine all other parts of life. . . . No violence, no pressure. Sexual life should be enjoyed and mutually respectful, with a good understanding between two partners." Sanjaya felt sad and even furious at times that she had not been able to experience such a sexual partnership, because of how her limp from surviving polio as a toddler had made her unmarriable in society's eyes.[23] Yet, she and others in her single women's support group, most of the rest of whom identified as lesbian, were animated in their discussions of the value of an egalitarian and mutually enjoyable sexual relationship.

POSSIBILITIES FOR LESBIAN AND QUEER LOVE

In her important *Queer Activism in India*, Naisargi Dave invites readers to conceptualize lesbian activism as creatively inventive, involving both the problematization of existing norms and the imaginative invention of heretofore unimaginable possibilities (2012: 8). I found this imaginative labor to be taking place in the small single women's support group I was invited to attend, in a bustling, working-middle-class neighborhood of north Kolkata, founded by Sanjaya and her two close lesbian friends, Ajay and Anindita.

Sana arrived at the support group one spring evening, her short black hair falling to just below her ears, in a modern style now popular among the more cosmopolitan women in the city. Eight women drifted in as the evening came on. We lit mosquito coils and brought in hot samosas from the neighborhood, as each woman, including me, shared her story as to why she had come that evening. Six of the eight women identified as lesbian, while the founding group saw its broader mission as the fight for rights—to property, income, independence, housing security, and more—for all kinds of single women in West Bengal. Sana was dressed in a *kurta*, a loose Indian-style shirt that can be worn by either gender, and light-washed jeans. She had a reserved demeanor, but she spoke openly and movingly when it came her time to speak.

"This is also my first time," Sana began. "I don't know anything about movements, but Mina invited me." Sana pointed to her friend next to her. Sana narrated: "When I was young, I lived at home with my parents and younger brother. He and I were close in age, and from a young age, I began to feel a real injustice—that he was treated differently than me, and no one seemed to notice or mind. For instance, he really liked yogurt, and so did I. Once I asked for some yogurt, and they said there was none. But I knew there was! Then my mother explained that the yogurt is for your brother. I felt there was such an injustice, and after that I never asked for yogurt again. Now I buy it and eat it, but I never again asked for yogurt in my parents' home.

"Then I also felt that my brother could do all these things that I could not do, like go out and fly kites with other boys in the fields, and I somehow began to feel that I perhaps should have been born as a boy. They also encouraged and supported his studying much more than mine. But it turns out that I was the one who succeeded more in school: I passed the class ten exams, and went on to higher secondary. But my brother didn't even pass class ten," Sana said with a small smile of satisfaction.

"Anyway, around the time that I was 15 or 16, I had a very close girlfriend (*bandhobi*),[24] and we were very close friends, and we began to fall in love and make love (*prem kora*). At the time—this was around forty years ago now [around 1978]—we had never heard of 'lesbian' or anything like that, so we thought, you know, that what we were doing was highly unusual (*asadharan*), unnatural (*asvabhabik*) even, and you know, like a—[pause]—sin (*pap*)." The others in the room nodded, and a few had filled in the word *pap* (sin) as Sana had paused. "We thought we were the only ones," Sana went on. "But we both felt that we couldn't live without the other.

"By the time I was in my young twenties, however, my family started thinking about my marriage. And we then had no idea of the possibility of not getting married. We thought there was no other way, and that we would have to get married. At the same time, we knew that without each other we couldn't live, so we resolved to somehow maintain our relationship (*samparka*), even though we had to get married. So, some families and boys came to look at me, and it was arranged that I would marry one man. It was all arranged, but just two days before the wedding, I felt that this is such a big mistake, I shouldn't go through with it. I would not be able to love him and give him what he wants—a relationship, and children, and family life (*shongshar*), and everything. So I told my family that it's a mistake and I can't go through with the marriage. But they said that we have already made the commitment, and so much expense has already been paid on both sides—all the arrangements for the wedding and gifts and everything—that we must go through with it. So the marriage happened.

"We were married for thirteen years. He, that gentleman (*bhadralok*), was a very good man. We became business partners also—he took me in as his business partner [in a printing and copying company], so I also began to have some money of my own. I was able over this time to maintain a relationship with my girlfriend. And with my money I ended up buying a small flat, and I decorated it, always dreaming that this is where my girlfriend and I could live together. Eventually after thirteen years, I said to the gentleman that we should separate. I couldn't tell him the reason why, but he was very good, and he accepted. And we have still maintained good relations with each other and are still business partners."

One can assume that their families did not as easily "accept" the divorce, given the importance of marriage in the larger kin group; but Sana's narrative that evening contained no mention of their families' reactions. The two had had no children, and I got the sense from Sana's narrative that perhaps she and her husband had not engaged in (regular? any?) sexual relations. This may be why her husband readily agreed to the divorce. Because Sana had not felt that her marriage had been genuine (as when she articulated, "I would not be able to love him and give him what he wants—a relationship, and children, and family life, and everything"), I feel that her life story resonates with those of other never-married women. Sana also never referred to the man she married as a "husband," but instead as "that man" and "that gentleman."

Sana continued: "My plan was that my girlfriend and I would be able to live together in my flat. But it turns out that over the years that I was married, she had fallen in love with a man—she had never told me—and they got married."

There was a collective sense of deflation in the room, and several let out breaths. "Is she still married?" we asked.

"Yes, she is, and they are happy, and they have a son." Sana paused, and continued softly, "That was very difficult for me, a very difficult time of my life.

"Then eventually after a few years, after looking on websites, and seeing a little news coverage on 'gay' and 'lesbian' issues after [the film] *Fire* came out, I learned about the concept of being a 'lesbian,' and I found the organization Sappho.[25] I received some support there. Through Sappho I met Mina, and we became friends, at first just friends, and then now our relationship is at a deeper level."

Someone asked where Sana lived. In the flat she purchased?

Sana replied, "No, for a long time, I couldn't stay in that flat. It was very painful for me. I had prepared it and decorated it so lovingly thinking of my girlfriend. It was very difficult for me to stay there."

Instead, Sana is living with some friends who treat her "like family"—an unusual arrangement for Bengalis, and something Medha herself had sought out for several years without success. Making a home with non-kin, except as a "paying guest" or in an institutional setting like a working women's hostel, is not common.[26]

Sana closed by mentioning softly that she is still not open to anyone about her 'identity'—not her family, nor the friends she lives with, nor people at work.

Scholars such as Ruth Vanita (2001, 2012) have revealed how a variety of sexualities and sexual practices were recognized in India's more ancient past. However, under British colonial rule, Section 377 of the Indian Penal Code banned all sexual activities "against the order of nature," including same-sex sexual acts, as "unnatural offences."[27] Portions of this 1860 law were struck down as unconstitutional in 2009, but were then reinstated in 2013. Finally, on September 6, 2018, the Supreme Court of India ruled unanimously that Section 377 was unconstitutional "in so far as it criminalizes consensual sexual conduct between adults of the same sex." Through this 2018 decision, the Supreme Court legalized gay sex (although not gay marriage).[28]

Among the women in my study, all over the age of 35, few mentioned any familiarity with or exposure to the concepts of lesbian or gay while growing up. For the four self-identified lesbian women, it was Deepa Mehta's *Fire*—and the enormous public reaction it provoked—that spurred their own awareness of lesbian and gay sexualities as a named identity. Mehta's 1996 film—often regarded as the first mainstream Indian cinema to explore homosexual love—features two sisters-in-law within a traditional middle-class joint-family household who become lovers. The film's unprecedented lesbian themes led to riots outside cinemas in India, with protesters arguing that the film showed things "not part of Indian culture" (S. Ghosh 2010; Nath 2016). Yet, the public controversy surrounding the film also spurred a broader feminist and lesbian social movement, leading many women to embrace publicly for the first time an "Indian and lesbian" identity (Dave 2011). Filmmaker Metha recalls in an interview: "That night after *Fire* was attacked, there was a vigil by candlelight at Regal [Cinema]. As far as the eye could see, there were women and men with placards that said, 'We are Indians and we are lesbians.' I was like, 'Holy shit, this is cool'" (Nath 2016).

Since *Fire*, LGBTQ+ public cultures and activist movements have become more visible and prominent in India, especially in large metros like Mumbai and Delhi. Still, homophobia does not disappear easily, and many find lesbian identities to be even more stigmatized than gay male identities. As Gayle Rubin argued in her classic "The Traffic in Women": "As long as men [and families] have rights in women which women do not have in themselves, it would be sensible to expect that homosexuality in women would be subject to more suppression than in men" (1975: 183). At the same time, since lesbian women can be legible to the public as homosocial friends, some find it easier to meet up with a lover in a café, rickshaw, or apartment, compared to the experiences of single heterosexual women, who find it socially impossible to socialize with a man for even just a cup of coffee, let alone for a visit to her home. Nonetheless, many lesbian women feel angry and isolated, contending with deep social pressures to keep their sexual identities invisible.

Cofounders of the single women's support group where I met Sana, Ajay and Anindita, now in their forties, were proud to have become increasingly public and activist around their lesbian identities beginning in the early 2000s, pushing against heteronormativity. Both from middle-class Kolkata families, they fell in love in their girlhood years. At around age 15 or 16, the two became intimate friends and began to make love before they had ever heard of the concept of lesbian, thinking they were the only ones, like Sana and her girlfriend in the story above. In college, Ajay recalls seducing numerous other women lovers in the girls' dormitories, while always frightened that they might be caught and expelled or, worse, arrested and imprisoned. All the while, Anindita had remained Ajay's primary partner and true love.

Ajay and Anindita each managed to avoid marriage, while remaining in their natal homes. Anindita's older sister had had an arranged marriage ending in divorce, a fact Anindita used in arguments with her parents against her own marriage. Ajay had begun in their twenties to express themselves in increasingly masculine terms, taking on a male name and dressing largely in masculine-style clothing.[29] These forms of gender expression have helped convince Ajay's family that Ajay is not really the marrying or marriable type.

Neither Ajay nor Anindita have directly "come out" to their families, while each spends a lot of enjoyable time participating in the other family's home life. Both Ajay's and Anindita's widowed mothers now praise their daughters for all the devoted parental elder care they provide.

Focusing on queer lives and kinship in Mumbai, Brian Horton suggests that we pay more attention to queer attachments to natal kinship, while heeding how queers in India may strategically employ forms of silence and nondisclosure— such as choosing *not* to come out, the act so valorized in universalizing models of queer rights and recognition—as acts of familial care. Horton suggests that "queers often inhabit heterosexual kinship networks through the interplay of contestation and submission" (2017: 1059), and he proposes that "inhabiting contradictions between queer and normative—failing to ever be fully one or the other—is perhaps the substance central to queer experience" (2017: 1061).

As lesbian activists, Ajay and Anindita first joined Sappho for Equality: The Activist Forum for Lesbian, Bisexual Woman, and Transman Rights after graduating from college, shortly after Sappho was founded in October 2003. Later, finding Sappho a bit too elite and snobbish, they founded, together with their disability-rights-activist friend Sanjaya, the small, alternative single women's support group I attended, welcoming of all single women of any sexual orientation, while catering especially to lesbians. In their smaller group, the women converse primarily in Bengali rather than in Sappho's English.

It is still not easy to live openly as a lesbian or queer couple in Kolkata. Negotiating overlapping possibilities and constraints, Ajay and Anindita have found ways to cultivate a lifelong relationship amidst warm kinship ties and a vibrant circle of single women and lesbian friends. Watching Ajay and Anindita together, I sense possibilities for women's queer love expanding. The couple now runs a printing company. While making deliveries, Ajay drives a motorcycle dressed in shirt and pants, while their partner Anindita rides in back, her long black hair and brightly colored scarves flowing behind her.

CONCLUSION

Single women's stories of sexuality and love invite us to consider the ways people forge lives out of intersecting conditions of possibility and constraint. The cultural logics of the dangers of female sexuality uncontained by marriage underlie the puzzle of why Bengali society makes it so difficult to be an unmarried woman— thwarting single women's access to housing, to respectability, to social belonging, to possibilities for embracing sexual desire. Single women are presumed to be either vigilantly asexual—a difficult life path, although one that can ultimately bring some respect; or, if they engage in any sexual activity all, dangerously hypersexual. Positioned outside the norm, single women maneuver around, succumb to, and dynamically critique such logics. Their stories help us see the ways agency for single women involves not only pushing against but also strategically conforming to resilient norms of sexuality. Describing the society that pushed her to remain celibate forever, Rinku asked, "But *who* makes society? *We* make it! We make it *bad!*" later adding, "But we can change."

Bearing witness to expanding public cultures of sexual liberation among the cosmopolitan elite in India's metro cities, this chapter's stories also reveal how profoundly differentiated across layers of class are single women's experiences of sexuality and love. Most of the new single women who are successfully seeking sexual experiences outside marriage and on their own terms are elites. It may be hard for these cosmopolitan elites, participating in what Ira Trivedi (2014) views as a groundbreaking sexual revolution sweeping through urban India, to change the ways Indians across classes experience love and sex in the future. Perhaps they will. We shall see.

6

Never-Married Single Moms

One lovely February day in 2019 while I was in Kolkata, Indrani invited me to come stay the weekend at her home. I could spend time with her vivacious, growing six-year-old daughter as well as Indrani's parents, who lived just below her in the first two stories of the family's three-story home on a sought-after, tree-lined Kolkata street. Indrani would also invite over a single-mother friend, Mithun, and her young daughter. The two girls could play together, while Indrani and Mithun would share with me stories of being single mothers in India. It sounded fun as well as enlightening. I always loved Indrani's home and company. I was happy to accept.

Among many other topics, Indrani and Mithun shared stories about how they and their daughters respond to persistent questions about the fathers. Both Indrani, who has never been married, and Mithun, who is divorced, had adopted their daughters. Mithun taught her five-year-old daughter Aanshi to reply to such questions by pronouncing, "My mom is both my mother and father." But recently some kids at school retorted, "That's impossible." Aanshi had cried.

Indrani and her daughter Nandini had then spoken about this problem for a while. "What should Aanshi say?" Nandini ended up making a lovely WhatsApp video message for Aanshi, which Aanshi had loved. Dressed in a bright yellow frock and smiling confidently, Nandini told her young friend, "Don't let those children bother you! . . . Also, if you speak in English, then no one will mind about the father issue." It seems that Nandini already realized the cultural capital that English proficiency can bring, which can also serve to silence other children not fluent in the language.

Enormous importance is placed on having children in Indian social worlds, and this chapter explores how it is possible to have a child on your own. Media stories are reporting an upsurge of single mothers in India, focusing on single celebrities and other elite cosmopolitans, while grouping together divorced, widowed, separated, and never-married women.[1] These stories are often upbeat and celebratory, like one titled "On Her Own: 3 Courageous Women Share What It Means to Be a Single Mother in India," featuring the byline "This International Women's Day, we introduce you to some truly incredible Indian women whose stories define resilience, courage, and inspiration" (Raja 2019). A United Nations Women report relates that 13 million, or 4.5 percent, of Indian households are now run by single mothers.[2]

Being a never-married single mom can also be very challenging, however, partly because of how strongly the society is set up for women with husbands and children with fathers. "Is It Easy to Be a Single Mother in India?" the *Times of India* asks, replying, "It's hard to fathom the magnitude of challenges that single mothers (widows, divorcees, separated, or single parent by choice) face every day in India," including financial struggles, stigma, sexual harassment, unending questions, and the difficulty of balancing work and childcare (Vajpayee 2019).[3]

This chapter focuses on the stories of three never-married single moms navigating diverse life paths. The first, Suravi, is a rural woman from a high-caste yet poor family who conceived her son through a relationship with a neighbor. She has managed to raise her son amidst much hardship and challenge, while continuing to fight for her and his legal rights and for social respect. The next is Indrani, my weekend host, an urban professional woman who adopted her daughter. The third, Kumkum, is a successful Kolkata author who conceived her daughter through IVF. Each of these single moms lives not only with her child, but also with extended natal kin.

No one trajectory of single motherhood emerges from these three stories. The women whose voices are heard here lead multifaceted lives, balancing the challenges and stigma of single motherhood with a range of motivating aspirations and opportunities. We will see how their stories illuminate not only the lived experiences of particularly situated individuals but also both changing and enduring configurations of kinship, gender, and sexuality in a wider Indian society.

NAVIGATING BEING AN UNWED VILLAGE MOTHER:
SURAVI'S STORY

Medha had been keen to show me her natal village, and we made the weekend trip together, described at the opening of chapter 3. One motive for the journey was to give me the opportunity to meet one of Medha's childhood friends, a woman she described in English as an "unwed mother." Medha had known the unmarried mother, Suravi, since girlhood, growing up together in the village just two years apart in age. Suravi had raised her son, now 21, with much difficulty in village society, and she continued to live there with her extended natal family.

Rising before 6 a.m. on my first morning in the village, I went out to take a brisk walk with Medha's sister-in-law, Boudi. Boudi and I complimented each other on our fast walking pace, while Boudi introduced me to neighbors carrying out their morning routines. She explained my research interest in unmarried women. "You have one of those," a neighbor woman said to Boudi in a tone conveying a hint of discussing something shameful, referring to Medha. Another female neighbor mentioned in hushed tones, "There's a woman who had a child outside marriage—would you be interested in that type of case?" Boudi replied that, indeed, Medha was planning to introduce me to her.

Shortly after, as we continued our walk, Boudi pointed out "the boy's" house, recalling how he and a village girl, "a *kumari*"—a term referring to an unmarried girl or daughter, sometimes translated as "virgin"—had fallen in love. They had even made love (*prem korechilo*) without being married! The girl got pregnant, "and then of course no one else would marry her," Boudi said. "The boy got married to someone else."

"And her child?" I asked.

"Yes, she's raising him—with much difficulty. When he was in school, he couldn't write his father's name [on the school forms]. Imagine! In this society. The mother's name doesn't matter at all—only the father's. And he can't write down his father's name."

Medha later added, as she, Boudi, and I were talking over a breakfast of hot milky tea and puffy luchi breads with spiced potatoes, "Imagine what suffering (*kashta*) she endured! In this village society."

Later that morning, Medha and I dropped in at the unmarried mother Suravi's home. While we waited for her to return from giving tutoring lessons to some village children, we met several of the household's family members, who offered us stools on a verandah of mud walls and thatched roof, facing the home's inner walled courtyard. Suravi still lives in the natal home where she was born and raised. With her now are two brothers, her mother, her married brothers' wives and three children, her own 21-year-old son, and her son's young wife and infant.

Arriving back from tutoring dressed in a fresh blue-and-green-checked cotton sari and her long black hair pulled into a knot, Suravi was happy to greet Medha after several years. I explained the research project and asked if Suravi would like to participate. Suravi agreed, asking, "Where should I begin? Right from my childhood, or from this episode of mine?"

Suravi's son, Srijesh, and the other women of the household gathered around us as we spoke, listening in and occasionally helping to fill in details. Throughout, Suravi's son would coach his mother, "Speak slowly/clearly, Ma (*aste aste bolo*). Let her write. Tell her carefully."

"Start from your childhood," Medha and I replied together. Then Medha added, "In your life story, when you first began to experience pain and suffering, tell all about that."

"Well, when I was very young," Suravi began, "when I was absolutely a young child, I didn't suffer at all."

"I also told Sarah the same!" Medha exclaimed.

"I absolutely didn't suffer when I was very little," Suravi reaffirmed.

I recalled other Bengali women's life narratives, which almost always emphasize a very early period of happiness and care within the natal family, receiving love and affection from parents and other relatives, with few responsibilities, constraints, or worries (e.g., Lamb 2001: 17, 24).

"Then as I grew up gradually, bit by bit, I became a little older," Suravi continued, "and so many little brothers and sisters came along. We were four sisters and three brothers, and I was the oldest. And Father was the only one earning. He was alone, and there was no one else to earn," indicating that they were not living in a joint family with other members to pool resources. "So, what happened is that, whatever was remaining of our land, our [agricultural] fields, Father sold to feed us. And then we became extremely poor."

They were a Brahman family, often deemed to be the "highest" caste, but caste intersects with class in varying ways. Although historically disadvantaged caste groups remain heavily concentrated in the lower economic classes, even Brahman families can suffer from poverty.

"I began working in other people's homes, in Kolkata," Suravi continued, laboring as a live-in domestic servant around eight hours away from her Medinipur village, undergoing an arduous journey by foot, bus, and train. "Whatever money I would earn, I would send back home, so that my brothers and sisters could eat."

In this way, Suravi's young life followed the familiar pattern of the oldest daughter in poor families working to support natal kin rather than marrying—like Nita in *Megha Dhaka Tara* and other women featured in chapter 3. Standard practice in Bengali families is that same-gender siblings should get married sequentially in order of age. But this did not happen for Suravi. "While I was gone in Kolkata," Suravi narrated, "one of my sisters got married, and then after I arrived back home, another sister's marriage happened. Then my youngest sister's marriage took place."

It was around this time, when Suravi would have been nearly 30 years old, that she started a relationship with a neighboring young man from a financially well-to-do, high-caste (but not Brahman) Kayastha family.[4]

"After that, after the last of my sisters married, a person who lived in a neighboring house—I'll tell you his name—let the name be there—when I'm telling everything else, then his name too should be there," Suravi asserted. We will come to see how Suravi's years of struggle for respect and social recognition have included striving to publicly proclaim her son's father's name. "Let the name be recorded," Suravi went on. "My son's father's name is Kalaparan Kundu.[5]

"The connection [or relationship, *jogajog*] was with him only." Suravi emphasized her overall sexual purity, that she had not engaged in romantic or sexual relations with anyone other than this one man.

"After the connection took place—." Suravi paused, so Medha jumped in, "A 'love affair' developed."

"Yes, it developed," Suravi added.

I interjected gently, "This happens in my country all the time."

"It really happens?" Suravi asked.

"Yes, in their country, all people's 'love affairs' are always happening!" Medha exclaimed.

"I see. So, then what happened," Suravi continued, "is that he adorned me with vermilion in a temple." Vermilion in the woman's hair parting is a key symbol of Hindu marriage. "And then, as we were preparing to go to the registry for an official marriage, after the marriage in the temple, I conceived a child."

We see here how important it was for Suravi to present herself as being married before she conceived the child. The groom's act of placing vermilion, or *sindur*, in the part of the bride's hair is a central ritual in Hindu weddings. Medha later explained, as did my Bengali research assistant working on transcribing this recorded interview, that unregistered and socially ambiguous marriages can occur this way—where a couple goes secretly to a temple to perform the vermilion-giving ritual. Whether or not a couple in fact goes to a temple, telling the story of performing a private vermilion marriage ritual within a temple is itself a performance aimed at giving the relationship legitimacy and symbolizing marital status. From then on, Suravi has worn red vermilion in her hair part, along with the red-and-white *shakha pola* bangles signifying marriage for Bengali women. Further, importantly, she does not see herself as unmarried. Medha later reflected further to me about Suravi's wearing the signs of a married woman and speaking about a temple wedding: "She presents herself as married. She fell into *such* danger, she faced *such* extreme humiliation by 'society,' that for survival, she needs to put on this disguise."

Suravi continued: "Then, assuring me that we would register our marriage, he escorted me to the registry office. But then what happened was that on our way there to the registry, he fled back." I surmised from Suravi's narrative here and my knowledge of Bengali village society that the groom would have been experiencing at this point a great deal of turmoil, knowing how tremendously disapproving his family would be were he and Suravi to marry—a marriage that his parents had not arranged, and with a woman older than their son, from a lower socioeconomic class, from a different (although socially-deemed higher) caste, and who was already pregnant (so, lacking in "good character").

"So, then I went to his home," Suravi recalled. "When I arrived, my mother-in-law and my sister-in-law began to beat me, and they threw me out into the road. They beat me up severely."

Medha interjected, "They beat her severely. Severely."

"Yes, they beat me up ruthlessly," Suravi described. "They tied these two hands of mine with a rope and threw me onto the road. . . . They attempted to murder my son, the son in my womb. They kicked my stomach with their feet, viciously, trying to kill him. Please write about this ruthlessness, this cruelty," she said to me.

"They dragged her thrashing down an unpaved road!—down this very unpaved road," Suravi's brother's wife shared.

"Then I came back to my home, right here. To my father's house. And my son was born here.

"When I was pregnant," Suravi went on to describe that trying time, "I would never eat for the whole day, the whole day. When this one was in my womb, I would weep the whole day. All I would do is weep the whole day long. I wouldn't eat for the whole day. I couldn't even eat one little bit."

Suravi recalled that around this time, the village council held a meeting to try to resolve the dispute between the two families. In some cases in West Bengal villages, if a woman becomes pregnant out of wedlock, a village council will intervene to persuade the two families to accept the couple's marriage, or require the male party to provide monetary compensation to the woman. "But since I have no money, there was no one to stand by me, to represent me," Suravi explained, and so she received no support.

Medha interjected, "Right! Write this down, Sarah. Make a note of this!"—how money plays a crucial role.

"I am impoverished," Suravi explained. "There was no one to support me. At that time, I was so poor, I didn't even have food to eat. Our financial condition was extremely miserable. My father by then had also had a stroke and was not well.

"So, once again, I came back to my father's house," Suravi continued. "After coming back, I struggled a lot. To earn money, I gave tuition [tutoring lessons] to children, even though I am not so educated."

Medha jumped in here to praise her friend: "She actually was really good in education. She passed up to the eighth grade. And that was a time when most girls here were not studying."

"Yes, and considering the state of education now, I can even put a tenth-grade student to shame," Suravi added proudly. "So, then, living like that, giving tutoring lessons in other people's homes, I slowly brought up this child with great difficulty."

"Did your family support you in this matter?" I asked. "Or did they blame you?"

Suravi, her son, Medha, and the others listening in all replied at once.

"Absolutely everyone blamed me as a bad woman!" Suravi exclaimed. "My father, my mother, absolutely everyone blamed me!"

"The neighbors all talked," Medha added.

"When a bad reputation occurs, it sticks on," Suravi's brother's wife stated.

"Everyone said bad things about me!" Suravi recalled.

"At that time, everyone called it bad," her son added.

"At that time, her mother, father, everyone—"

"My father, my mother, absolutely everyone blamed me," Suravi emphasized. "But then, could they throw me out? They could not throw me out."

"Even though they all showered abuses, does any parent want their own daughter to struggle with pain and hardship?" Suravi's sister-in-law queried.

"My father was still alive at that time," Suravi recalled affectionately. "Father died when my son was just four years old. But until then, Father raised this son of mine, taking him in his own lap and carrying him on his back."

Suravi then told of her ongoing "war" (*juddha*) and "struggle" (*sangram*) with her son's father and his family, and with the state, to achieve justice and legal recognition of her son's paternity. From birth certificates, to voter identification and ration cards, to admission cards to appear for school examinations, to bank accounts and passports, the father's name must be provided in almost every official document needed by Indian citizens. Some of these rules are slowly changing, as courts come to recognize the increased prevalence of single mothers in India. For instance, in 2015, the Supreme Court ruled that single women could legally claim sole guardianship of their children without naming the father or needing his consent (Joshi 2018)—quite a momentous change. In 2016, the Ministry of External Affairs passed a new rule stating that the name of only one parent on the passport is enough (Dabas 2016).[6] Yet, as Srijesh was growing up, the father's name was required. At the same time, Srijesh's father and paternal grandfather worked hard to block Suravi from entering the father's name on her son's legal documents. Starting when the boy was an infant, Suravi recounted, "I lodged a lawsuit [to force Srijesh's father to acknowledge paternity]. But even in the case of a lawsuit, there was no one on my side, because I had no money."

"No, it's because you were a woman—a woman!" several others listening in interjected.

"Well, I informed the Women's Commission, too," Suravi said.[7] "In Kolkata," her son added.

"But there, too, money can hush up things," Suravi explained, suggesting that her son's father's family had provided a bribe to stop the complaint.

Then, when Suravi's son was preparing to appear for his major tenth-grade Madhyamik exams, having provided his father's name on the school forms, his father went to the High Court in Kolkata to lodge a case to have his name deleted from the boy's papers. Srijesh related, "My father made a lot of efforts to remove his own name from the school board forms, but by the grace of God, it never happened."

"What happened? Did he lose?" I asked.

"Yes, by losing I mean," Suravi replied, "what I did then with great hardship is that I hired a lawyer and restarted a case in the Kolkata High Court. I had no money alright, but I was convinced that God is there. Even if no one [person] was there with me, God was there. I said I would conduct a DNA test. He [my son's father] was even applying to the Election Commission to cancel my own ID card [where Suravi had listed him as husband]. So, then the BDO [Block Development Officer from the rural local government] came and conducted an enquiry. And the BDO gentleman learned the truth and left."

Medha added indignantly, "Because he is powerful, because he has money, and being a man, you can see he is harassing her in so many ways! He has no right to go to the court! Only Suravi has the right to go to court—she and her son. They have the right."

I asked Srijesh, "Did you ever face any bullying or difficulties in school?"

Suravi clarified, "Because of your father?"

"Yes," Srijesh replied pensively. "I mean, I used to feel upset in the sense that everyone else had one thing—everyone else, all my classmates, all the other kids, would call their father 'father' (*baba*). But I couldn't call my father my father. From this there was pain. One other point was that I had to express my identity (*porichoy*) with great difficulty. I mean, the open declaration that here is my father—it was always difficult for me to reveal that identity." Boys and young men in this village society are very often introduced by their father's names, as so-and-so's son.

"And have you told how that man has married again?" Medha encouraged Suravi to relate.

"Yes, he has married again," Suravi replied.

"And he has fathered a son also," Srijesh added. "That son resembles me a lot."

"They look exactly the same!" Suravi added. "I mean, both look just like their father. Neither looks like each one's mother."

"And if my father, myself, and that brother were made to stand in one place, then all three of us would appear as sons of one father—as if we were three brothers, looking just the same! We all look exactly the same," Srijesh proclaimed.

Srijesh went on to express, however, how much he loves and admires his mother. "I want to draw your attention to one point," he said to me. "That is, whatever I never received from my own father, my mother compensated for that. She never let me feel lacking for what my father did not give me."

Other family members concurred, offering their praise. "Whatever his father was supposed to have done, his mother fulfilled it all."

The family women gathering around—the young man's mother, aunts, and grandmother—all praised Srijesh, using the diminutive *tui* second-person pronoun to call him affectionately such a good boy; a nice, kind, and loving boy; a generous, considerate, and intelligent boy. "All is well that ends well," one proclaimed, while another offered the young man blessings: "You grow old and live a long life."

We see in this narrative and Suravi's other stories how she navigates strategies for survival and respect in a social environment highly condemning of unmarried motherhood.[8] First, she presents herself as married, even when not legally or widely socially recognized as such. She wears all the signs of a Bengali Hindu married woman, tells of how her son's father married "again" and "a second time," and emphasizes how she had been married in a Hindu temple before conceiving the child.

Second, Suravi worked hard to claim a legitimate father for her son—initiating legal cases demanding the father to accept paternity, freely pronouncing the man's name, and having her son observe all the *ashauch* (death-impurity) rituals of an ordinary male lineage member when anyone in the father's family dies.[9] Death-impurity rituals vary by gender and kinship connection to the deceased, and Suravi underscored how her son Srijesh observes the full set of rituals of a regular male lineage member of his father's family: "When someone dies in their family, we too perform the rules of *ashauch*. I make him [Srijesh] shave his head, cut his nails, perform the rituals, do everything."

Third, Suravi lived an impeccably sexually pure life after that one incident. No one in the village could claim that she had ever taken up with any other man. Fourth, she was able to maintain good relations with her natal kin. Although they severely criticized her at first for becoming pregnant, they never disowned her, and the large joint family continues to eat together and care well for each other. Each smaller family unit funds their own major expenses—food, clothing, and so on—but Suravi described how they all eat food cooked from the same hearth, sit down together for shared meals, and offer each other emotional support and love. Finally, Suravi drew on her intelligence and education to find ways to financially support herself and her son, by offering tutoring lessons and securing a modest salaried job with the UNICEF-funded Integrated Child Development Services.

Because it is so important to Suravi that she present herself as married, I have been reluctant to label her in this writing as "unwed," a category that goes against Suravi's own assiduously crafted public and inner persona. At one point during our interview conversation, Medha turned to me and instructed, "Please write down that all the signs that a Bengali 'married woman' uses, she wears all of those." However, "unwed" (in English) and "*abibahita*" (unmarried) were terms others in the village regularly used to describe Suravi. Then, after taking me to meet Suravi, Medha posted on her Facebook page a photograph of me while talking with Suravi and her son, a notebook open on my lap, labeling the post: "Sarah interviewing an unwed mother with her son in my home village."[10] One of Medha's Facebook friends, a Bengali man who can easily recognize the visual signs of a Bengali Hindu married woman, commented: "I just noticed the woman wearing shakha pola [married woman's bangles]—trying to think what dynamics might have prompted 'an unwed mother' to do so, if she is 'outed' as unwed anyway?!" Medha posted her reply: "She has to show the society, a village society, that the person who cheated her, married her secretly in a temple. She took this disguise to protect herself and her son so that she can live at least."

I admired Suravi's sense of resilience and pride, and the feminist outlook she and her kin seemed to employ to blame other people and forces in society rather than the single mother herself. They critiqued the injustices of class and wealth inequalities, disapprovingly describing the father's family as "extremely comfortable materially" and "very affluent." They also blamed gender inequalities woven into the legal system, arguing that Suravi could not prevail in her legal disputes not just because she was poor poor, but also because she was a woman. Suravi's whole household also forcefully criticized not only the one responsible man but also his father: "His father, too, is an extreme rascal (*prochur bodmas*)!" "Right, that grandpa of mine—" Srijesh jumped in. Others completed Srijesh's sentence: "*He* is the one at the root of all evil."

Yet, despite her resilience, Suravi shared toward the end of my visit that she still often feels ill, has trouble eating, and has difficulty sleeping night after night, "from enduring all this hardship (*kashta*)." I commented softly, "There's a lot more hardship in women's lives, compared to men's." Suravi concurred: "Tremendous hardship."

ADOPTING AS A SINGLE MOTHER: INDRANI'S STORY

Indian adoption rules have long allowed single parents of either gender to adopt a child. The Hindu Adoptions and Maintenance Act of 1956, still basically in effect, states that any male or female Hindu may adopt a child if the parent is sound of mind, not a minor, and has the capacity to care for a child—provided that a male parent, if married, has the consent of his wife, and that a female parent is *not* married, "or, if married, whose marriage has been dissolved or whose husband is dead or has completely and finally renounced the world or has ceased to be a Hindu or has been declared by a court of competent jurisdiction to be of unsound mind."[11]

More recently, in 2015 and 2017, India's Central Adoption Resource Agency (CARA) instituted updated and more transparent adoption procedures, acclaimed for making adoption a little easier for single parents, whether never-married, divorced, widowed, or separated.[12] The adoption regulations of 2017 delineate that "any prospective adoptive parent, irrespective of marital status and whether or not he has a biological son or daughter, can adopt."[13] Some restrictions pertaining to gender and marriage exist, including that single males may not adopt girl children (while "a single female can adopt a child of any gender"), and that "no child shall be given in adoption to a couple unless they have at least two years of stable marital relationship."[14] Further, the new guidelines aim to fast-track adoptions for financially secure single women over the age of 40, to facilitate their success in being matched with a child before they reach the 45-year-old age limit for adopting a child under age four (Dhar 2017; Khan 2020).[15]

Public media report that single-parent adoptions are on a steady rise in India. One report reads: "A sizeable number of people, both single women and men, are opting to don the role of a parent by going in for adoptions. Adoption agencies, which earlier showed a staunch bias against unmarried men and women, are now more prepared to consider them as prospective parents" (Nair 2018). Another story reports that single adoptive mothers have varying motivations for taking the step, "the underlying theme being that they didn't see motherhood and marriage as connected experiences" (Khan 2020).

Statistics indicate a pronounced rise in single people, especially women, seeking to adopt in India. In just three years, from 2015–2016 to 2018–2019, the number of single women registering to adopt through CARA grew from 286 to 589 (Khan 2020). The numbers for single men seeking to adopt are also on the rise, although much lower, jumping from 21 in 2015–2016 to 71 in the first quarters of 2019–2020 (Khan 2020).

A smaller fraction of prospective adoptive parents ends up receiving a child, however. The *Economic Times* reports that only 75 single women adopted a child through CARA in 2015–2016, 93 in 2016–2017, 106 in 2017–2018, and 121 in 2018–2019 (Bhatt 2019). Stories also abound in public media that adoption agencies are still biased against single parents for not fitting into standard heteronormative molds, persistently querying prospective single mothers, "Why didn't you marry?" And single fathers, "Are you gay?" (Bhatt 2019; Khan 2020).

Having trouble falling asleep one evening while in Kolkata, I rose from bed to check my email and came across this remarkable message from Indrani. This was toward the beginning of my research project on single women, about five years before my weekend invitation to Indrani's home.

> Just writing very quickly to say hello and that I am very much looking forward to seeing you again! I got your brief note from Kolkata [last year] just before you returned to the States, and there was a lot going on in my life at that time, and there was no short way of describing it to you. I had actually been in the queue for adoption for over three years and it was going nowhere. Although it's legal for single women to adopt in India (and has been so for at least a generation), there are a lot of biases, as I found out. Every step of the way I had to explain why I was not married and I could not give any answer that was acceptable to them.
>
> It all ended happily, eventually, and that allows me to look back and think of the horrendous experience as some kind of test I needed to pass. I can tell you more when we meet. But mainly I didn't/couldn't write back because there was so much uncertainty about the outcome, it was a bit like holding my breath for something and not being able to do or think of anything else. In the end [the adoption] happened just one day before I would have been legally outside the [45-year-old] age limit for this application!

Indrani had returned to India several years earlier to build a flat and live above her parents, after receiving a PhD in electrical engineering in the United States and holding for several years a high-salaried job in New York City. She returned to Kolkata when her grandmother became ill, having had enough of US corporate life and wishing to be with her grandmother during her dying days. With a shipload of furnishings from the United States, Indrani created a lovely flat with a roof garden above her parents, while securing another meaningful and prestigious job in Kolkata working with green and alternative energies. She never gave too much thought to marriage while pursuing her education and career. But as she approached her forties, she began to long intensely for a child.

When she and I met up, Indrani told me more: "My mother used to say that love can happen even at 97, but there is a time for having a child. I also very much longed for a child." Indrani and her parents passed through many adoption agencies over the emotionally intense three-year period. "Why aren't you married? Why didn't you get married?" the adoption agencies always asked. "'I was just studying all the time,'" Indrani reported replying. "You know, presenting myself as a real nerd. 'I was just studying all the time, and I didn't think of it, and then time passed.'"

The agents would turn to glare at Indrani's mother, she recalled: "Well, a daughter may be able to forget such things as marriage, but a mother never should!" Indrani said she would motion to her mother to not say anything, but just sit there looking guilty.

Some of the adoption agency women interviewing Indrani over the years found her too pushy, or not demure enough, or in need of counseling. So Indrani, with her parents, went to several counseling sessions, and returned to report that they had completed the counseling.

Finally, Indrani was approved as fit to adopt, with an agency in the neighboring state of Bihar—due to Indrani's good professional position and the fact that she lives with her parents. So, she is not really entirely "single." True singlehood in terms of living on one's own without parents or other kin makes it difficult to be approved, as there is a strong sense that no one can raise a child alone, and that a child needs a family.

But would there be an infant available before Indrani aged out? The last weeks were very stressful. Finally, Indrani received notice that there was an infant, and could she and her mother come right away? There was one other family also being summoned—a younger husband and wife couple who had been infertile. The agency would meet with and interview both groups and decide to which the child should go. When Indrani and her mother arrived, though, the person who was supposed to interview them was not there; it turns out she had gone out of station and would return the following Monday. Indrani and her mother hadn't expected to spend the night and had brought no traveling bags with them. Plus, the following Monday was dangerously close to Indrani's 45th birthday. What if the woman didn't turn up again? Indrani was quite frantic. She made phone calls and sent emails. Isn't there anyone else who could do this interview? Also, couldn't they please select Indrani for this infant, as the other couple is still young and would have other chances to adopt, but this is Indrani's *very last chance*. If it doesn't happen this time, it cannot ever happen.

Finally, Indrani reached a woman in the adoption agency who was sympathetic, a single woman herself who had adopted a child. So, just a day before her 45th birthday, Indrani was given a child! The infant was six weeks old. They named her Nandini, "daughter who brings joy." Nandini has emerged into a beautiful, healthy, loving, smart, and energetic little girl, beloved to both mother and maternal grandparents. A photo album depicts as many happy, beaming photos of growing Nandini with her grandparents as with her mother, Indrani.

Indrani's father, now 80 and with a tall stature, gentle smile, and warm twinkling eyes, explained to me how he had arranged all the papers legally so that his daughter fully owns the upstairs flat that she had built, so that there will be no problems later on. "It's completely in her name, all hers," he emphasized. One central life duty of an Indian father is to ensure that his children are settled and taken care of for the next generation. For a daughter, this usually means arranging her marriage, but setting up a daughter with a secure home accomplishes many of the same objectives. Indrani's case shows how fathers can and often do care for their unmarried daughters, even when brothers do not. Indrani's brother once complained that their parents were giving so much help and attention to Indrani and her child, but their mother reportedly replied, "Look, you have help raising your children and running your household—from your wife. No one can raise a child alone."

Indrani's upstairs flat, beautifully constructed with fine, tasteful, sturdy materials, contains two spacious bedrooms with baths, a large living and dining area, a lovely modern kitchen, and verandahs at both the front and back. The real gem is the roof, which Indrani's mother also enjoys and maintains. The roof level is full of plants—some flowering, some edible—a bamboo-latticed pavilion, a wooden swing, sitting chairs, and the sky open to the moon and stars at night and warming sun in the winter months. Right off the roof garden is Indrani's office, constructed also as her daughter's play room, with low cabinets filled with toys and children's books, and a soft rug and futon mat on the floor. Nandini sleeps at night mostly with Indrani's mother, who felt that Indrani's sleeping habits—staying up working far into the night—were not good for a child. Once when Indrani thought maybe Nandini should sleep with her, her mother missed Nandini so much that Indrani returned the girl. A gentle male domestic worker, whose daughter the family educated and is now attending college, brings Nandini up to her mother in the mornings after the child has awakened and had her milk.

Indrani wonders how her daughter's unusual background will impact her life. People ask Indrani continually, "Are you married?" "No," Indrani replies simply. Then they wait for an explanation as to how there could be a child. Indrani says little and leaves them guessing. But she worries about when Nandini can understand more. Indrani also protests how Indian identification systems—for school IDs, high school exams, driver's licenses, passports—all normally require providing a father's name, in this patriarchal setting.

Indrani sometimes suggests that she might still like to marry, if it can happen. She seems to indicate that if she married, it would be to a man. She had participated in a few awkward match-making situations, including a singles event for forty-plus persons. Now, she says that if she can find someone naturally, OK; if not, not. She related how the adoption agency counselors would ask her whether she planned to marry, seeming to prefer that she promise not to marry, as dating and marriage could jeopardize the child. Indrani would reply firmly, "If I marry, it will be a package deal—me and my child. If a man won't accept both of us, then I wouldn't marry him; this would disqualify him." She added to me, "Of course, I wouldn't marry a man who wouldn't accept both me and my daughter!"

Indrani commented that most of her female Indian colleagues in the engineering field are also unmarried, having become too highly educated, professional, and career oriented to be attractive to Indian men as marriage partners.

Indrani's story highlights a vibrant life, replete with meaningful work, economic security, friends, and a successful quest to create and sustain intimate ties of love and kinship beyond marriage and patriliny. In December 2019, after the passing of the Citizenship Amendment Act, which excludes Muslim immigrants from pursuing paths to Indian citizenship, Indrani, her mother, and her daughter were active, going to protests. One attendee snapped their photo together as each held up protest signs, posting the photo on social media with the label: "Three generations of aware and responsible citizens."

Over that weekend I spent at Indrani's home, she told me how a neighbor woman around her parents' age whom she hadn't spoken with in years suddenly asked Indrani the other day, "So, there is no husband? You never married?" "No," Indrani replied. "Well, that's fine," the older woman responded after a brief pause. "If you marry, your life is rubbish; and if you don't marry, life is rubbish." As I relay it on paper, this snippet of dialogue sounds a bit grim; but Indrani reported the exchange to me with a smile. Her sense was that the older woman was intending to convey the reality that, whether married or unmarried, a woman's life falls under the patriarchal structure; and in this way, she voiced support for Indrani's progressive choices as a single adoptive mother.

EMBRACING UNMARRIED IVF MOTHERHOOD: KUMKUM'S STORY

Kumkum had looked forward to being a mother ever since she was a young girl. As she reached her late thirties still unmarried, she recalls thinking, "One can get married after 50, but you cannot have a child then—at least not a child from your own egg and womb. That's what I wanted." So Kumkum began the process of searching for a fertility doctor in Kolkata who could help her conceive a child through IVF.

Kumkum grew up as the only child of well-to-do parents in a spacious three-story home on a quiet lane in the sought-after Ballygunge neighborhood of south Kolkata. In college, while studying to be a journalist and creative writer, Kumkum recalls how so many boys and men were interested in her, finding her very beautiful.

"I delighted in this attention," she recalled, "and I found it very fun! But like a woman in a sari store—facing so many beautiful saris—it was hard to choose! Plus, I'm afraid I wasn't very sensitive about their feelings. I was young and didn't understand many things."

Eventually, Kumkum did move in together with another man, a fellow artist. Her parents highly disapproved. The two were heady in love with each other and their creative work, becoming successful in publishing and art shows. They introduced themselves in public—such as to neighbors and travel agents—as a married couple. Yet, gradually Kumkum found herself insufficiently attracted to him, while also describing herself as "too demanding," "reluctant to compromise," and "difficult to live with." So, the relationship lasted no more than several years, and Kumkum moved back in with her parents. Her elderly father died a few years later.

It took Kumkum two years to find a fertility clinic and doctor who would accept her as an IVF patient. No formal policies or laws prohibit single women from conceiving through IVF, but individual doctors are often reluctant to take on single women. Similar to their experiences in the adoption approval process, single women seeking motherhood through IVF in India tell of persistent questions: "Why didn't you marry?" "Why don't you marry first, and then come back?"[16] Once Kumkum even attempted to disguise herself as a married woman, putting vermilion in the part of her hair and donning the typical red-and-white bangles of Bengali married woman. "But the doctor asked me to bring my husband along to the next meeting," Kumkum said. It also helps if an unmarried woman comes to the IVF clinic with family members, to demonstrate a wider family support system. However, Kumkum wanted to take this journey on her own, without her mother's help. Her mother, further, was not always approving of Kumkum's decisions. Finally, Kumkum found a doctor who would accept her, and she gave birth to a wonderful, healthy daughter at the age of 40.

Kumkum and I hung out together on several occasions at her colorfully decorated home—enjoying tea, hot pakoras, mutton curry, domestic red wine, and conversation, sometimes joined by her three-year-old daughter and mother. A few themes stood out to me from our conversations. One concerns sexuality. Kumkum's experiences reveal how much the sexuality—or, really, asexuality—of the single woman becomes socially enforced as a matter of public concern, playing out through experiences surrounding IVF.

At one point, I asked Kumkum if she thought Indian society looked rather favorably upon IVF single mothers as sexually pure, because they were conceiving and bearing a child through a kind of intercourse-free "virgin birth." Kumkum laughed doubtfully at my theory. She delineated all the ways that people kept trying to regulate her sexuality while displaying their suspicions regarding her sexual propriety.

First, it was a problem that her sperm donor was known to her. "I'm revealing this news to you," Kumkum remarked, "because you're a foreigner and won't judge me." But she felt that she generally had to keep this information secret from those in Bengali society "because some things just wouldn't be accepted."

Her sperm donor had been a close friend of Kumkum's in her college years, and he had loved her then, but she had not gone for him. However, they had stayed in touch. He was an amazingly talented artist and now a brilliant professor. He had been the first one to inspire Kumkum to pursue her passion in creative writing. She asked if he would consider being a sperm donor, and he agreed. Kumkum told of the day of the IVF procedure:

> When he was supposed to give the sperm [at the clinic], I was all ready. My body was ready. I had taken medicine to produce more eggs. But his father was dying right then; it was difficult for him to get away. Also, he is a reserved fellow, and I think he was feeling awkward. So, I was worried that he wouldn't come. But, finally, he came and was able to produce the sperm! I was so grateful that I kissed him on the cheek, right in the clinic! Now, in Indian society, this is not done—a public display of affection between a man and a woman. Although it was on the cheek and not on the lips—but, still this is not done. So, he was a bit surprised, and I'm sure the doctor and others in the clinic were, too!

Kumkum told also of how when she was once discussing the IVF process and the identity of her sperm donor with a few close relatives, an aunt told her to stop sharing such "indecent" information. Now, Kumkum rarely divulges having any kind of personal relationship with her sperm donor, to avoid being construed as sexually inappropriate. Social mores suggest that to exchange sperm in a medical clinic is too sexually intimate an interaction for an unmarried couple.

Kumkum went on to explain how difficult it had been to get her daughter admitted to a top nursery school due to doubts about her sexual morality. "At our first school interview, the principal asked me, 'So, why didn't you get married, and why did you have a child this way?' They demanded that I produce the birth certificate and medical records to prove that there was no father." If the school could become convinced that the child was not conceived sexually out of wedlock, OK, but they were suspicious. News media on single IVF mothers report similar stories: "Despite furnishing a birth certificate, a letter explaining how her son was born, and the hospital's discharge certificate, officials at [one top-notch Kolkata school] asked [single mother] Anindita to provide an affidavit stating that 'the child has no father and that he was born through IVF'" (Wangchuk 2020).

One neighbor man, seeing me coming and going from Kumkum's house, mentioned to me how concerned he is for the daughter, as the girl gets older—how everyone, in school, in society, in official documents, will be constantly asking about her father. Kumkum herself complained how people are continually asking her about the father, criticizing how there is "such emphasis in this society on having a father."

Importantly, like the other single moms featured in this chapter, Kumkum lives not only with her child, but also with natal kin—in this case, her mother and the family's long-term live-in domestic *kajer meye*, or "work-girl," Rina, who helped to raise Kumkum herself when Kumkum was young. Kumkum's mother and Rina are the primary caretaker of the newest family member while Kumkum is out working. Kumkum believes that Rina disapproves of her manner of giving birth, however, and that Rina would treat Kumkum with more respect if she were married. Kumkum and her mother also often quarrel. However, Kumkum says that she cannot imagine moving out, leaving her widowed mother alone, and depriving her daughter of her grandmother's love and care. She also feels that her decision to bear a child is one of the most meaningful of her life.

MAKING KINSHIP WITHIN AND BEYOND LINEAL MASCULINITY

In diverse ways, Suravi, Indrani, and Kumkum—three single mothers raising children without a husband—are reconfiguring patrilineal conventions to expand forms of gendered kinship and reproduction. In thinking about these women's kinship strategies, I find useful the concept of "lineal masculinity" developed by Diane King and Linda Stone. Lineal masculinity is "a perceived ontological essence that flows to and through men over the generations," and a fundamental feature of patriliny in many societies, including widely in South Asia and the Middle East (2010: 323). For Hindu Bengalis, the concept of *bongsho*, or lineage (literally "bamboo") is at the heart of conceptualizations of patriliny. According to conventional patrilineal discourse, father and son form central, structuring parts of the continuing lineage. Like bamboo, with its series of linked and growing nodes, the *bongsho* is conceptualized as a continuing succession of males—linked fathers and sons—passed on through semen and shared blood, a male line of descendants from a common "seed" ancestor (*bij-purush*). King and Stone find that notions of lineal masculinity are frequently undergirded by semen-as-seed and womb-as-soil metaphors (2010: 331). Leela Dube writes that the seed–soil metaphor for procreation is found "almost all over patrilineal India. . . . The seed is contained in semen, which is believed to come from blood; hence, a child shares its father's bloodline. . . . Males are the transmitters of the blood of a patriline. The mother's role is to nourish and augment what her womb has received" (1997: 76).

One everyday practical consequence of such patrilineal models in India is the requirement to provide a father's name on myriad social and legal documents. I have noted that recent court challenges are loosening a few such rules, including now permitting a mother's or other legal guardian's name to appear in lieu of a father's name on a passport. However, paternity remains a powerful form of social and legal identity in endless contexts.

Suravi, Indrani, and Kumkum expand possibilities for gendered kinship both within and beyond lineal masculinity in several core ways. First, a woman as a wife would ordinarily provide the womb to nurture her husband's seed but not the core essence of the lineal or familial identity for her child. Yet, by being in a sense "both the mother and father" to their children, these single mothers are reproducing the next generation in some novel ways. Could one say that these mothers pass on their own (father's) patrilineal identities to their children, through a sort of matrilineal patriliny? It is difficult to answer this question strongly in the affirmative, based on only three cases and varying circumstances. Recall that Suravi worked hard to define her son socially and legally as part of his biological father's patriline rather than her own. Srijesh had assumed his father's surname, observed the same death rituals that his father's family observed, and attempted to provide his father's name on all his legal documents. Yet, Indrani's and Kumkum's children had no sense of having a different father, and they shared their mothers' and maternal grandfathers' surnames. As more unmarried Indian women choose to have children, it will be meaningful to investigate whether they and their families consider the possibility that unmarried daughters can extend their own patrilines of birth by bearing and raising children without marrying.

Further, it may be *because* they are raising children that each of these single mothers' relationships within their natal families is so secure, because of how the single mother's parents and wider kin become so attached to and invested in the child. Becoming a mother may be one way for an unmarried woman to buttress her natal family relationships.

Thinking through these materials on single mothers who are challenging norms of conventional lineal masculinity has also helped me see how single Bengali men—such as gay men who shun heterosexual marriage—in certain respects face even more familial pressure to marry than women. Amy Brainer also explores widespread understandings among queer communities in Taiwan that men face even more family pressure than women to marry and carry on the patriline (although Brainer complicates this public sentiment, not wishing to suggest that lesbian women face no family pressures). As one gay man Brainer interviewed articulated, "If a woman can't find a suitable husband, the family will be like, 'It's OK, don't worry; we'd rather you be single and happy and have a good job than marry into a family where you have to work very hard and have a more difficult life" (2019: 44).

At first, I had trouble recognizing the immense reproductive pressures non-marrying men can face in India, because of the way a single woman's sexuality is such a crucial matter of family and public concern. Parental conversations conveying the sexual dangers of leaving a child unmarried and vulnerable to disgraces like pregnancy out of wedlock, for instance, center on daughters and not sons. We saw how Suravi's male lover had no problem getting (re)married, while Suravi's (re)marriage was out of the question in her rural context.

However, I gradually came to see that—in relation to *ideals of lineal masculinity*—it is men who face even more pressure to marry, and how then both men and *married* women face the immense pressure to produce progeny. Given norms of patrilineal kinship in most of India, it is not surprising that for married men and women both, experiences of infertility can entail immense stigma and pain (although it is still women who bear the most social blame for being "barren") (Bharadwaj 2003, 2016; H. Singh 2016). In Egypt, Marcia Inhorn (1996, 2006, 2015) explores similarly how men who are deficient in patrilineal reproduction due to infertility may experience a great threat to their masculinity. Susan Greenhalgh explores how non-reproduction impacts experiences of masculinity among involuntary bachelors in China, known as "bare sticks" (*guanggun*) and "not real men" (2012, 2015).

Because of my focus on women, I had little contact with single gay men during my fieldwork, but Jayaprakash Mishra's ethnographic research with thirty-two self-identified gay men from the neighboring eastern Indian state of Odisha reveals how failure to conform to the heterosexual marriage imperative can cause men to experience massive feelings of guilt (2020). The men interviewed from semi-urban and rural areas of Odisha poignantly conveyed a powerful sense of the inevitability of marriage out of indebtedness to parents and to continue the family lineage. At the time of the interviews, 12 of the 32 respondents (aged 27 to 42 years) were married to women. Among the rest (unmarried), six were searching with their families for marriage alliances with women, and two were engaged to women (J. Mishra 2020: 357). One unmarried interlocutor articulated, "I know deep down somewhere in the back of their mind, they [my parents] still expect that someday I will find a suitable girl, will get married, will have kids and will uphold their family lineage" (362). Another interlocutor remarked: "Moreover, I want to get married, as I am the only son in the family. Somebody has to take the family lineage forward" (361). Emphasizing the tremendous significance of the family lineage, Mishra describes how "fathers, in particular, regard their sons as extensions of themselves" (360). Exploring queer attachments to natal kinship in Mumbai, Brian Horton tells of how Ram, a gay male activist working for LGBTQ+ inclusion, recalled, "When I came out to my mother, she called me *vansh mrityu*, the death of the clan" (2017: 1060).[17]

So, despite the near ubiquitous obligation for both genders to pursue marriage and heterosexual reproduction as central dimensions of adult personhood, we can see how—by not being the core bearers of the ontological essence of lineal masculinity—single women may enjoy a *certain* flexibility regarding potential kinship paths that some men find even more challenging to achieve.

CONCLUSION

The flurry of new media on single mothers in India paints a celebratory picture of women transcending entrenched forms of gender inequality. "Meet the Choice

Mothers: Single Women Who've Opted for Parenthood without a Partner" proclaims: "Even a decade ago, families and society would have judged these women. But times have changed" (Mathew 2019).

However, three women's stories highlight how enduring challenges interpenetrate novel opportunities for never-married single motherhood. These challenges include, first, that to conceive a child sexually out of wedlock remains extremely stigmatized. Second, the wider society strongly expects every child to have a father. Further, although single women are legally permitted to adopt and to conceive children through IVF, they face enormous uphill challenges to be approved for parenthood, while continuing to need to socially demonstrate that they acquired these children in sexually chaste, that is, in asexual, ways. Additionally, access to adoption and especially new reproductive technologies for single mothers is largely restricted to the most cosmopolitan, urban elite. Whether these elite single mothers will usher in enhanced scripts for gender, kinship, and reproduction across social classes, time will tell.

7

Pleasure, Friendships, and Fun

About five years into my fieldwork, Medha and I made a trip together by train from Kolkata to the lovely university town of Shantiniketan, sharing an Airbnb cottage. We had started making the trip about once each year. This time, I planned to use the town as a base to do research in nearby villages, while Medha was looking forward to simply getting away and to purchasing items to decorate her new apartment. Each Saturday, Shantiniketan attracts many weekend visitors to its large, festive outdoor market featuring vibrantly colored local handicrafts.

The trip also coincided with Medha's birthday, and on that very morning, her brother called to convey his birthday greetings. This surprised Medha. They had not spoken in many months, maybe even a year. Medha had not visited her natal home since the event when she had overheard her brother's wife, Boudi, complain about having to cook for Medha, asking, "Does she think this is a hotel?"—an exclusionary utterance which continued to disturb Medha. Medha and her brother spoke briefly and pleasantly, and then the two hung up.

Medha had long felt hurt by Boudi, and I had seen how Medha's hurt and anger can eat away at her, a topic she broached as we sat enjoying our breakfast. I brought up the Jewish holiday of Yom Kippur, a day of prayer and fasting during which individuals strive to apologize to and seek forgiveness from those we have hurt, as well as to forgive those we have harbored anger against. I described how many people find these acts of forgiveness to be freeing and healing. Maybe it would be helpful for Medha to try to see things from Boudi's perspective and to forgive her?

We talked. Of the two of them, Boudi was the one leading the socially conventional life, meeting prevailing norms of gender through her fifty years of marriage and well-established sons, and receiving respect from her local village community. Yet, to Boudi, it is Medha—the unmarried, single, professionally successful woman—who is the one having fun and opportunities. Boudi was married at age 13. From then on, she had been responsible for cooking for the household, including for six-year-old Medha. While Boudi had been carrying out the standard norms of femininity for a rural woman—marrying young, cooking, bearing and raising children, deferring to her parents-in-law and husband—Medha had been studying first at home, then going off to live in a college hostel, then getting her PhD from a Kolkata university, then landing a job as a well-paid professor. She was able to use her earnings to travel the country and world, including Egypt and Europe, buy a car, meet an American friend whom she escorted to her natal village for fun, go on meditation retreats, and go out to movies and to restaurant dinners. Boudi had never done any of that.

Medha thanked me for introducing a new perspective. She called her brother back and asked to talk to Boudi. The two did not become close after that point, but Medha no longer harbored so much hurt and anger.

This exchange helped me see a blind spot in my own and some others' thinking. In focusing on hardships in the lives of single women who are not traveling on conventional social paths, I and my interlocutors often implicitly and explicitly imagined married women to be experiencing multiple advantages. Yet, women outside of marriage—especially those who have achieved economic independence—seem often to have more opportunities to express and experience fun and pleasure in their daily lives.

Cross-cultural scholarship on singlehood often emphasizes such themes, too, suggesting that single individuals may be better able than married people to make and maintain friendships, engage with their communities beyond the home, pursue pleasures of their own choosing, and have fun.[1] Natalia Sarkisian and Naomi Gerstel find that in the United States "being single increases the social connections of both women and men" (2016: 361).

At the same time, cultural contexts and social inequalities powerfully shape gendered possibilities for forming friendships and having fun. In India, adult women can face tremendous barriers to pursuing pleasures, friendships, and public fun, barriers which are often heightened for single women, particularly for those beyond the most elite social classes. Obstacles to single women's capacities to experience enjoyment in their everyday lives in India include the following: (1) women are taught to please and serve others rather than seek pleasure for themselves, (2) friendships for adult unmarried women can be strikingly difficult to fashion, and (3) fun for women in public—especially for non-elite and solo women—runs counter to idealized images of gendered respectability. In these ways, many of my interlocutors experienced tremendous barriers to having fun, especially as women alone.

Exploring the ways my interlocutors experience and express enjoyment, pleasure, and fun in daily life, as well as the obstacles they face to having fun, is key to understanding women's singlehood, I came to realize. Jonathan Shapiro Anjaria and Ulka Anjaria argue that we should treat *mazaa*—a Hindi-Urdu word that can mean "fun," "pleasure," and "play" (*moja* in Bengali)—as an important theme in social analysis (2020). Shilpa Phadke writes of fun as "any activity that produces a visceral sense of enjoyment" (2020: 283) and argues for regarding claims to fun as "central to a feminist politics in the twenty-first century" (281). Nida Kirmani suggests that "focusing on the pursuit of fun and enjoyment as an area of academic inquiry can be an important way to show how women push against and challenge patriarchal boundaries" (2020: 319). Brian Horton advocates for not only telling stories of abuse and marginalization when studying queer lives, but also thinking of queer joy, pleasure, and fabulousness as important analytic and political projects (2020).

Exploring pursuits of pleasure, friendships, and fun in my interlocutors' daily lives, I examine pleasure and fun as domains in which normative ideals of gendered respectability and femininity are both produced and contested. I witnessed how single women felt governed by ideologies restricting their fun, while at the same time many succeeded—in both subtle and rebellious ways, both purposefully and less consciously—to realize enjoyment and pleasure.

CONTENDING WITH THE PLEASING SYNDROME

On the topic of pleasure and gender, many women told of how they were raised as girls and women to care for others rather than themselves, and thereby to suppress or deny their own desires. Recall Sana's poignant narrative from chapter 5: "Once I asked for some yogurt," she recollected, "and they said there was none. But I knew there was! Then my mother explained that the yogurt is for your brother. . . . After that I never again asked for yogurt in my parents' home."

Recall also Medha's comment, when discussing how seeking and expressing sexual pleasure and desire is so forbidden for single women: "But one thing in this society that you have been seeing—women are not supposed to pleasure themselves! Not for sex, or anything! You are supposed to focus on your family! Sexual pleasure is for having children—and especially for a son!" (chapter 5).

Aparajita articulated the same theme: "We as women have been socialized to care for others and not ourselves."

In *Chup: Breaking the Silence about India's Women*, author Deepa Narayan describes such ideologies as making up "the pleasing syndrome" (2018a: 122): "The internalized rule to always take care of others locks a girl into ignoring her own self, her own needs and wants. Slowly it becomes a deeply ingrained habit. . . . Pleasing is in essence training to forget yourself, because if you have your own needs and preferences, it interferes with the total focus on serving others" (2018a: 94–95). Sarah Pinto explores similar insights expressed by a professor and activist for women's rights in India who argues that the dependent position of women within the family fosters "a state of identity that distances women from their own desires" (2014a: 246). Deepa Narayan tells of how little girls are socialized into not developing preferences in the first place. Ginny, 25, with a degree in finance, recalled how she used to love soda as a young girl and would ask for it, until her parents told her to stop: "What will people think? . . . She is so shameless" (D. Narayan 2018a: 95). Narayan goes on to reflect how "the pleasing syndrome . . . keeps women half-alive to keep on serving others and half-dead to serve themselves. Pleasing as a moral life principle simply means do not exist for the self but exist only for others" (2018a: 122–123). This principle impacts subjective senses of self-worth: who is allowed to have desires and who isn't?

Operating in the lives of both married and single women, this pleasing syndrome can feel particularly constraining for women who cannot use their families as channels for some of their desires. So, it is OK for a woman to purchase and prepare delicious foods if her children or husband or parents-in-law will (also) be enjoying them. It is acceptable for a woman to buy consumer goods for her home—maybe a nicer fridge, a large color TV, a washing machine—if her children and husband need and want them, too. Smitha Radhakrishnan explores how young professional IT women in urban India think about their new access to consumption stemming from their professional incomes. In many of these women's eyes and the eyes of their families, "materialism . . . must begin and end in the family. . . . The deeply troubling kind of consumption . . . was not the consumption of consumer goods per se, but rather consumer spending that is disconnected from family life" (2009: 204–205).

Medha recognized these ideologies about women and pleasure, and criticized how everyone is always asking a single woman for money, if she has a job. "If she were married," Medha explained, "they wouldn't think of asking her for money, because they would believe that her family needs it. But if she's single, they can't fathom that she would spend the income on herself."

Medha at one point decided to use some of her income to buy a car, a luxury and convenience she enjoyed at first, until her various family members—her brother, nephews, grandnieces and grandnephews—all kept asking her to loan or give the car to them, conveying their skepticism about a single woman needing or wanting a car for herself. Due to all this haranguing, Medha ended up selling the car within just a few years.

Women's consumption, pleasure, and value is expected to be channeled into the reproduction of the family, whether natal or marital; but women cannot easily claim pleasure and value entirely for themselves. This is a theme we saw also in chapter 3 on a daughter's and sister's care, and in chapter 4 while exploring how some single women successfully learn to cultivate pleasurable and sustaining forms of self-care.

A deep, internalized sense of obligation to please and serve others rather than oneself emerged in my fieldwork interactions in several ways, very often simply as an unarticulated mode of being in the world. For instance, when I would bring small gifts from my home, such as dark chocolates and roasted specialty nuts, my single women interlocutors often could not accept indulging in the treats themselves. Rather, they would promptly open the gifts to offer to any others around, or tell me that they would give the treats to their household deity, who would be delighted. However, women also maneuvered with the obligation to please, finding ways to nurture the self while still maintaining a moral, pleasing, feminine persona.

On this latter point, my research assistant Madhabi and I were struck by how many single women seemed to care for themselves by virtue of caring for Gopal, the cute, infant form of Krishna. Malobika, Hanvi, and Ashapurna were three who found much meaning in caring for the baby deity Gopal in their household shrines. Hanvi, from an old, well-off north Kolkata family who now lives all alone in her sixties, the one who asserted her own self-care when experiencing cancer, explained that many single women find a particular attachment to Gopal—divinity in the form of an infant they never had. Ashapurna said, "I used to really long for a son, and Gopal has fulfilled that longing." It is a practice in Hindu worship to provide daily care, or *seva*, for the images (*murti*) of deities by clothing, bathing, and feeding them. Then, the caregivers may consume the deities' leftovers as holy *prasad*. So, the women who cared for Gopal could ultimately eat treats like special chocolates or nuts, and other delicious and nourishing meals, by first affectionately and reverently offering the foods to their beloved deity, Gopal. I would ask Hanvi sometimes when we met up, just as a matter of small talk, "What did you eat today?" She would reply, "Well, Gopal has to eat, so I cooked up some rice and vegetables for him and fed him, and so I ate a little, too."

Malobika, the working-class woman in her fifties residing in the Government of West Bengal Working Girls' Hostel, almost never ate anything without first offering it to Gopal. Fortunately for her, she related, Gopal absolutely loves milk and milk products like butter and yogurt, and she herself absolutely loves milk, too! (Legends of the baby Krishna are replete with stories of his loving milk and butter.) Malobika was disappointed that I myself cannot have milk in my tea, due to lactose intolerance. It would have been really hard for her to take her own tea with luxurious milk while giving me merely black tea, except that Malobika could prepare milk for Gopal as well, who loves it so much. "I'll warm the milk up for him, and then I'll put a little in my tea, too," she would say—signaling her moral goodness as a single woman not unduly indulging in her own pleasures. Through Gopal, Malobika and Hanvi were also able to experience the simple human pleasure of sharing food, even while living without kin.

As Medha came to realize when comparing her life path to that of her married sister-in-law, however, single women can in other ways experience greater freedom than married women to pursue pleasures, especially if they have independent income. Some of my more elite interlocutors had deliberately worked as solo women to transcend the gendered pleasing syndrome, striving to learn to feel free to pursue pleasures of their own choosing, such as by going out alone, decorating their homes with lovely items, and traveling. This is a topic I explore in this chapter's final section, after first considering two further obstacles to enjoyment in single women's lives vis-à-vis their quests to form friendships and to have public fun.

TACKLING THE OBSTACLES
TO FORGING FRIENDSHIPS

Cross-cultural literature on singlehood often highlights the importance of friendships in single people's lives.[2] Elyakim Kislev optimistically generalizes that "friendships are something that singles excel at. Recent studies show that singles in many countries have more friends and are better at maintaining their friendships than married people" (2019b). Kislev also suggests that "friendship can serve as a basic building block for the future of the single lifestyle" (2019a: 164). Rebecca Traister, in *All the Single Ladies*, writes that "female friendship has been the bedrock of women's lives for as long as there have been women" (2016: 97). Now that more and more women are marrying late or not at all, "women find themselves growing into themselves, shaping their identities, dreams, and goals not necessarily in tandem with a man or within a traditional family structure, but instead alongside other women. Their friends" (Traister 2016: 97). However, one must be attentive to the ways local cultural contexts and social forces shape the possibilities for forming friendships in diverse and situated ways.

In India, friendship is another important form of pleasure and belonging that can come with serious obstacles for unmarried women because of the ways fashioning friendships across marital-status and class divides is so difficult, and because of how unfamiliar it is to co-reside intimately with non-kin. Sanjaya, Ajay, Anindita, and the others in their single women's support group had successfully established a wonderfully sustaining and enjoyable circle of friends by working hard to find and recruit other unmarried women who felt comfortable identifying as "single" and who shared a similar middle-class, non-elite status. It was often difficult to recruit non-elite women who felt comfortable identifying as "single," though. Many would voice objections like "I'm not that kind of woman"—perceiving "single" as a kind of radical or sexualized identity. Ajay and Anindita had earlier joined a different, more public-facing support organization for single and lesbian women, but found the English-speaking members there too elite and snobbish. Among other interlocutors, cases of strong friendships existed as well, as I get to at the chapter's end. However, more often I witnessed serious obstacles to friendships faced by adult single women.

These obstacles come in several forms. First, in this marriage-centric society, married and unmarried women tend to become quite separated in divergent social worlds. The concept of "friend" (*bondhu*) for women is often interpreted to mean a childhood or college "girlfriend" (*bandhobi*), generally conceived to be a young woman or girl not yet married. When I would ask adult single women if they had any friends (using the more generic, gender-neutral *bondhu*), they would frequently reply something like: "No, not any more. I used to have girlfriends (*bandhobi*) when young and in school, but now they're all married. None of my other girlfriends remained unmarried like me." Single women told of how these married girlfriends are now tied up with household/family life (*shongshar*) and cannot go out. Women often have only limited access to their sisters once married, and the same holds for married former girlfriends.

These barriers are class based to a large degree, as several of my most elite interlocutors had close friends with whom they would go out for coffee and shopping, talk on the phone, and get together for drinks or a meal. However, as mentioned in chapter 5, even these elite women tell of how married women among their professional colleagues and former friends often avoid inviting single women to mixed-gender social events, worried that their husbands might be tempted by the single woman's presumed sexual availability.

Social class distinctions also pose a barrier to forging new friendships. Just as it is difficult to marry across social classes, forming close friendships across class divides is challenging and rare. Only one of my fifty-four interlocutors, Sana, whose story I tell in chapter 5, lived with friends. Keen to find other single women friends with whom she might be able to live or at least spend time, Medha eagerly accompanied me on various research appointments to meet other single women. But few friendships really worked out, in part because none of the women shared precisely Medha's same class makeup—an obstacle, it turns out, to friendship as well as marriage. With her rural village background, Medha was excluded from the circles of elite Kolkata women. At the same time, her PhD and high professor's salary made most working-class and rural women feel that she was in a different league.

One might think that those living in the working women's hostel where I conducted fieldwork could form good friendships there, but differences of age and social class got in the way in the hostel, too. Malobika told of how she has no one she can really mix with at the hostel. In her fifties, she was older than many of the other women, and she also felt a little embarrassed about her lack of education. Each resident had her own distinct class position; some had gone to college, and others not; some spoke English well, and others not; and each woman's form of employment carried a different level of income and prestige. Sukhi-di, my other key interlocutor from this hostel, told of having friends there in the early days, when she moved in as a younger woman in her forties, but now, in her seventies, she had become too old, and she also found the new generation of working women there not educated or respectable (*bhadro*) enough for her tastes.

In this hostel, I also witnessed a general sense of unfamiliarity with the idea that one could live very intimately with people who are not kin. As I note in chapter 1, it is not common in India for friends simply to set up an apartment with one another. I would notice the hostel residents' vigilance about maintaining a sense of separateness through protecting their own living, cooking, and dining spaces. Each woman lived two or three to a small room. The practice was that each cooked for herself. The rooms contained no formal kitchens, but each woman would set up her own small kitchen cabinet and cookstove in her own corner of the room or out on the long open-air corridor outside the room, careful not to trespass into her roommates' spaces. There was also the unspoken and spoken (when necessary) rule not to sit on a roommate's bed, such as when a resident is entertaining outside guests. Instead, all guests will sit closely together on their one host's bed, even if the other roommates are out for the evening or away for several weeks. The hostel women say that one is lucky to have a roommate who will offer tea when one is ill, but that most residents do not become close friends.

Interestingly, I have noticed some close and mutually caring friendships develop among residents in old age homes, and this seems partly driven by the fact that most Indian elder-home residents eat food cooked and served from the same hearth, often together in a shared dining room. Because of this commensality, some elder-home residents tell me that their home is like a large joint family, or literally a "one-rice family" (*ekannaborti poribar*) of old (Lamb 2009: 153, 288n28). Even when Sukhi-di first moved into the West Bengal Working Girls' Hostel during the 1980s, the women residents were all served food as part of the hostel accommodations, eating together in a common dining hall on the ground floor. Sukhi-di attributed this earlier commensality to her ability to form some close friendships in those early days. Now, for some years, group meals were not offered, and each woman resident needed to fend for herself. Further, even the old age home example here highlights how Bengalis often foreground metaphors of family rather than friendship to signify relationships of co-residential intimacy and support.

#WHY LOITER: RECKONING WITH RESPECTABILITY
AND BARRIERS TO PUBLIC FUN

The ability of single women to achieve a sense of well-being and enjoyment in daily life is also impacted by the ways having fun in public spaces counters prevailing ideologies of women's respectability. In "Defending Frivolous Fun: Feminist Acts of Claiming Public Spaces in South Asia," Shilpa Phadke analyzes how engaging in fun in public spaces in India "troubles the boundaries of what is acceptable behavior for women" (2020: 283–84). "When women claim fun in public spaces, they produce in others not happiness but anxiety, born out of the desire to restrict women in order to control their sexuality" (2020: 283). Katherine Twamley and Juhi Sidharth similarly explore how both middle-class and poor young women in Indian cities contend with shared discourses of gendered respectability that curtail women's access to non-privatized spaces for purposes other than work, education, or shopping (2019; see also Phadke 2020: 281). Phadke and colleagues' pathbreaking book *Why Loiter?* and the ensuing Why Loiter movement has led to increased public recognition that women as fellow human beings should have the right, as men do, to hang out in public spaces just for fun—or to "loiter," as this is often called in India.[3] *Why Loiter?* argues that the right to loiter is no more and no less than the right to everyday life in the global city, and that "the inextricable connection of safety to respectability . . . does not keep women safe in public; it effectively bars them from it" (Phadke, Khan, and Ranade 2011: 31).

Such important dialogue on women's access to public spaces for fun in India has not focused on single women per se, but my fieldwork data highlights how the problems Phadke and others describe for women in general are magnified for women alone, particularly outside the elite classes. Many of my non-elite interlocutors experienced tremendous barriers to going out to have fun—*especially as women alone*—despite their desires to be outside, enjoy public spaces, go to movies or plays, enjoy some street food, sip tea, or sit on a park bench.

Expensive cafés and malls are one site where elite single women can feel comfortable simply hanging out alone. Upscale cafés have been flourishing in India's cities over recent years, providing spaces for upper-middle-class and elite women (and men) to feel normal and safe spending public time in casual, unproductive ways, whether alone or in a group, and whether talking, sipping tea, people watching, writing in journals, reading, browsing on laptops, or engaging in other activities of "loitering." Compared to what one finds in the trendy neighborhoods of Delhi, Mumbai, and Bangalore, however, in Kolkata it is still more common to see café patrons hanging out in friend groups or as couples rather than solo. For this reason, even some of my elite interlocutors, like Aarini, would never go out alone in Kolkata, and she would be tremendously eager to engage in fun café hopping with me each time I came to town.

Further, for the many single women in my study who could not afford such cafés (where a single cup of tea costs twenty to thirty times the price at an outside stall), who did not have kin with whom they could go out, and who faced barriers to forming friendships for the kinds of reasons described above, going out for pleasure was experienced as practically impossible.[4] Recall Medha, Nayani, and Nita talking over the Valentine's Day lunch (chapter 1) about how much people talk if they see unmarried women going out. Other urban working-class and rural women conveyed similarly how they found it virtually impossible as unmarried women to go out from the home at all, unless traveling directly and vigilantly straight between work and home, viscerally underlining their legitimate purpose going from point A to B, moving determinedly, their eyes gazing down. Phadke, Khan, and Ranade similarly observe the ways women in Mumbai learn to comport themselves in public: "Every little girl is brought up to know that she must walk a straight line between home and school, home and office, home and her friend or relative's home, from one 'sheltered' space to another" (2011: vii).

Married women in my fieldwork also in different ways often face tremendous barriers to going out, especially if their husbands or parents-in-law prefer that they not do so. I do not expect to be able to go out "loitering" with young married women from rural areas. One afternoon, Roudri and I decided just for fun to slip out during siesta time when her husband and teenage daughters were napping. We talked while walking around the village lanes and then spontaneously went to have a cup of tea at the roadside stall. By the time we got back to her home just about forty-five minutes later, Roudri's husband was up and agitatedly waiting for his own cup of afternoon tea. According to the two daughters, who were teasing him, their father had awoken and become increasingly agitated the longer we were out: "Where is my wife? Who is going to make me tea? How long do I have to wait for tea?"

Some single women did point out a double standard, though: while performing being a good housewife and devoted mother caring for children, middle-class housewives will often spend the whole school day hanging out chatting together on the sidewalks in front of their children's schools, sitting on small mats brought from home. If this is not an example of socially acceptable loitering practiced by married women, then what is? Kumkum asked. In *Why Loiter?*, Phadke, Khan, and Ranade point out how "marriage, especially coupled with appropriate gender performance, often gives women greater access to public space. In comparison, single women tend to be policed more stringently" (2011: 34).

Malobika, who lived in the working women's hostel and who cared lovingly for Gopal, confessed to how much she loves to go out and do things, but told of how she cannot go out, since she has no one to go out with. After her mother died, with whom she had shared a rented flat, Malobika moved in briefly with her married sister. The two of them really enjoyed going out together, visiting places, and seeing movies. Those excursions ended when Malobika moved into the hostel. Malobika still talks by phone with her sister, but her sister's in-laws don't like her heading out alone to meet up with Malobika.

Learning of how much Malobika enjoys going out, my research assistant Anindita and I invited her to meet up with us one day at the popular open-air Dakshinapan Shopping Complex near her hostel. Malobika was delighted to accept, and she fondly prepared a beautiful picnic for us, saying that she preferred to hang out in the open air on the complex's broad cement steps rather than spending money in one of the shops. She laid out a brightly colored cotton picnic blanket and pulled out stainless steel tins of meticulously prepared foods, including puffy luchi breads, *aloor dum*, or spiced baby potatoes, and boiled eggs. Malobika said this was the first time she had gone out for fun in over a year, and we talked, laughed, lingered, and enjoyed our time together.

After the picnic, Anindita and I wished to treat Malobika to tea at the popular Dolly's Tea Shop, where I frequently (often without reflecting on my own privileged class status) joined other moneyed women patrons, writing fieldnotes, chatting with a research assistant or friend, or simply hanging out, taking a break from the bustling streets. I mistakenly assumed Malobika would also enjoy the treat. But she was visibly ill at ease. Anindita and I sensed her class discomfort as a working-class woman. She knew she did not "fit" there. She looked around uncomfortably while speaking in hushed tones. She also vehemently objected to our spending 200 rupees on a cup of tea when one could get perfectly fine tea outside for just 10 rupees. On our way back to Malobika's hostel, she proudly treated us to fried battered eggplant and hot tea from a crowded street stall—which we relished eating as three women together claiming fun in a public space.

Some women seemed to accept without overt critique the restrictions of patriarchal culture limiting women's access to public spaces. Others engaged in critique, humiliation, and struggle, and what Phadke describes as "an inordinate amount of subterfuge and strategizing" to access fun in public space (Phadke 2020: 282–283)—examples of "rebellious bodies of women who refuse to stay within limits defined by a patriarchal culture" (290).

Focusing here on her desire to be able to smoke for pleasure alone in public as a woman, Sanjaya pronounced that "women still can't really be free in Kolkata. . . . For instance, I do smoke," Sanjaya declared. "I enjoy smoking. I even smoke on the road. But I feel very uncomfortable." She told of how she smokes anyway, to resist unequal gendered norms. "But then, if I light up a cigarette outside, I'm immediately stared at by 150 people. They will almost force me to throw out my cigarette into the road. You feel so humiliated. Maybe another five or ten men will even be smoking right there, on the same road, and no one will look at them! Even those very same five men will look at *me* critically." Her voice conveyed her anger. "They will say, 'Oh, seeing you smoking looks so bad.'"

In such daily ways, single women strategize to access public fun, while being pressed to enact appropriate femininity and respectability again and again each time they enter public space.[5]

As a conclusion to this section on public fun and pleasure, let us consider Rituparno Ghosh's award-winning 2000 Bengali film *Bariwali* (*The Lady of the House*), which exposes the crude reality of oppression faced by a lonely, repressed, never-married woman who is cloistered away from pleasure and sociality amid conventional systems of propriety. The quiet drama centers on Banalata, a middle-aged single woman who has lived a solitary existence as the only surviving lineage member in her ancestral home ever since her husband-to-be died from a snake bite on the eve of their arranged wedding. Banalata's solitary and drab existence livens up briefly when she agrees to allow a film crew to shoot in a wing of her aristocratic mansion on the outskirts of Kolkata. Suddenly her household is filled with movie stars and glamorous people, including the charismatic director, Dipankar, who flirts with Banalata and persuades her to act in a bit part in the film. Banalata tells the director, matter-of-factly conveying the cloistered nature of her unmarried woman's life: "Actually, I don't go out (*baire*) anywhere at all. I don't mix with anyone" (R. Ghosh 2000: 1:10). Yet, amid her monotonous days devoid of pleasure, Banalata still yearns for erotic love. She is overcome while watching her young maid being caressed by her suitor in the garden below, and she dreams of the filmmaker slowly removing an elaborately embroidered quilt from her body as she lies writhing in passion on her bed's white linen, her feet twisting together, decorated with the vibrant red *alta*, symbolizing feminine attractiveness, auspiciousness, and fertility.[6] However, once the film crew departs, things at the estate return to the same grueling tedium as before; only now Banalata feels the isolation and monotony of her life all the more acutely.

The other women in the film with the potential for marriage are portrayed as lively, attractive, and optimistic. In contrast, the unmarried Banalata moves slowly and hesitantly, her appearance drab and somewhat disheveled, her craving for marriage never dissipating, and evoking the viewer's pity. As an unmarried woman, she maintains the conventions of feminine propriety, never actualizing a relationship with the filmmaker and never leaving the confines of her domestic space; but the filmmaker depicts her world as almost unlivable. Rohit Dasgupta and Tanmayee Banerjee describe how the film "brings the ostracized figure of the spinster to the center, . . . pulling back the veneer of social norms to expose the crude reality of exploitation lying underneath, [and] . . . throwing the conventional sense of propriety into question" (2016: 44–45).

CAN SINGLE WOMEN REALLY HAVE FUN? PURSUING PLEASURE, FRIENDSHIPS, AND FUN IN DAILY LIFE

Amid all these social and cultural constraints upon pleasure and enjoyment in single women's lives, *can* single women also have fun? The women in my study most able to achieve fun and enjoyment in daily life were mainly middle class and higher who had incomes of their own and who either lived apart from natal kin (such as alone or in the working women's hostel) or whose natal kin supported their sense of independence regarding daily movements, activities, and spending. Several women in these groups conveyed how learning to enjoy life on one's own contributed to an important sense of empowerment and self-worth, contrasting their society's negative messaging about singlehood.[7] For these women, sources of enjoyment, pleasure, and fun included the following:

- Enjoying delicious foods
- Focusing on one's own self, health, and body—such as by exercising (daily walking, yoga, calisthenics), using self-nurturing body products (lotions, hair oils), and purchasing attractive clothing
- Decorating and purchasing nice items for one's home
- Traveling (either solo or with friends)
- Cultivating friendships (despite the obstacles)
- Growing flowers and vegetables in balcony pots or in the ground
- Going out to plays and movies (by oneself or with friends)
- Reading for pleasure
- Pursuing meaningful activities, like important social justice projects and a fulfilling career
- Learning to enjoy one's own company
- Developing positive attitudes, such as accepting one's singleness and life as it is

The narratives of the mostly elite single women from India's metros shared in Kalpana Sharma's 2019 *Single by Choice: Happily Unmarried Women!* convey many of these same strategies for pursuing enjoyment and pleasure. Note how the performative exclamation point in the title pronounces and celebrates the potential for happiness in singlehood.

Travel especially was a favorite practice of pleasure enthusiastically embraced by many single women in my study. Sukhi-di's roommate in the West Bengal Working Girls' Hostel, Mita—a middle-class never-married woman in her forties—articulated how being single enhances a woman's opportunities to engage in the delights of travel: "I love to travel! If you get trapped in household/family life [*shongshar*, that is, by marrying], then you can't do anything like that. But we can travel freely." Mita travels by train a few times per year with two of her childhood girlfriends who also never married and now live in the same working women's hostel.

Some women among my interlocutors were also bold and adventurous enough to travel alone, like Medha and Aarini. Recall, however, Aarini's difficulties in finding accommodations as an unaccompanied single woman, and her strategy of booking rooms in advance by saying that she would be traveling with her aunt (chapter 5). Because of such hassles, women were always on the lookout for other single women with whom they might be able to travel and have fun.

Sanjaya, the survivor of childhood polio, had purposefully developed techniques for her and other single women to cultivate a sustaining and fun community of friends with whom to hang out, offer mutual support, and have fun. Seen by her family and semi-urban natal village community as unmarriable due to her limp, Sanjaya had made the decision after completing college and a master's degree to move out from the demoralizing environment of her natal home to establish her own apartment in a working-middle-class neighborhood of Kolkata. Her work founding an activist organization geared toward training and supporting women with disabilities connected her with like-minded colleagues around the world. She also organized the informal, vibrant support group for other single women who mostly identified as lesbians, although Sanjaya saw herself as heterosexual. This group of about ten women became fast friends who offered each other a lot of support while also having fun together—sharing tea and hot street foods at their weekly Friday evening meetings; traveling once or twice per year by train to destinations where they share hotel rooms, drink, and laugh with one another; and agreeing to count on each other in times of sickness and other need.

In addition to avidly pursuing social justice causes, mentoring her university students, exercising, and reading novel after novel, Medha had cultivated the enjoyment of partaking in an elite cosmopolitan lifestyle and aesthetic, pleasures that she had only earlier fantasized about while growing up poor and first reading about the wider world from a remote village library. Even now, she is amazed at how comfortably her salary supports her, allowing her to purchase expensive organic foods, attractive clothing, and modern accessories like iPhones and a washing machine. She (and others, like Aarini, Nayani, Kumkum, and Indrani) also loves to decorate her home with beautiful, brightly colored handmade curtains, colorful throw pillows, pleasing lights, and bountiful plants.

My own fieldwork with single women was also often so pleasurable for me—fun!—as I myself love to be out of the home, go out and do things, travel, loiter in cafés and outdoor parks, and have fun in public spaces. Never before conducting fieldwork for any other project have I had so many opportunities to hang out and do fun things with the people I was also "studying." Such hanging out was made possible by the unique freedom from family/household life experienced by many single women.

Perhaps the pinnacle of fun in my fieldwork experiences was the Himalayan trip four of us embarked on in November 2018. Aarini, Medha, and I recruited one additional never-married woman from Delhi, an old friend of mine. It turned out, sadly, that Medha and Aarini had to drop out from the Himalayan trek part of the journey due to concerns over the challenging nature of the planned route and other issues. But we started our trip together on the airplane and train, and for the first night in a lovely hill lodge, talking and laughing over dinner and breakfast. From there, Aarini went off on a solo pilgrimage, and Medha joined her new male friend and a few of his friends to go on a road trip in the mountains. My Delhi single friend and I took the most amazing weeklong Himalayan trek (figure 5). It is difficult to imagine pulling this journey off if she and the others had been married.

FIGURE 5. Pleasure, friendship, and fun in the Himalayas. Photo by author.

CONCLUSION

This chapter's materials highlight pleasure and leisure as domains carved up differently for married and single women. Middle-class and elite single women with independent incomes can be successful at pushing boundaries to create meaningful spaces of pleasure and fun in daily life. Recall how Medha proclaimed exuberantly, as reported in chapter 4: "I finally realize now that compared to other Bengali women, I have so much privilege! I have a salary, education, a meaningful job, respect, and freedom. I say to myself each day inside: 'I am a happy soul. I am a peaceful soul.' . . . I've had an absolute transformation! . . . All the times I cried with you before—now what a transformation. I'm having fun (*moja*)! And I'm really happy!"

Yet, the chapter has also had to convey just how difficult it is to have fun and to pursue pleasure as a single woman in India. Others may envy the single woman, imagining how much fun, freedom, and adventure singlehood can offer; but being outside the norm as an unmarried woman also creates a wealth of barriers to friendships, to access to public spaces, to pursuing pleasures, to having fun.

It would be enjoyable to write a chapter on pleasure, friendships, and fun that highlighted only delightful fun. But to meaningfully understand the nature of fun and pleasure in singlehood, I have found that I must consider both the possibilities for, and barriers to, achieving pleasure and fun in daily life.

Conclusion

There is no smoothing out all the diverse stories of single women into a simple narrative, but some things have become clear. Increasingly, more women are choosing a single life in India, and new opportunities for education and advancement are thrusting singlehood upon more women. Yet, while single women may enjoy greater access to education, work, and leisure than their married counterparts, they are also more often than not subjected to more stigma, expected to sacrifice their sexuality, and left to fend for themselves.

The experiences of and possibilities for being single in India form part of a global trend of rising singlehood. Today, the majority of the world's population lives in a country with falling marriage rates.[1] Global delays and declines in marriage have been characterized as one of the major social transformations of our time, with profound impacts on women, gender, and sexuality. An upswell of recent books highlight this global trend, including Joanna Davidson and Dinah Hannaford's (2022) *Opting Out: Women Messing with Marriage around the World*, Marcia Inhorn and Nancy Smith-Hefner's (2021) *Waithood: Gender, Education, and Global Delays in Marriage and Childbearing*, Rebecca Traister's (2016) *All the Single Ladies: Unmarried Women and the Rise of an Independent Nation*, Roseann Lake's (2018) *Leftover in China: The Women Shaping the World's Next Superpower*, and Elyakim Kislev's (2019a) *Happy Singlehood: The Rising Acceptance and Celebration of Solo Living*.

Pushing this global trend of rising singlehood are several key forces illustrated in this book's stories. These include increasing educational and employment opportunities for women, which are providing more ways for women to assert their agency and secure independent forms of economic and social security beyond marriage. We also see a rise in alternatives to family-based housing across many of the world's metros, such as single-person households, senior living arrangements, and (in India) hostels for working women. Living outside marriage is also made possible by expanding paradigms for sexuality, intimacy, and reproduction beyond conventional marriage, connected to modern ideals of sexual freedom and agency, and increased global recognition of feminist and LGBTQ+ rights. To the extent we can understand singlehood for some people as a matter of choice, living singly outside marriage also signals agency and aspiration, opportunities for pushing beyond many gendered norms in pursuit of personal development, freedom, and equality.

Yet, despite what can be seen as a major social transformation taking place around the world regarding the rise of socially accepted singlehood, it is important to note that in the majority of cultural contexts "(a) marriage is still a given, (b) childbearing is still expected within the bounds of marriage, and (c) both are closely linked to the achievement of social adulthood" (Inhorn and Smith-Hefner 2021: 394). We see all three givens in the stories of never-married single women in India.

My research with Indian single women also reveals just how profoundly socially and culturally situated are forms of single personhood. The marriage imperative takes different shapes, is grounded in different reasons, exerts different impacts, and possesses varying degrees of flexibility and constraint within each social-cultural context. As the growing scholarship on singles studies develops, one of its key agenda items must be to examine the unique ways possibilities for singlehood play out in particular locales. There is no one global, uniform "happy singlehood" (Kislev 2019a). Being single in North America or western Europe is not the same as singlehood in, say, China (Fincher 2014; Lake 2018), or Iran (Babadi 2021), or India. Further, even within any one national-cultural context, distinctions and inequalities tied to the identities of social class, race, caste, gender, sexuality, and forms of embodiment and ability play a powerful role.

In offering a few closing reflections, I wish to highlight further the ways social class and gender so powerfully intersect to shape women's marital choices and possibilities in India, a theme that has run throughout this book. I then turn to contemplate the ways experiences of single women shed light on the problem of marriage itself.

ON SOCIAL CLASS AND SINGLEHOOD

"India is in the middle of an independence movement. For women," Deepa Narayan asserts (2018a: 4). One feature of this women's independence movement is the expanding possibility for women to say no to marriage. But for whom is opting out of marriage really a choice? And in what ways? What models of subjectivity and personhood underlie public conceptualizations of women's life choices?

To delve into the issue of how social class profoundly shapes marital choices for women in India, let me turn to a weekend experience Medha and I shared in the midst of my fieldwork. One evening while Medha and I were visiting Shantiniketan, I was invited to an evening gathering at an outdoor restaurant with around a dozen other women academics, both married and unmarried, Bengali and foreign, and I was eager to bring Medha along to introduce her to a wider community of scholars and friends. We all talked animatedly, mostly in English. We ordered Indian beers along with the food. It was an elite gathering, and this was the first time Medha had tried beer. On our way back to our guesthouse, walking through the moonlit lanes, we were both feeling a little tipsy, talking and laughing, when suddenly we could hear approaching a group of about four or five young men. Medha and I were both apprehensive, two women alone at night on a dark deserted road, but Medha immediately took charge, talking with the young men in a maternal, professorial tone, telling them that we were both professors, chatting in a manner as if they were her students and asking them to help show us the way with their flashlights. When we arrived to our guesthouse and closed the door safely behind us, Medha hugged me and exclaimed how proud she was at how she had "saved us!"

We then got to talking more about the evening. Medha had become enamored with Shoumi, a geologist who had attended the event. Shoumi was graceful and self-assured, had chosen not to marry, and seemed so strong and genuinely happy with her life. We had learned over dinner that Shoumi had been a successful professor, but had quit, tired of university and department politics. She still researches, publishes, and does contract work for the government, but on her own terms. Shoumi was likely around 50, near our age. Medha urged me to please email and message the others I knew better at the dinner to ask for Shoumi's number so we could meet up again.

The plan worked, and the next afternoon, Shoumi, Medha, and I gathered to have green tea and conversation on Shoumi's verandah. It was during this gathering, though, that Medha came to realize that Shoumi was in an entirely different class league, meaning they would not be able to be close friends. Medha divulged to Shoumi that she had been thinking that maybe she should also quit her university job, retiring early and living off the pension, to give her more freedom in life. Shoumi responded firmly yet affectionately to Medha, "You must not take me as a role model." She explained how her world—her access to wealth, her upper-class background—gives her so much freedom and security that Medha would not be able to create on her own. Shoumi told us about how she spends half the year in her family's hill-station home with her longtime lover, and the other six months moving between a lovely home she has access to in Shantiniketan, and her large family house in Kolkata where her widowed father, a retired London-trained surgeon, still lives. In the evenings in Kolkata, she and her progressive wealthy father sip whiskey together (an elite practice for women), and her father's name remains on the plaque outside their Kolkata home, giving Shoumi social legitimacy and kinship protection. She urged Medha to keep her job.

Medha was a bit crestfallen as we walked back to our place that evening. Another potential friendship that would not work for her. "Shoumi's right," Medha said. "Her world is entirely different from mine." Then, after a pause, "What vast social class differences we are witnessing through your research, Sarah!"

Just a few days earlier, Medha and I had gone together to an utterly impoverished village near her university to meet with single women on a list of needy women provided by a charitable NGO. These women were mostly widows, in a village where the men were all dying in droves from drinking locally crafted alcohol made from mixing chemicals together. In addition to the widows, we located a few women who had never married because of poverty. These never-married women included the sisters Nabami and Srabani, introduced on several occasions above, and their aunt, who lived in a tiny hut made of crumbling mud walls and a blue plastic tarp for the roof, not tall enough to stand up inside. One unmarried woman we met there had not had anything at all yet to eat that day, by midday, and she told us of how terrifying worms appear from her nose at night, yet she has no money to seek out a doctor for a diagnosis or medicine.[2] Medha and I returned the next day bearing a huge carload of fresh vegetables to disperse, and some cash for medical treatment for this one woman, but this was not near enough to make even a small dent in these women's poverty and suffering.

Then there was Shoumi. And all the women we had met in between. Medha remarked that all of the intimate mixing with women from such vastly different class backgrounds, which we were engaging in through my fieldwork and Medha's concurrent search for single women friends, is something that normally no one individual Bengali person would ever experience.

I could reflect now that maybe all these women of radically different social classes should not be regarded as part of the same topic, should not be in the same book. Yet, in important respects, these women are living together in overlapping physical and social spaces. I am convinced that it is worth looking at such disparate class experiences, as a way to better understand the workings of both social class and gender in India, and at how class and gender so powerfully intersect to impact experiences of singlehood.

Even with all the hype about expanding opportunities for women to opt out of marriage, such as in the 2019 *India Today* cover story "Brave New Woman," I must highlight again that it is mostly only women from highly privileged, educated, and cosmopolitan class backgrounds who are able to embrace singlehood as a distinctive lifestyle emerging from a sense of freedom of choice. Recall that the overall number of never-married women remains strikingly low in India, currently at less than 1 percent of the population of women aged 45 to 49, one of the lowest non-marriage rates in the world.[3] As I have mentioned, recent media stories and anthologies celebrating the rise of single women in India focus also almost exclusively on the cosmopolitan, highly educated classes—and these stories seem often aimed more at promoting new ways of thinking about women and marriage than at reporting actual widespread societal transformations taking place beyond the most elite.

True to the public narratives, though, women among the most cosmopolitan, educated classes like Shoumi's do seem to be experiencing a relative degree of freedom from prevailing societal norms of gender, sexuality, and marriage that allow them more flexible life paths. Especially when the elite single women in my study were successful at establishing professional careers, which provide both economic security and societal respect, they are often able to craft secure, pleasurable, and socially respected lives beyond marriage. Further, because members of the elite participate in a cosmopolitan public culture emphasizing what they see as modern ideals of sexual freedom, and due to their privileged access to private spaces such as independent apartments, a few among this elite group in my study were successful in creating satisfying romantic and sexual relationships outside of marriage. Others, like Hanvi (chapter 4), seem very content to be unpartnered.

At the same time, we have seen how women across social classes in West Bengal contend with many similar norms of gender and sexuality. One is the ongoing near ubiquitous expectation that women (and men) will marry. I met no woman of any social class who had not faced forceful social and familial pressure to marry. Many women of all social classes also feel and internalize painful forms of stigma and exclusion directed at them by neighbors, colleagues, and kin due to their being unmarried.

As just one more example of how exclusions tied to being never-married operate in all kinds of ordinary, everyday interactions, I share how Indrani's mother described to me her own challenging efforts to legitimize her single daughter's and adopted granddaughter's nonnormative kinship as she negotiates with relatives and friends. For instance, wedding hosts treat and address a guest, including through the kinds of gifts and blessings bestowed, based on the guest's marital and adult status. Many of the family's relatives and associates call Indrani's mother to ask what should be done about Indrani and her daughter Nandini. If Indrani attends the wedding as an unmarried daughter, then she would be treated one way—basically as an attachment to her parents. Indrani's mother replies, "No, treat her the way you would any other independent adult attending." Yet many of their associates, all moving in elite circles, are flustered and don't follow through, choosing instead to treat Indrani as an unmarried daughter/child and failing to offer Nandini the same kinds of gifts and blessings they would give to a descendant of a married couple.

Other pervasive gendered norms that single women across social classes contend with concern ideals of feminine respectability—such as that single women should not spend time having fun in public spaces or be sexually active (so, even elite women tend to be discreet if they have partners)—and ideals of heteronormativity preventing lesbian women from living openly together or marrying. And as we have seen, single women across social classes can find it difficult to find housing, to obtain permission to adopt or bear a child, and to gain their child's admission to schools. To forge a life path outside of marriage is not, at this point, straightforward or simple for women of any social class in India.

For women not born into the most elite, educated classes, the avenue of education and work can open up viable possibilities for non-marrying, as evident in the stories of Medha and Subhagi. Yet, I would not want readers to come away with the impression that Subhagi, the Scheduled Caste rural laborer who chose not to marry in order to stay with and support her natal kin, is a typical or common example of what is happening among the laboring classes in India today. I had to search hard to find never-married women from non-elite families in urban, semi-urban, and rural contexts. In Subhagi's whole large village of around five thousand residents, only Subhagi and one other woman, born with congenital dwarfism, had forged the path of never marrying. In Medha's natal village, which she took me to visit, we were able to locate two other women who had never married. One was Suravi of chapter 6, who had become pregnant out of wedlock and was then deemed unmarriable; the only other never-married woman from this village, in her mid-forties, lived with her widowed mother. This woman's father had died when she was only 15, leaving the family near penniless and without money to fund the daughter's wedding and dowry. Medha could be said to be the third unmarried woman of this village. One could deem that she had achieved a remarkable success story, as the first girl from her village ever to graduate from class ten, let alone to then go on to receive a BA, MA, PhD, and prestigious job as a tenured professor. But Medha's ensuing mismatched class status—born into a poor, rural family but now with the education and professional position of an urban elite—made her highly unusual, virtually unmarriable, and often feeling socially cut loose and in limbo.

In her examination of changing cultures of gender and sexuality in India, Deepa Narayan writes that she chose to focus on highly educated urban elite women "because these are the groups that can bring about change" (2018a: xvi). Whether more women across social classes, rural-urban contexts, and generations will choose the life path of non-marriage in coming years, time will tell.

ON THE PROBLEM OF MARRIAGE

Another goal of this book has been to probe the fundamental question of *why* it is that a society such as India's—like so many societies around the world—erects so many obstacles and deterrents to being an adult unmarried woman. At the same time, this book's stories highlight problems with marriage itself. As I note in the introduction, I came to realize through my fieldwork that in some ways single women were not the real or primary problem of my research, but rather marriage was—or the ways gender inequality is so intertwined with the institution of marriage in Bengali Indian society. As such, the book's stories contribute to the emerging field of critical heterosexuality studies, aimed at examining the often taken-for-granted assumptions that surround dominant heterosexual institutions such as marriage.[4]

While writing this book, I came across lines penned in 1925 by the celebrated Bengali poet, writer, composer, and painter Rabindranath Tagore in an English essay titled "The Indian Ideal of Marriage." Near the close of the essay, Tagore reflects: "That is why, in every country, marriage is still more or less of a prison house for the confinement of woman—with all its guards wearing the badge of the dominant male" (qtd. in Lal 2015: 300).

This discovery from the 1920s resonates with Sarah Pinto's reflections in studying women in settings of psychiatric care in India: "Against an overwhelming popular discourse that said that Indian marriages are strong and Indian society (and minds, souls, and families) strong because of them, was a fierce counterdiscourse that saw oppression, control, and dependency in marriage" (2014a: 216). Srimati Basu, in her ethnography of lawyer-free family courts mediating cases of domestic violence in India, reflects similarly: "We can contemplate the categorical trouble of marriage itself: an institution fused with 'trouble and strife,' . . . persistently associated with conflict, deprivation, and exclusion" (2015: 3).

John Borneman critiques anthropology more broadly for rarely examining the relation of marriage "to the assertion of privilege, to closure, death, abjection, and exclusion" (1996: 215), and for often failing to consider that not all people follow an "eternal, putatively cross-cultural sequence of birth, marriage, death" (221).

We have seen in single women's stories their perspectives on the profound gendered vulnerabilities and confinements that marriage can produce. Moreover, we have seen how a woman cannot be made "free" of constraining social institutions and conventions simply by not marrying. The catch-22 is that if it is not easy to be married for a woman in India, it is also not easy to be unmarried. In this way, single women's stories make transparent the broader social-cultural and political-economic forces that impact both single and married women's experiences and subjectivities in situated and often painful ways.

ON POSSIBILITY

Finally, though, in striving to represent single Indian women's lives, I find it important analytically and politically not only to tell stories of suffering and exclusion. One evening, as Indrani and I were socializing at her home, I sought her advice in interpreting themes from this project's fieldwork. There were so many themes of difficulty and constraint—stigma, loneliness, suffering, exclusion. Indrani was fascinated by anonymized stories I shared of other single Bengali women's lives, while she also helped me understand various materials. At the end, though, Indrani made a warm appeal: "Please don't make the book only about gloom and doom. That will be too depressing." Her eyes twinkled as she spoke.

She was right to urge me to keep my eyes open to the possibilities for well-being and pleasure in single women's lives, and to acknowledge how many women—even while underlining the difficulties in their lives—would not trade their single-hood for marriage. Indrani also insists that singlehood in India is in many ways easier than in the West, such as in the United States where she lived for several years and witnessed the tremendous societal emphasis placed on being coupled up. The stories of Indrani and others make clear how and why, despite the challenges, many women are intentionally making the choice to live singly in India and often remaining confident in their decisions.

In doing research on unmarried women in the United States for *All the Single Ladies*, Rebecca Traister interviewed Anita Hill, now also my esteemed colleague in Brandeis's Women's, Gender, and Sexuality Studies Department. Anita has chosen not to marry and commented to Traister: "I want everyone to understand that you can have a good life, despite what convention says, and be single. That doesn't mean you have to be against marriage. It just means that there are choices society should not impose on you" (in Traister 2016: 256–257).

Although the ideal of free choice is never as straightforward as it seems, many Bengali single women across social classes strongly articulate a clear desire for expanded choices and life possibilities—to be able to pursue alternative paths toward economic security, intimacy, social belonging, and living well—in ways not tied to marriage. And some are making it work.

I close by sharing my latest news from Medha, arriving by WhatsApp during the final stages of my writing this book: "I have been selected as a governing member of my college. The first female member of its 150-year history." Medha and others have helped me see that to analyze single women's stories only in terms of precarity and oppression would elide much of their content and force. This book's stories invite us to actively reflect on the ways people forge meaningful lives out of intersecting situations of both constraint and possibility. I suggest—as does Rebecca Traister in her exploration of the rising tide of single women in the United States (2016: 240)—that never-married single women in India, by circumstance and by choice, through argument and just through daily existence, are pushing the country to expand to make new spaces for them. Indian single women's narratives help us begin to imagine what it can mean for anthropologists, and for our interlocutors, to decenter marriage as an unquestioned norm.

Acknowledgments

This book has emerged from collaboration with countless people from its first days to its last. I am incredibly grateful for the creative insight, knowledge, and camaraderie I have received from my interlocutors, colleagues, friends, and family both in India and the United States. As I approach the final days of writing this book, I am almost disappointed to see the process come to an end, as the project has enriched my life immensely for the past seven years, and even sustained me emotionally and intellectually during the long pandemic days.

I am most grateful for the ethnographic process itself, which enabled innumerable encounters with people who entrusted me with stories and experiences close to their hearts. The book would not have been possible without the generosity of the many people in India who valued my fieldwork, offered me hours of interviews and conversations, imparted their insight, and welcomed me into their homes and lives.

Madhabi Maity, PhD, Anindita Chatterjee, PhD, and Hena Basu, MA, were amazing research assistants and true collaborators on the project. Each helped me locate single women to interview and often accompanied me on interview and fieldwork encounters, making the fieldwork interactions more fun, lively, natural, and productive. They each also continued to share illuminating insights and interpretations both in person and over email. Conversations and time spent with the wise and perceptive Madhabi Maity have enriched every page of this book. Anindita Chatterjee read each page of the draft manuscript, offering her sage advice and marginalia. As a specialist in language and discourse, Anindita was also instrumental in encouraging me to gain permission from interlocutors to switch on our recorders even for informal, everyday conversations (often the richest interactions) and not only for formal interviews. As she did for my *Aging and the Indian Diaspora* project, Hena also provided me with relevant news and popular cultural, film, and literary sources. Both Madhabi and Hena—strong, single, independent, and inspirational women in their own lives—were foundational in inspiring me to embark on this project from the beginning.

In Kolkata and wider West Bengal, I have also benefited tremendously from the illuminating conversations and hospitality received from so many friends and mentors in Indian and Bengali culture. I offer my profound thanks especially to Mahamaya Banerjee, the late Purnima Banerjee, Kumkum and Ranjit Bhattacharya, my "Boudi" Basanti Chakraborty and her sons and daughters-in-law, Anubha and Manoj Kumar Chatterjee, Kuhu Das, Khushi Das Gupta, Sanjukta and Anjan Dasgupta, Anindita Dutt, Reshmi Ganguly and her sisters Manjuri and Arna and daughters Baisakhi and Srabani, Nayantara Kayal, Bandana Lohar, Bhagyabati Lohar, and Arunava Mondal. In Delhi, Ira Raja and her family offered amazing hospitality and many eye-opening conversations. The director and staff at the American Institute of Indian Studies in Kolkata welcomed me into my favorite home away from home, and taught me through our everyday conversations. These persons include Subir Sarkar, regional officer, the language teachers, and the outstanding staff, Soumen Bhattacharyya, Subrata (Brundaban) Behra, and Biswajit Mondal. Aditi Nath Sarkar was my first Bengali language instructor years ago at the University of Chicago, and he has continued to enlighten me through conversations in Kolkata.

I am deeply grateful to my numerous colleagues who have contributed to this project's thinking and writing in rich ways. Tanya Luhrmann, the Ethnographic Studies in Subjectivity series editor, and two reviewers for the University of California Press, Lucinda Ramberg and one anonymous reader, offered highly insightful suggestions for the manuscript, helping me sharpen several lines of thought. Other colleagues who offered close readings and illuminating conversations at various stages of the book's development include Jonathan Anjaria, Jennifer Cole, Joanna Davidson, Elizabeth Ferry, Michele Friedner, Michele Gamburd (who read especially many chapters in their early form), Dinah Hannaford, Brian Horton, Marcia Inhorn, Faris Khan, Caitrin Lynch, Janet McIntosh, Diane Mines, Shilpa Phadke, Ira Raja, Martha Selby, Harleen Singh, Tulasi Srinivas, and Kimberly Walters. My colleagues at Brandeis University in Anthropology, South Asian Studies, and Women's, Gender, and Sexuality Studies have provided a sustaining abode, fostering me and my writing through their friendship, collegiality, and intellectual engagement.

The book benefited tremendously from the capable research assistance and close reads of chapter drafts provided by Brandeis graduate students Medha Asthana, kimcraig, and Meera Kulkarni. Brandeis MA student Patrick Harhai was one of the first to encourage me to situate this project partly within queer studies.

Several aspects of the book were presented to audiences at the University of Chicago's Department of Comparative Human Development, Brandeis's Women's Studies Research Center, and the American Anthropological Association, via the

"M.N. Srinivas Centenary Panel" organized by Tulasi Srinivas and the exciting comparative panel "Opting Out: Women Evading Marriage around the World," organized by Joanna Davidson and Dinah Hannaford. The feedback I received during these engagements was highly beneficial. Earlier versions of some of this research were published first in *Ethos* (Lamb 2018), and as chapters in the edited volumes *Waithood: Gender, Education, and Global Delays in Marriage and Childbearing* (Inhorn and Smith-Hefner 2021), and *Opting Out: Women Messing with Marriage around the World* (Davidson and Hannaford 2022).

Generous financial support from the Theodore and Jane Norman Fund for Faculty Research at Brandeis University and a Brandeis University Senior Faculty Research Leave enabled me to conduct fieldwork in India in 2018 and 2019. A fellowship from the Andrew Carnegie Foundation funded fieldwork in India in 2020 focused on aging and care, providing the basis for chapter 4.

I am tremendously grateful to my University of California Press editor, Kate Marshall, for her support of this project from the beginning, and to Enrique Ochoa-Kaup and Julie Van Pelt for seamlessly shepherding the book through production. I also thank my invaluable and perceptive copy editor Sue Carter, my indexer Alexander Trotter, and the entire UC Press team for bringing this book to fruition.

Finally, I offer profound thanks to my family and friends, who sustain me in so many large and small ways, and who have unfailingly cheered me on and encouraged my career in anthropology. These include my parents, stepparents, and parents-in-law: Sharon Rowell, Doris Black, Sydney and Susan Lamb, and Bob and Barbara Black; my amazingly wonderful and inspiring daughters Rachel and Lauren; and my lifelong best friends Jenny, Katie, and Tamar. A special note of gratitude to Lauren, who was really interested in the materials on obstacles to pleasure, friendships, and fun, encouraging me to develop them into a chapter! To my life partner Ed: to be buoyed by you is an immeasurable gift.

NOTES

INTRODUCTION

1. Here and elsewhere, I use single quotes to indicate English words, such as 'patriarchal,' inserted into otherwise Bengali dialogue. Most conversations reported in this book took place in Bengali, alt hough sprinkled as is common with English terms. To protect privacy, all names of research participants are pseudonyms.

2. For demographic figures on the rise of single living, see Kislev 2019a: 4, 14 and Klinenberg 2012: 3–5.

3. For scholarship on women evading marriage around the world, see Davidson and Hannaford 2022; Inhorn and Smith-Hefner 2021; Lesch and van der Watt; Sharma 2019; Traister 2016; Trimberger 2005. In China, the government popularized the derogatory term *sheng nu* ("leftover women") to describe the rising trend of educated, professional women remaining unmarried into their late twenties and thirties (Fincher 2014; Howlett 2021; Ji 2015; Lake 2018; Lewis 2020; Qian 2018; Shlam and Medalia 2019; To 2013).

4. "Meet the 5 Kinds of Single Women," *Times of India* (Kuriakose 2014).

5. For recent news stories on single celebrity parents, see S. Chakraborty 2019; Dutt 2017; P. Singh 2018. Chapter 6 also examines recent media on single parenting in India.

6. See https://www.happilyunmarried.com/ and https://www.bbc.com/news/business -18164049. The joke came from a plaque on an earlier Happily Unmarried website from November 2016.

7. Amazon.com review, "So glad this book got written," posted July 28, 2019, https://www.amazon.com/Single-Choice-Happily-Unmarried-Women/dp/9385606220/ref=sr_1_1?dchild=1&keywords=single+by+choice+kalpana+sharma&qid=1600092735&sr=8-1.

8. From the B. C. Sen Jeweler's Facebook page, accompanying a bridal gold jewelry ad: https://www.facebook.com/bcsenjewellers/photos/3490267504404288, accessed January 25, 2021.

9. "I'm 29. Single. Woman. Indian," by Rutu, February 16, 2016, https://byrslf.co/i-m -29-single-woman-indian-81786b6794f1, accessed January 29, 2021.

10. Ibid.

11. This cartoon image can be found in Qamar's 2017 *Trust No Aunty* book and by scrolling down within this essay on the artist: https://www.cbc.ca/arts/trust-no-aunty-and -listen-to-hatecopy-instead-1.4240410.

12. For instance, anthropologist Claude Levi-Strauss, in *The Elementary Structures of Kinship* (1969 [1949]), proposes that marriage and the "exchange of women" beyond closely related kin is what links together various groups into one broader whole: society (although see Gayle Rubin's famous 1975 critique of Levi-Strauss's theory, explored briefly in chapter 1).

13. In *Zenana*, Laura Ring discusses reasons English words are used by Urdu speakers across social classes in Pakistan, as "a practical recognition that something is happening or being constructed that eludes Urdu categories" (2006: 83).

14. In Bengali: *meyeder biye hoe, chelera biye kore, ma-babara biye dae* (daughters'/girls' marriage happens, sons/boys do marriage, parents give marriage).

15. See also DePaulo, Moran and Trimberger 2007 and DePaulo and Morris 2005. Mariam Slater also notes how "a kind of marriage-ism has dulled our lens for studying single women" (1986: xxii).

16. Notable works on subjectivity in anthropology include Bakke 2020; Biehl, Good, and Kleinman 2007; Desjarlais 2016; Gammeltoft 2014; Jackson 2012; Ortner 2005; and Parish 2008.

17. Other works exploring autobiographical stories and songs in fashioning (individual and intersubjective) identities and asserting forms of agency include Becker, Beyene, and Ken 2000; Carlisle 2012; Craig 2011; Davidson 2019; Lamb 2001; Linde 2000; Lomsky-Feder 2004; Rainbird 2014; Seligmann 2009; and Wekker 2006.

18. On queer theory, see more below, and Nikki Sullivan's articulation of the practice of queer theory: "to make strange, to frustrate, to counteract, to delegitimize, to camp up heteronormative knowledges and institutions, and the subjectivities and socialities that are (in)formed by them and (in)form them" (2003: vi).

19. See, for instance, Boellstorff 2007; Horton 2017; Luna 2020: 18, 65; Sullivan 2003: vi. Heteronormativity denotes a worldview that assumes two natural, binary genders drawn toward heterosexuality as the normal sexual orientation, often in unarticulated and taken-for-granted ways.

20. My choice of the terminology "reproductive futurity" takes off from Lee Edelman's "reproductive futurism," referring to societal fixation on children and the next generation (2004: 14).

21. See chapter 1 for more on the intersections among the body, appearance, femininity, and marriage; see also N. Ghosh 2016.

22. For foundational work on critical heterosexuality studies, see Fischer 2013, and Dean and Fischer 2020. As Nancy Fischer articulates, critical heterosexuality studies "makes heterosexuality more visible, including the ways it is institutionalized, operates symbolically, and how it is practiced and shapes gender and sexual identities" (2013: 507), while probing the ways normative heterosexual status "is presumed and accrues privilege, and is regarded as 'natural,' 'normal,' and 'morally superior,' and often not in need of explanation" (2013: 502). For foundational earlier texts, see Judith Butler's 2002 "Is Kinship Always Already

Heterosexual?" and John Borneman's 1996 "Until Death Do Us Part: Marriage/Death in Anthropological Discourse."

23. See, for instance, Olga Khazan's 2017 essay, "We Expect Too Much from Our Romantic Partners," based on her interview with Eli Finkel, author of *The All-or-Nothing Marriage*.

24. See also DePaulo and Morris 2005, and Buddeberg and DePaulo 2015. Singles studies scholar Bella DePaulo and colleagues expose how "singlism"—stereotyping and discrimination against single people of all genders—is prevalent in largely unrecognized, unnamed, and unchallenged ways in the United States.

25. Tine Gammeltoft makes this same point beautifully in *Haunting Images* (2014: 15).

26. Important works in anthropology on practice theory include Ahearn 2001; Bourdieu 1977, 1992; Mahmood 2005; Ortner 1984, 1996, 2006.

27. I am inspired here by Sara Dickey's examination of how residents of Madurai, Tamil Nadu, work to gain and maintain recognition as middle class, as they aspire to belong, to be "worthy of recognition," and to "count in the social body" (2013: 234, 238, 219).

28. I am inspired here by arguments developed by Tine Gammeltoft 2014 and Saba Mahmood 2005.

29. For critical investigations of the notion of the friendship in ethnographic fieldwork, see Driessen 1998 and Magnarella 1986.

30. These other projects mostly concerned gender and families, but with a focus on aging rather than singlehood (e.g., Lamb 1997, 2000, 2001, 2009, 2017).

31. Two recent anthologies celebrate India's new genre of single women, focusing on the elite, well-educated classes (Kundu 2018; Sharma 2019). Media stories on India's cosmopolitan single women appear periodically throughout the book.

32. Christians make up the third largest religious group in India, at about 2.3 percent, while Muslims make up India's second-largest religious group, constituting over 13 percent of India's population and 25 percent of West Bengal's population (https://censusindia.gov .in/census_And_You/religion.aspx). My own research in West Bengal over the past thirty years has focused on Hindu communities. Some of what I describe here applies broadly within both Hindu and Muslim communities, such as the immense social pressure to be married and to contain sexuality within marriage. However, more research is needed on singlehood in Indian Muslim communities for the commonalities and distinctions to be meaningfully understood.

33. In Bengal, a historical social class division between the *bhadralok* ("respectable" people) and *chotolok* (lowly or literally "small" people) still sometimes enters into discourse today. The *bhadralok* emerged as a new middle-class social group during the British colonial era, the first to gain entry to urban professional occupations (Ganguly-Scrase 2013). For more on social class categories in India, see Aslany 2019; Brosius 2010; Dickey 2016 (33–37 and passim); Fernandes 2006; and Sridharan 2004. Note that "class" refers to socioeconomic status and is distinct from, although intersecting with, "caste" in India. Like class, caste operates simultaneously as a form of identity and social inequality.

34. For parallels between caste and race in India and the United States, see Berreman 1972 and Wilkerson 2020.

35. As Bengali names all have meanings, I select pseudonyms that fit my sense of each person. *Medha* means "intellect" and is associated with Saraswati, the Hindu goddess of knowledge, wisdom, and learning.

36. This was the fieldwork that resulted in the book *Aging and the Indian Diaspora* (Lamb 2009).

1. ON BEING SINGLE

1. Again, I use single quotes to indicate English terms inserted into otherwise Bengali dialogue.

2. Ever since the horrific gang rape of a young woman on a Delhi bus, which made its way into the world media, the intensity and volume of depictions and debates about rape "indicate an urgency, a sort of crisis in the life situation of Indian women," as Himani Banerjee examines (2016: 3).

3. The useful concept of habitus as developed by Pierre Bourdieu refers to dispositions, schemes of perception, habits, gut feelings, intuitions, attitudes, skills, and ways of being in the world—basically, the ways individuals perceive and act in the world around them. These ways of being, perceiving, and acting are to a large extent shared by people with similar backgrounds (social class, region, nationality, etc.) while also individually embodied and practiced (Bourdieu 1977, 1987, 1992).

4. In Bengali: *meyeder biye hoe, chelera biye kore, ma-babara biye dae* (daughters'/girls' marriage happens, sons/boys do marriage, parents give marriage).

5. For critical investigations of the notion of the key informant and friendship in ethnographic fieldwork, see Driessen 1998; Magnarella 1986; and Rabinow 2007 [1977].

6. Conventionally in West Bengal, girls and young women begin wearing saris regularly once married, and unmarried women also switch over largely to saris once perceived as adult. Now, especially within more elite circles in the metros, adult women can choose a range of clothing options, including saris, salwar-kameez, kurtis and kurtas, long skirts, and jeans.

7. Sanjaya's words here call to mind Uma Narayan's compelling opening narrative in *Dislocating Cultures*, in which she reflects on how her early witnessing of oppressive gender roles and domestic violence within the family led to her feminist awakening (1997: 6–11).

8. The English phrase "live in" is used in cosmopolitan circles to refer to couples who sleep together or live together without being married.

9. See, for instance, Goldstein and Kenney 2001; Inhorn and Smith-Hefner 2021; Jones 2007; Mukhopadhyay, Chapnik, and Seymour 1994; Raymo and Iwasawa 2005; and Sabbah-Karkaby and Stier 2017.

10. On increasing opportunities for education and work for women in India, see chapter 2, and Fernandes 2006 (162–168); Radhakrishnan 2011; and Waldrop 2012.

11. For more on experiences of sexuality, femininity, and marriage for disabled women in India, see N. Ghosh 2016 and 2018. Michele Friedner explores how many deaf individuals in India seek love marriages with other deaf persons, even though their families often oppose such matches (2015: 134, 152, 155, 169n3).

12. In India, the category of transgender often refers to hijras (e.g., Reddy 2005); however, Ajay used the term in a contemporary global, less culturally specific, sense.

13. Scholarship on the sexual double standard in the United States and other societies is extensive and includes works such as Allison and Risman 2013; Asencio 1999; Farvid, Braun, and Rowney 2017; and Fasula, Carry, and Miller 2014.

14. From episode 1 of *Made in Heaven* (Mehra, Akhtar, et al. 2019); see also "16 Powerful Moments from 'Made in Heaven' that Stay with You Long after You've Binge-Watched It," by Srishti Magan, https://www.scoopwhoop.com/entertainment/made-in-heaven-moments/.

15. For media stories and anthologies celebrating the new wave of Indian single women, see this book's introduction and Kundu 2018, Sharma 2019, Sinha 2019.

16. This woman's brother and father had also turned to a spiritual life, and the three lived together in a temple as caretakers.

17. See Zinnia Ray Chaudhuri, "'Happily Unmarried': An Online Project Reminds Indian Women to Celebrate Singlehood," Scroll.in, Internet Culture, October 21, 2018, https://scroll.in/magazine/896455/happily-unmarried-an-online-project-reminds-indian -women-to-celebrate-singlehood.

18. See also Joanna Davidson and Dinah Hannaford's *Opting Out: Women Messing with Marriage around the World* (2022), and John Borneman's critique of anthropologists for "presuming that birth, marriage, and death constitute a serial trinity at the center of the human life course" (1996: 216).

19. For more on implicit bias against singles in the United States, see DePaulo 2007; Morris, Sinclair, and DePaulo 2007.

20. See P. Mishra 2018 and Tilche and Simpson 2018. According to the population census of 2011, the sex ratio in India measured at 940 females per 1,000 males. The state of Haryana had the lowest sex ratio in the nation, at 877 females to 1,000 males, while the state of West Bengal fared slightly better at 950 females per 1,000 males. See Census 2011, "Sex Ratio in India," https://www.census2011.co.in/sexratio.php.

21. Susan Greenhalgh explores similar phenomena in rural regions of China facing sex-ratio imbalances, examining the plight of involuntary bachelors characterized as "bare sticks" (*guanggun*) and "not real men" (2012, 2015).

22. *Indian Matchmaking*, a Netflix original series, https://www.netflix.com/title /80244565 (Mundhra 2020). Aditi Sangal of CNN writes critically of how "the show presents brutal truths about Indian culture: the emphasis on being 'fair'; the enormous pressure to wed; the focus on caste and class; the stigmatization of independent, working women. But the show fails to contextualize or even question these problematic beliefs when they're brought up by its characters, presenting them instead as the status quo" (2020). See also Pathak 2020.

23. Chapter 5 further explores how concerns over protecting caste purity connect to social controls over unmarried women's sexuality. Goli, Singh, and Sekher (2013) examine the low rate of marriage across caste, religious, and economic groups in India and the troubling rise of "honor killings" of young women and men in intercaste relationships who marry against the wishes of their families.

24. *Kakima*: father's younger brother's wife; *jethima*: father's older brother's wife; *pisima*: father's sister; *masima*: mother's sister; *mamima*: mother's brother's wife.

25. See the National Family Health Survey (NFHS-4) 2015–16, https://dhsprogram .com/pubs/pdf/OF31/India_National_FactSheet.pdf. This report indicates that child marriage rates for girls decreased from 47 percent in 2005–2006 to 27 percent in 2015–2016 ("India-Key Indicators," 3). See also UNICEF 2019: 4–6.

26. The Bengali term *meye* (plural *meyera*) can be translated as "girl," "daughter," or "young woman." It is the most common term used to describe young women

or girls in the context of considering marriage. *Mohila,* "woman," would most often refer to an adult woman already married, or more generically to female persons of any age, such as in "ladies'" (*mohila*) compartments on trains. *Meye manus,* literally "girl-person," can also be used to refer to female persons of any age or to convey "womankind" more broadly.

27. Chapter 4 explores this recurrent question posed to and by single women: "Who will care for you/me?"

28. Of course, sexual harassment and assaults are prevalent in the United States as well, as the #MeToo movement taking off virally in 2017 helped expose.

29. As other materials in this book reveal, people do also worry also about the non-marriage of men, tied to concerns about achieving "normal" masculinity, reproducing the family line, and securing care in old age. Dilip's own cousin-brother (male cousin with whom he was raised) did not marry, and while this cousin continued to have social status in the village, live in a secure household with both his parents, and enjoy his mother's cooking and domestic care labor, now that he was approaching 60 and his parents 80, the family had begun to worry more about how the cousin would manage after his parents passed away.

30. *Laws of Manu* dates from approximately the second century BCE to the third century CE. Ira Trivedi refers to Manu as "the high-priest of prudish values" (2014: 31) and writes of how the *Laws of Manu* was just one of India's ancient texts, "but through the British, Manu became the ultimate voice of authority, deeply infiltrating contemporary Hindu culture, building into it many negative assumptions about lower castes and women that sharply restricted their freedom, regulated their behavior, and blocked their access to social and political power" (2014: 31).

31. For more on the rise of market-based senior living in India, see chapter 4 and Lamb 2009, 2013; Lamb and Kavedzija 2020: 115–119; and Samanta 2021.

32. For more on working women's hostels in India, see Melkote and Tharu 1983, Pothukuchi 2001, and Joseph 2016. See also "Scheme for Working Women Hostel" from the Ministry of Women and Child Development, https://wcd.nic.in/sites/default/files/Working%20Women%20Hostel_about_revised_about.pdf; and "Guidelines for Allotment and Boardership in the Working Women's Hostels under the Control of the Housing Dept. Government of West Bengal," https://wbhousing.gov.in/templetes/templete1/pdf/Womenshostel/Guide-line-for-allotment-of-seat-in-Working-Women's-Hostel.pdf.

33. In *Aging and the Indian Diaspora,* I explore in depth older Bengalis' attitudes about living alone, and my fieldwork did find some older people living singly who quite accepted the situation (Lamb 2009).

34. I occasionally spent the night in Medha's guest room-cum-study, giving me the opportunity to meet her hired companion.

2. EDUCATION AND WORK

1. "Zamindar" (or *jomidar* in Bengali) refers to a holder or occupier (*dar*) of land (*zamin,* a term of Persian origin, or *jomi* in Bengali). In the late eighteenth century, the British government regularized the zamindar system, further entrenching a landed aristocracy in Bengal that lasted until the beginnings of West Bengal land reforms in the late 1970s. Medha was born in 1960.

2. Chapter 1 delves further into ideologies of the body and appearance in single women's experiences.

3. See Chaturvedi and Sahai 2019. According to this *Time* story, by 2018, 95 percent of girls ages 11–14 across India were in school.

4. My numerous fieldwork conversations in West Bengal across social classes and rural-urban contexts over the past decade support this generalization; see also Chaturvedi and Sahai 2019.

5. These reports indicate that around 20 to 26 percent of working-age women in India received income for their work in 2018–2019 (Jose 2020; UN Women 2019: 121). See also Mazumdar and Neetha 2011. Readers should keep in mind, however, that many women in India work in the informal sector, not easily captured by large-scale economic studies.

6. See also the sections "Marriage Plays the Spoiler" (75) and "Women Want Work—Depends on Husbands/in-Laws" (84–85) in Chaturvedi and Sahai (2019).

7. Other Backward Class (OBC) is a category used by the Government of India to classify castes which are educationally or socially disadvantaged, one of several official classifications of the population of India, along with General Class, and Scheduled Castes and Scheduled Tribes (SCs and STs).

8. Note here how education and salaried employment are tied to notions of class and societal "respectability" (see P. Chatterjee 1989; Karlekar 1986; and note 16, below).

9. Other studies on expanding educational opportunities for women in India and the impact of education on women's empowerment and marriage include Bhat 2015, Chaturvedi and Sahai 2019, and Mukhopadhyay and Seymour 1994.

10. Mamata Banerjee was born in 1955. In 2012, *Time* magazine named her as one of the one hundred most influential people in the world.

11. The project's name, Kanyashree, coined by Mamata Banerjee, combines *kanya*, "daughter," with *shree*—signifying respect and, when applied to women, beauty, while also connoting the goddess Lakshmi, goddess of wealth, prosperity, and good fortune.

12. See the Kanyashree Prakalpa webpage, which reports a "unique beneficiaries" running list: https://www.wbkanyashree.gov.in/kp_4.0/index.php.

13. In the UN Public Service Award competition, Kanyashree was ranked highest among 552 social sector schemes from across sixty-two countries nominated for the coveted award. See Singh and Dutta 2017.

14. To see Kanyashree Prakalpa posters, see Singh and Dutta 2017 and www.wbkanyashree.gov.in.

15. See the introduction, note 3, for more scholarship on China's "leftover women."

16. Partha Chatterjee (1989), Malavika Karlekar (1986), and Tanika Sarkar (2002) analyze these same developments and ideologies in colonial Bengal, when formal education became not only acceptable but a requirement for the new *bhadramohila*, or respectable, educated woman. Nonetheless, the central place of this new educated woman was still to be in the home, and her education levels were not to equal those of men.

17. See also Gold 2010 on why fathers will not send their rural northern Indian daughters to school and the northern Indian herding girls' own rich and varying perspectives on schooling.

18. "Oscars: India-Set 'Period. End of Sentence' Tackles Taboos around Menstruation," *Hollywood Reporter*, February 24, 2019, https://www.hollywoodreporter.com/news/oscar

-winner-period-end-sentence-tackles-taboos-around-menstruation-1190295, accessed May 7, 2019.

19. National Family Health Survey statistics show that the number of women in West Bengal married before age 18 dropped from 53.3 percent in 2004–2005 to 40.7 percent in 2015–2016, although this is still above the national average of 26.8 percent (Singh and Dutta 2017).

20. See press release on "The Thirteenth Annual Status of Education Report (ASER 2018)," https://img.asercentre.org/docs/ASER%202018/Release%20Material/aser2018press releaseenglish.pdf.

21. The expense and extent of such gifts and dowry materials vary by caste and class, but can add up to a formidable sum even or especially for a laboring-class rural family. In 2019, laboring-class families gave me a figure of around 100,000 rupees, or nearly US$1,500, as the cost of a daughter's wedding, which for them is a huge sum.

22. See also Dickey 2016 (focusing on South India) and Sayer 2005 (drawing on social theory and moral philosophy), who explore the critical significance of class as a form of recognition and belonging.

23. For more on women, work, and social class in India, see also Radhakrishnan 2011; Vijayakumar 2013; and Waldrop 2012.

24. See Bourdieu 1977, 1987, 1992; and Mauss 1979 [1935].

25. I explore these themes surrounding nonfamily housing options further in chapters 1 and 7.

3. A DAUGHTER'S AND SISTER'S CARE

1. As mentioned in chapter 2, Medha's and Dada's family were of the same Mahishya farming caste as the zamindar's family, so social class is what mattered in this case rather than caste.

2. Lamb 2000: 83–88 further explores such kinship patterns, including Bengali ideas about how marriage makes a daughter "other" and why older parents cannot depend on a married daughter for support. Inden and Nicholas 1977: 12–14 examine how marrying transforms a Bengali woman's natal kin from her "own people" to "relatives." On women's ties to natal kin, see also Basu 1999; Dube 1988; Raheja and Gold 1994: 73–120.

3. On this theme, see also Chaturvedi and Sahai 2019: 84–85, who explore how "husbands and in-laws determine whether [married women] can work or not."

4. *Meghe Dhaka Tara*, commonly translated as *The Cloud-Capped Star* (or *The Star Veiled by Clouds* [Bagchi and Dasgupta 2006: 219]), was written and directed by Ritwik Ghatak and released in 1960. The film was inspired by the short story "Chena Mukh" (A Familiar Face), by Shaktipada Rajguru, who later developed a novelistic version of Ghatak's screenplay also titled *Meghe Dhaka Tara*, published after the film was released (P. Chakraborty 2018: 173, 209n14).

5. See, for examples, Bagchi and Dasgupta 2006: 5; Chakraborti 2009; P. Chakraborty 2018: 1, 165–213; and Raychaudhury 2004.

6. The film times provided in parentheses are approximate. Translations from Bengali to English come from a combination of the film's English subtitles provided in the YouTube version (https://www.youtube.com/watch?v=jxZXBMvwnwY) and my own

translations. For translations and language choice, I also consulted the partial screenplay reprinted in Bagchi and Dasgupta 2006: 219–231, translated by Sudeshna Chakrabarty, and P. Chakraborty's compelling analysis and partial retelling of the film (2018: 165–213).

7. Bengali Brahmin Kulin polygamy was practiced widely until the early 1900s by the highest-ranking Kulin (aristocratic, noble) Bengali Brahmans. Kulin Brahmans practiced strict hypergamy—Kulin daughters could only marry Kulin men. The ensuing surfeit of Kulin daughters "resulted in multiple marriages for Kulin men, many of whom left their brides with their natal families, and visited them only rarely" (McDermott 2011: 84; see also Karlekar 1995; Mitra 2020: 180–181, 183–188).

8. *Di*, short for *didi*, or "older sister," is a sign of both kin-like closeness and respect. Bengalis generally add kin terms to names when addressing persons senior to them.

9. Sukhi-di's story is explored further in this chapter's last section.

10. For more on Bengali patrilineality, see "Making Kinship within and beyond Lineal Masculinity" in chapter 6 and Dube 1988.

11. Rachel McDermott describes Uma as "the universal Bengali daughter of every house" (2011: 86). Bengali songs about Uma often "emphasize the sorrow of mother and daughter, or the plight of young girls" (McDermott 2001: 9), and the anticipation of unbearable loss as a daughter leaves in marriage to a family of strangers (McDermott 2011: 85). The fact that Nita's little sister Gita remains in her father's home after marriage is an exception not focused on in the film. Viewers might imagine Sanat's own natal family situation as insecure in this refugee context.

12. Most kinship systems in South Asia are patrilineal, although several matrilineal exceptions exist (e.g., Abraham 2010: 123–124, 126; P. Das Gupta 1984; Sebastian 2016).

13. For the living arrangements of this study's participants, see table 2 in chapter 1.

14. The idea of marriedness as the prime form of women's property, Basu explains, "is buttressed by two popular notions of ways in which women get property: the phantom equivalence of dowry with inheritance, and the idea that women 'get' affinal property" (1999: 224).

15. Like many other scholars, I have earlier focused on labor and power dynamics between mothers-in-law and daughters-in-law in Indian families (e.g., Lamb 2000).

4. WHO WILL CARE FOR ME?

1. For more on perceptions of decline in family-based old age care in India, see Cohen 1998; Lamb 2009, 2013, 2020; and Samanta 2018.

2. On the concept of elder orphans, see Carney et al. 2016, and the May 2015 CNN story "The 'Elder Orphans' of the Baby Boom Generation," https://www.cnn.com/2015/05/18 /health/elder-orphans/index.html.

3. See, e.g., Kislev 2019a: chapter 2, "Happy Singlehood in Old Age"; Klinenberg 2012: chapter 6, "Aging Alone"; and Bella DePaulo's April 23, 2017, online essay with links to further reading, "Older Single People: Here's What We Know," http://www.belladepaulo .com/2017/04/older-single-people-heres-know/.

4. For detailed information on rates of co-residence with children among seniors aged 60 and above in India, see Lamb 2020: 472, 487–488n14.

5. *Briddhashram* is the Bengali term, often translated into English as "old age home" and meaning literally "shelter" or "refuge" (*ashram*) for elders or old people (*briddha*). Loving Respect is a pseudonym akin in sentiment to Medha's home's real name and to the names of many other senior residential homes in India, such as Amazing Love Home in Chennai, Snehodiya (Giving Affection) Old Age Home in Kolkata, Sraddha (Respect) Old Age Home in Kolkata, and Bhalobasa (Love) Senior Citizens Residency in the Kolkata suburbs.

6. Medha has such high expectations for herself and others that it is difficult to truly impress her. She would later tell me that the managers are trying hard although imperfectly running the place. She introduced me via video call to the owner and central manager, who seemed very warm and sincere, and who expressed that they are trying hard, but not experts.

7. For more on the rise of market-based senior housing in India, see Lamb 2009, 2013; Lamb and Kavedzija 2020: 115–119; and Samanta 2021.

8. Personal communication, and see also Sandesara 2017. *Gharaḍa ghar* is the Gujarati phrase Sandesara glossed as "home for geezers," seeking to convey the derogatory tone with which his Gujarati interlocutors referred to such institutions.

9. The Naxalite movement grew out of a 1967 peasant uprising in the village of Naxalbari, West Bengal, leading to the formation of the Communist Party of India (Marxist-Leninist) two years later. West Bengal was originally the epicenter of the movement, and the colleges of Kolkata (then Calcutta) and Delhi became a hotbed for Naxalite activities.

10. The short story makes explicit parallels to Ritwik Ghatak's film *Meghe Dhaka Tara*, described in chapter 3. When the new wife of one of Bordi's brothers, Nitu, asks why Bordi was never married, Nitu is startled. "This question had never struck Nitu's mind! No, Nitu has no memory whether an attempt was ever made to arrange a wedding for Bordi. Is it that Ma intentionally never thought of getting Bordi married? Because Bordi was indispensable to the household? Because it was Bordi's hard physical work day and night that was essential in sustaining the disoriented household after father's sudden death? Only the other day, Nitu had hosted a Ritwik Ghatak Film Festival. . . . There, one of the speakers commented, 'Especially in the East Bengali refugee families, *Meghe Dhaka Taras* [that is, women like the film's heroine Nita] lay scattered everywhere.' That one exists in Nitu's own house had never before entered his mind!" (Bhattacharya 2017: 925, translated by my research assistant Hena Basu and SL).

11. See Malhotra 2019 and the Silver Talkies website, https://silvertalkies.com/about/.

12. Of the 100 elder home residents I interviewed for *Aging and the Indian Diaspora* (Lamb 2009), 13 women and 9 men were never married. One female resident with no kin with whom she could reside was only 38 years old. She had chosen the old age home as a safe place to live. She commuted to and from the old age home for work, and helped care for her many resident "aunts." In Lamb 2001, I also compare the stories of never-married old age home residents to those of widows (2001: 26–27).

13. Ideologies about activity as an ideal for a healthy and good old age have recently begun to circulate in India, as around the globe (Lamb 2019a; Lamb and Kavedzija 2020).

14. For US aspirations of old age independence and the myth of autonomy, see, e.g., Buch 2018; Gawande 2014: 55, Klinenberg 2012: 170–171; and Lamb 2014, 2019b.

15. In 2020, monthly fees for old age homes in West Bengal ranged from about 5,000 INR (or about $67) at the low end up to about 35,000 INR ($470) at the poshest institutions.

(To provide a point of comparison, the monthly salary in Kolkata for a part-time domestic worker who would wash dishes and cook ranged in 2020 from around 2,000 to 3,500 rupees.) Many retirement homes also require a substantial security deposit or (at the upscale places) an additional purchase of an apartment that could cost up to about 8 lakh rupees, or $10,000. Sukhi-di reported that her home's monthly fees come to 5,500 rupees, paid for by her siblings. (Sukhi-di's rent at the Government of West Bengal Working Girls' Hostel had only been 150 rupees per month, although excluding food and care.)

16. See more on this theme in chapter 7, "Contending with the Pleasing Syndrome."

17. Global media on self-care for singles, in order of reference: "One Isn't the Loneliest Number," Right as Rain, February 18, 2018, https://rightasrain.uwmedicine.org/mind/well-being/one-isnt-loneliest-number-self-care-singles; "4 Self-Care Tips for Single Women," *Elephant Journal*, February 12, 2018, https://www.elephantjournal.com/2017/07/4-self-care-tips-for-single-women/; "10 Ways to Take Better Care of Yourself While You're Single," Your Tango, October 15, 2019, https://www.yourtango.com/experts/lianne-avila/self-care-ideas-tips-how-to-take-care-of-yourself-be-happier-being-single.

18. Self-care pieces from the *Times of India*, in order of reference: "Self-Care Is the New Empowerment," March 17, 2019, https://timesofindia.indiatimes.com/life-style/health-fitness/de-stress/self-care-is-the-new-empowerment/articleshow/68406498.cms; "5 Ways to Practice Self-Care in 2020, February 26, 2020, https://timesofindia.indiatimes.com/life-style/health-fitness/de-stress/5-ways-to-practice-self-care-in-2020-without-spending-a-lot/photostory/74319017.cms; and "Happily Self-Partnered," December 22, 2019, https://timesofindia.indiatimes.com/life-style/relationships/love-sex/happily-self-partnered/articleshow/72886505.cms.

19. See table 2 in chapter 1: "Living Situations of Single-Women Participants."

20. In 2017, in a first, Chief Minister K. Chandrashekar Rao of the state of Telangana announced a Rs. 1,000 monthly pension for women who are "unmarried, single and aged over 30" from households with annual incomes of less than 1.5 lakh in rural areas and 2 lakh in urban areas (Ali 2017; S. B. J. Singh 2017). Indian inheritance laws also give daughters an equal birthright to inherit joint Hindu family property, but see chapter 3 and note 21, below.

21. See chapter 3 and Srimati Basu's analysis of the contemporary workings of property law in India, as she details how few women in practice lay claim to natal family assets, even when the law permits it (1999).

22. See "Young and Affluent, Women Too Drive Car Sales Now," *Economic Times*, February 8, 2020, https://auto.economictimes.indiatimes.com/news/passenger-vehicle/cars/young-affluent-women-too-drive-car-sales-now/74019874.

23. For the gendered concept and problem of "loitering" in India, see chapter 7 and Phadke, Khan, and Ranade 2011.

24. For more on the popularity of solo living in the United States and Europe, see Kislev 2019a; Klinenberg 2012; and "Singles Housing, and Living Solo as a Unique Form of Personhood" in chapter 1.

5. SEXUALITY AND LOVE

1. "February 15: Singles Awareness Day," NPR, February 15, 2019, https://www.npr.org/2019/02/15/695054803/feb-15-singles-awareness-day. Since the 1990s, Singles' Day,

originally called Bachelors' Day, has also been celebrated in China—on November 11 (11/11), the date consisting of four 1's, representing four singles. Online retailer Alibaba began offering Singles' Day discounts in 2009 and has since turned the event into a bonanza of online shopping.

2. One of anthropology's goals is to "make the familiar strange and the strange familiar." See, e.g., Myers 2011 and The Familiar Strange, https://thefamiliarstrange.com/everyday -anthropology/.

3. "Single" here refers specifically to unmarried people. One exception to studies suggesting that single or unmarried people have sexual relations more often than married people in the United States comes among those who identify as asexual. Many asexual persons prefer to be single, and neither want or need sexual contact with another person to feel fulfilled (Cerankowski and Milks 2014).

4. As in previous chapters, I use single quotes to indicate an English term inserted into an otherwise Bengali conversation. As noted first in the introduction, the use of English terms can signal a category's perceived unfamiliarity. Many Bengalis also prefer using English terms to refer to private matters of sexuality, often having been socialized that the Bengali versions of such terms are vulgar.

5. For more on cultural ideologies about women and pleasure, see "Contending with the Pleasing Syndrome" in chapter 7.

6. On lesbian in/visibility in India and im/possibilities for public relationships, see also Dave 2012: 13; Phadke, Khan, and Ranade 2011: 154–155; and Seizer 1995.

7. Kaivanara 2016 examines a similar rise in hymen restoration surgery (hymenoplasty) rates among young women in Tehran, Iran.

8. Other scholars have exposed and critiqued similar assumptions about women's sexuality, including Dewey 2009; D. Narayan 2018a; and Puri 1999. See also Durba Mitra's (2020) incisive examination of how British officials, European scholars, and elite Indian intellectuals deployed ideas about deviant female sexuality in the colonial era.

9. For more on the figure of the sex worker or prostitute in India, see Mitra 2020; Mokkil 2019; Walters 2016, 2022.

10. Shilpa Phadke, Sameera Khan, and Shilpa Ranade (2011) provide an incisive exposé of such ideologies at work, barring women from freely accessing public space, often in the name of "safety" and concerns surrounding caste and class purity (17).

11. In the early twentieth century, sociopolitical reformer B. R. Ambedkar (2014 [1916]) famously advocated for intercaste marriages as key to ending caste-based discrimination, as did Periyar through southern India's Self-Respect Movement, arguments which are still debated and of concern today (e.g., Prajwal 2018).

12. I first wrote about "Mithu's" pregnancy and its consequences briefly in Lamb 2000: 189, 197.

13. See Thomson Reuters Foundation, "The World's Most Dangerous Countries for Women 2018," https://poll2018.trust.org/. The United States came tenth on the list, behind (in this order) India, Afghanistan, Syria, Somalia, Saudi Arabia, Pakistan, Democratic Republic of Congo, Yemen, and Nigeria.

14. See, for instance, BBC's "Is India Really the Most Dangerous Country for Women?," June 28, 2018, https://www.bbc.com/news/world-asia-india-42436817. One theory is that countries making progress toward publicizing sexual violence, such as through the

#MeToo movement, may end up higher on the list of dangerous countries due to greater awareness.

15. The "Priya's Shakti" story is by Ram Devineni and Vikas K. Menon; the art is by Dan Goldman; https://www.priyashakti.com/priyas_shakti/. See also Flood 2014.

16. See more on skin color perceptions in chapter 1.

17. Steamed cabbage and boiled peanuts are not at all standard Bengali breakfast foods, but as I mention in chapter 4 reflecting on self-care, Medha had developed a passion for preparing only very healthful, plant-based, and organic foods.

18. See note 7 in chapter 3 for a discussion of Bengali Brahmin Kulin polygamy.

19. See Dickey 2016: 145; Grover 2018; Trivedi 2014: 1, 175; "5 Reasons Why Arranged Marriages Are Still Successful in India," *Times of India*, May 14, 2019, https://timesofindia .indiatimes.com/life-style/relationships/love-sex/5-reasons-why-arranged-marriages-are -still-successful-in-india/photostory/69309141.cms; and "Benefits of Love Marriage," *Times of India*, December 23, 2017, https://timesofindia.indiatimes.com/astrology/others/benefits -of-love-marriage/articleshow/68205887.cms.

20. Two unmarried Brahman village men I know now in their sixties and seventies tell of having fallen in love with village girls of a lower caste whom they could not marry as their reason for never marrying; and one working-middle-class Kolkata shopkeeper I knew for many years had fallen in love with a visiting American scholar and felt he could never marry even after the American woman ended the affair.

21. For more on asexuality as a sexual identity, see Cerankowski and Milks 2014. An asexual movement emerged in the early 2000s with the goal of establishing asexuality as a legitimate sexual identity, such as through the Asexual Visibility and Education Network (AVEN).

22. Essay posted April 6, 2018, https://www.facebook.com/thikanashimla/ (translation from the Bengali is mine). See also Datta 2017.

23. See more on disability, appearance, and the body in chapter 1.

24. *Bandhobi* is the female form of *bondhu*, "friend," and in ordinary usage does not imply a romantic or sexual relationship.

25. Sappho for Equality: The Activist Forum for Lesbian, Bisexual Woman and Trans-man Rights was established in 2003 in Kolkata (http://www.sapphokolkata.in/). I discuss Deepa Mehta's 1996 film *Fire* below.

26. See more on the unfamiliar notion of living without kin in chapter 1: "Singles Housing, and Living Solo as a Unique Form of Personhood."

27. See "Section 377: Here Is Everything You Need to Know," *Economic Times*, September 7, 2018, https://economictimes.indiatimes.com/news/politics-and-nation/sc -delivers-historic-verdict-heres-everything-you-need-to-know-about-section-377/article show/65698429.cms?from=mdr.

28. See "Consensual Sex among Adults in Privacy Does Not Harm Public Decency, Morality: Supreme Court," *Economic Times*, September 6, 2018, https://economictimes .indiatimes.com/news/politics-and-nation/consensual-sex-among-adults-in-privacy -does-not-harm-public-decency-morality-supreme-court/articleshow/65708151.cms; and "Full Text of Supreme Court's Verdict on Section 377," September 6, 2018, *The Hindu*, https:// www.thehindu.com/news/resources/full-text-of-supreme-courts-verdict-on-section -377-on-september-6-2018/article24880713.ece.

29. It is for this reason that I choose the gender-neutral "they" as an English pronoun for Ajay, as I note in the introduction. Bengali's third-person pronoun *se* is already gender neutral.

6. NEVER-MARRIED SINGLE MOMS

1. The flurry of recent media stories on single mothers in India include Bagchi 2018; Dutt 2017; Gupta 2019; Joshi 2018; Khan 2020; Mathew 2019; A. Mukherjee 2015; Raja 2019; P. Singh 2018; Vajpayee 2019; Wangchuk 2020; and Yengkhom 2015. See also Mehrotra 2003 for an earlier study, and Sarah Pinto's portrait of a single divorced mother (2014a: 240–241).

2. This UN Women report figure includes widowed, separated, and abandoned, divorced, and never-married women leading households with children under age 18 (UN Women 2019). One can glean from the report's other data that the majority of these single mothers are widowed and separated or abandoned women, while fewer are divorced or never-married. The report relates that "in India, while the number of divorcees has doubled over the past two decades, still only 1.1 percent of women are divorced, with those in urban areas making up the largest proportion" (2019: 56). See also Dommaraju 2016. Regarding never-married women, the study reports that, in India, less than 1 percent of all women aged 45 to 49 have never married (UN Women 2019: 54). See also Gupta 2019 and Vajpayee 2019, who report on this study.

3. See also "13M Single Moms in India, Yet Taboo against Them Is Unchanged" (Gupta 2019).

4. In West Bengal, Kayastha is a large caste group often deemed ideologically to be next in rank to Brahmans.

5. Like other names in the book, Suravi's son's father's name here is a pseudonym. I choose surnames reflecting a similar caste background to the participants' real names.

6. See also HuffPost 2017 and "Father's Name Not Mandatory for Passport, Rules Court," Press Trust of India, May 21, 2016, https://www.ndtv.com/india-news/mothers-name -sufficient-for-passport-high-court-1408568.

7. Suravi is referring to the West Bengal Commission for Women, which "has helped numerous women get help, counselling, and relief from the torture or injustice that they were being subjected to." Cases coming under the purview of the commission include the categories of Illicit Relationships, Divorce and Maintenance, Family Disputes, Rape and Molestation, Dowry Torture, Sexual Harassment at Workplace, and more (https://www .wbcw.co.in/).

8. Jordal, Wijewardena, and Olsson 2013 examine similar strategies employed by unmarried young women who become pregnant in urban, semi-urban, and rural Sri Lankan communities.

9. For more on Bengali Hindu death-impurity rituals (*ashauch*), see Lamb 2000: 164–169, 230.

10. Shortly after, per my request, Medha took down the post for privacy reasons.

11. See the Hindu Adoptions and Maintenance Act of 1956, https://tcw.nic.in/Acts /Hindu%20adoption%20and%20Maintenance%20Act.pdf. Note that "Hindu" in this act refers to Hindus, Sikhs, Buddhists, and Jains, while excluding Muslims, Christians, Parsis, and Jews. India's secular state has aimed to allow different marriage and family laws to be

practiced by different religious communities. The gender distinction in this 1956 law gives authority to the male partner in a married couple, while a woman would ordinarily only become a legal adoptive parent if not married. Note that a male adoptive parent need not get the consent of his wife if she is officially unavailable, unsound, or no longer Hindu.

12. See, e.g., Bhatt 2019; M. Das Gupta 2017; Dhar 2017.

13. See item I.5.2 of the Ministry of Women and Child Development Notification, New Delhi, January 4, 2017, Adoption Regulations as Framed by the Central Adoption Resource Authority, http://cara.nic.in/PDF/Regulation_english.pdf.

14. Ibid., items I.5.2 and I.5.3.

15. To adopt a child less than four years old, the maximum composite age is 90 in case of a couple and 45 in case of a single parent. For adopting a child above four years old, the maximum composite age for a couple is 100 while the maximum age for a single parent is 50 years. For adopting a child between 8 and 18 years, the maximum age is 110 for a couple and 55 for a single parent (ibid., item I.5.4). See also Choudhury 2021.

16. For news media exploring the experiences of single mothers choosing IVF in India, see Bagchi 2018; Joshi 2018; Mathew 2019; A. Mukherjee 2015; Yengkhom 2015.

17. The Hindi term for lineage here, *vansh*, is the equivalent of the Bengali term I have transliterated above as *bongsho* (to approximate the way the term is pronounced in Bengali), which can also be transliterated as *vansha*. Horton goes on to examine how queer identities and desires intersect with the urge to care for others in the family, developing the concept of "agonistic intimacy" to explore how the competing desires of queerness and kinship interpenetrate. Horton writes: "While some strands of queer critique conceptualize the relationship between kinship and queerness antagonistically, [I] deploy the concept of agonistic intimacy outlined in [Bhrigupati] Singh's *Poverty and the Quest for Life* (2015) to consider how queers might inhabit heterosexual kinship networks through the interplay of contestation and submission" (2017: 1059).

7. PLEASURE, FRIENDSHIPS, AND FUN

1. Studies exploring the potential social and pleasurable benefits of singlehood include DePaulo 2017a; Hauser 2016 (e.g., p. 53); Kislev 2019a; Sarkisian and Gerstel 2016; Sharma 2019; and Trimberger 2005. However, other studies continue to suggest that sense of well-being and happiness are higher among married or coupled people (e.g., Perelli-Harris et al. 2019; Raymo 2015).

2. For scholarship on singlehood and friendships, see Kislev 2019a: 164–169, 2019b; Klinenbeg 2012: 97–98; Maeda 2008; Sarkisian and Gerstel 2016; Traister 2016: 96–122; Trimberger 2005.

3. See Phadke, Khan, and Ranade's *Why Loiter?* (2011) and the Why Loiter movement (#WhyLoiter and http://whyloiter.blogspot.com/).

4. A single cup of tea at the highly popular upscale cafés in Kolkata will cost about 200 to 300 rupees, 20 to 30 times higher than the cost of tea at an outside stall at 10 rupees. For US readers, think of spending $32 to $48 for a small coffee at a chic café rather than $1.59 at Dunkin' Donuts.

5. For more on enacting respectability as defined by the gendered division between public and private spaces, see Phadke, Khan, and Ranade 2011: 24–26; and Seizer 2000.

6. *Alta* is a red dye applied to the feet of women during religious festivals and weddings, and as an everyday adornment. The vibrant red is thought to bring out the beauty of the feet, and a Bengali bride is visually incomplete if her feet are not colored with alta. This particular dream is only one in a remarkable dream sequence in which Banalata envisions the never-to-materialize events of her own wedding and conveys her never-ending craving for marriage and erotic fulfillment (S. Mukherjee 2016: 92–96; Dasgupta and Banerjee 2016).

7. These themes resonate with those in chapter 4, "Strategies for Self-Care."

CONCLUSION

1. See Inhorn and Smith-Hefner 2021: 394; and Ortiz-Ospina and Roser 2020.

2. We conducted a little online research when we got back to Medha's flat, deciding that this unfortunate woman must have been infected with ascariasis, the most common roundworm infection worldwide, concentrated in tropical and subtropical areas with poor sanitation. The *ascaris lumbricoides* is a large nematode (roundworm) that infects the human gastrointestinal tract. The adults can reach over twelve inches in length and emerge through the nose, mouth, or rectum. The infection can be easily treated with oral medication in the early stages, but can require more complicated interventions including surgery if left untreated.

3. UN Women 2019: 54; I also discuss India's extremely low non-marriage rates in "The Gendered Marriage Imperative" section of chapter 1.

4. For foundational work on critical heterosexuality studies, see Fischer 2013; Dean and Fischer 2020; and note 22 of the introduction. See also Basu 2015; Basu and Ramberg 2015; and Satalkar 2012 for critiques of marriage in India.

REFERENCES

Abraham, Janaki. 2010. "Wedding Videos in North Kerala: Technologies, Rituals, and Ideas about Love and Conjugality." *Visual Anthropology Review* 26(2): 116–127.

——. 2015. "Contingent Caste Endogamy and Patriarchy: Lessons for Our Understanding of Caste." In Srimati Basu and Lucinda Ramberg, eds., *Conjugality Unbound: Sexual Economies, State Regulation, and the Marital Form in India.* Pp. 161–189. New Delhi: Women Unlimited.

Abu-Lughod, Lila. 1990. "The Romance of Resistance: Tracing Transformations of Power through Bedouin Women." *American Ethnologist* 17(1): 41–55.

——. 2008. *Writing Women's Worlds: Bedouin Stories.* 15th anniversary ed. Berkeley: University of California Press.

Agarwal, Bina. 1994. *A Field of One's Own: Gender and Land Rights in South Asia.* New York: Cambridge University Press.

Ahearn, Laura M. 2001. "Language and Agency." *Annual Review of Anthropology* 30: 109–137.

Ali, Roushan. 2017. "30 and Single: Hyderabad Women Give Career Priority, Lead the Flock." *Times of India,* February 20. https://timesofindia.indiatimes.com/city/hyderabad /30-and-single-hyderabad-women-give-career-priority-lead-the-flock/articleshow /57242335.cms?from=mdr.

Allison, Rachel, and Barbara J. Risman. 2013. "A Double Standard for 'Hooking Up': How Far Have We Come toward Gender Equality?" *Social Science Research* 42(5): 1191–1206.

Ambedkar, B. R. 2014 [1916]. "Castes in India." In Vasant Moon, comp., *Dr. Babasaheb Ambedkar: Writings and Speeches.* Vol. 1. Pp. 3–22. New Delhi: Dr. Ambedkar Foundation, Ministry of Social Justice and Empowerment, Government of India.

Anjaria, Jonathan Shapiro, and Ulka Anjaria. 2020. "*Mazaa*: Rethinking Fun, Pleasure, and Play in South Asia." *South Asia: Journal of South Asian Studies* 43(2): 232–242.

Asencio, Marysol. 1999. "Machos and Sluts: Gender, Sexuality, and Violence among a Cohort of Puerto Rican Adolescents." *Medical Anthropology Quarterly* 13(1): 107–126.

Aslany, Maryam. 2019. "The Indian Middle Class, Its Size, and Urban-Rural Variations." *Contemporary South Asia* 27(2): 196–213.

Babadi, Mehrdad. 2021. "Between Cynicism and Idealism: Voluntary Waithood in Iran." In Marcia C. Inhorn and Nancy J. Smith-Hefner, eds., *Waithood: Gender, Education, and Global Delays in Marriage and Childbearing.* Pp. 249–268. New York: Berghahn.

Bagchi, Jasodhara, and Subhoranjan Dasgupta, eds. 2006. *The Trauma and the Triumph: Gender and Partition in Eastern India.* Kolkata: Stree.

Bagchi, Shrabonti. 2018. "Two's Company: Single Women in Search of Motherhood." *Mint*, October 20. https://www.livemint.com/Leisure/PfWgIPTXJMcTvSGaitskwM/Twos -Company-Single-women-in-search-of-motherhood.html.

Bakke, Gretchen. 2020. *The Likeness: Semblance and Self in Slovene Society.* Oakland: University of California Press.

Banerjee, Himani. 2016. "Patriarchy in the Era of Neoliberalism: The Case of India." *Social Scientist* 44(3/4): 3–27.

Banerjee, Madhuri. 2011. *Losing My Virginity and Other Dumb Ideas.* New Delhi: Penguin Random House India.

Barrett, Liz Cox. 2006. "*Newsweek* Discovers Doomed Spinsters Marrying." *Columbia Journalism Review*, May 30. https://archives.cjr.org/behind_the_news/newsweek_discovers _doomed_spin.php.

Basu, Srimati. 1999. *She Comes to Take Her Rights: Indian Women, Property, and Propriety.* Albany: State University of New York Press.

———. 2015. *The Trouble with Marriage: Feminists Confront Law and Violence in India.* Berkeley: University of California Press.

Basu, Srimati, and Lucinda Ramberg, eds. 2015. *Conjugality Unbound: Sexual Economics, State Regulation, and the Marital Form in India.* New Delhi: Women Unlimited.

Becker, Gay, Yewoubdar Beyene, and Pauline Ken. 2000. "Memory, Trauma, and Embodied Distress: The Management of Disruption in the Stories of Cambodians in Exile." *Ethos* 28(3): 320–345.

Berreman, Gerald D. 1972. "Race, Caste, and Other Invidious Distinctions in Social Stratification." *Race* 13(4): 385–414.

Berry, Kim. 2014. "Single but Not Alone: The Journey from Stigma to Collective Identity through Himachal's Single Women's Movement." *Himalaya* 34(1): 43–55.

Bharadwaj, Aditya. 2003. "Why Adoption Is Not an Option in India: The Visibility of Infertility, the Secrecy of Donor Insemination, and Other Cultural Complexities." *Social Science and Medicine* 56(9): 1867–1880.

———. 2016. *Conceptions: Infertility and Procreative Technologies in India.* New York: Berghahn.

Bhat, Rouf Ahmad. 2015. "Role of Education in the Empowerment of Women in India." *Journal of Education and Practice* 16(10): 188–191.

Bhatt, Stephali. 2019. "Despite a Favourable Law, Why Do Single Women and Men Struggle to Adopt a Child in India." *Economic Times*, August 11. https://economictimes.india times.com/news/politics-and-nation/despite-a-favourable-law-why-do-single-women -and-men-struggle-to-adopt-a-child-in-india/articleshow/70621618.cms.

Bhattacharya, Sunanda. 2017. "Naxaler Didi Ebong Iswariccha" [Elder Sister of a Naxalite and Wish of God]. In Bijit Ghosh, ed., *Naxal Andolaner Galpa* [Naxalite Movement Stories]. Vol. 2. Pp. 921–931. Kolkata: Punascha.

Biehl, Joao, Byron Good, and Arthur Kleinman. 2007. *Subjectivity: Ethnographic Investigations.* Berkeley: University of California Press.

Boellstorff, Tom. 2007. *A Coincidence of Desires: Anthropology, Queer Studies, Indonesia.* Durham, NC: Duke University Press.

Borneman, John. 1996. "Until Death Do Us Part: Marriage/Death in Anthropological Discourse." *American Ethnologist* 23(2): 215–238.

Bourdieu, Pierre. 1977. *Outline of a Theory of Practice.* Translated by Richard Nice. Cambridge: Cambridge University Press.

———. 1987. *Distinction: A Social Critique of the Judgement of Taste.* Translated by Richard Nice. Cambridge, MA: Harvard University Press.

———. 1992. *The Logic of Practice.* Translated by Richard Nice. Stanford: Stanford University Press.

———. 2004. "Gender and Symbolic Violence." In Nancy Scheper-Hughes and Philippe Bourgois, eds., *Violence in War and Peace: An Anthology.* Pp. 339–342. Malden, MA: Blackwell.

Brainer, Amy. 2019. *Queer Kinship and Family Change in Taiwan.* New Brunswick, NJ: Rutgers University Press.

Brosius, Christiane. 2010. *India's Middle Class: New Forms of Urban Leisure, Consumption and Prosperity.* New York: Routledge.

Buch, Elana D. 2015. "Anthropology of Aging and Care." *Annual Review of Anthropology* 44: 277–293.

———. 2018. *Inequalities of Aging: Paradoxes of Independence in American Home Care.* New York: New York University Press.

Buddeberg, Rachel, and Bella DePaulo. 2015. "Do You, Married Person, Take These Unearned Privileges, for Better or for Better?" Truthout, January 14. https://truthout.org/articles/do-you-married-person-take-these-unearned-privileges-for-better-or-for-better/.

Butler, Judith. 2002. "Is Kinship Always Already Heterosexual? *differences: A Journal of Feminist Cultural Studies* 13(1): 14–44.

Carlisle, Steven. 2012. "Creative Sincerity: Thai Buddhist Karma Narratives and the Grounding of Truths." *Ethos* 40(3): 317–340.

Carney, Maria T., Janice Fujiwara, Brian E. Emmert Jr., Tara A. Liberman, and Barbara Paris. 2016. "Elder Orphans Hiding in Plain Sight: A Growing Vulnerable Population." *Current Gerontology and Geriatrics Research*, October 23: 1–11.

Cerankowski, Karli June, and Megan Milks. 2014. *Asexualities: Feminist and Queer Perspectives.* New York: Routledge.

Chakraborti, Basudeb. 2009. "The Essentials of Indianness: Tolerance and Sacrifice in Indian Partition Fiction in English and in English Translation." *Rupkatha Journal on Interdisciplinary Studies in Humanities* 1(1) (Summer Issue): 3–32.

Chakraborty, Paulomi. 2018. *The Refugee Woman: Partition of Bengal, Gender, and the Politcal.* New Delhi: Oxford University Press.

Chakraborty, Shamayita. 2019. "Kolkata's Unwed Moms Welcome Ekta Kapoor's Choice." *Times of India*, February 3. https://timesofindia.indiatimes.com/city/kolkata/kolkatas-unwed-moms-welcome-ekta-kapoors-choice/articleshow/67807122.cms.

Chakravarti, Bithi. 2006. "Becoming the Breadwinner." In Jasodhara Bagchi and Subhoranjan Dasgupta, eds., *The Trauma and the Triumph: Gender and Partition in Eastern India.* Pp. 150–154. Kolkata: Stree.

Chakravarti, Uma. 1993. "Conceptualizing Brahmanical Patriarchy in Early India: Gender, Caste, Class, and the State." *Economic and Political Weekly*, April 3: 579–585.

Chatterjee, Anindita. 2019. "Everyday Talk and Gendered Labour: An Ethnography of Action in Interaction between Domestic Servants and Middle-Class Bengali Women in Kolkata and Delhi." PhD diss., Jawaharlal Nehru University, New Delhi.

Chatterjee, Partha. 1989. "Colonialism, Nationalism, and Colonialized Women: The Contest in India." *American Ethnologist* 16(4): 622–633.

Chaturvedi, Gitanjali, and Garima Sahai. 2019. "Understanding Women's Aspirations: A Study in Three Indian States." *Antyajaa: Indian Journal of Women and Social Change* 4(1): 70–91.

Choudhury, Disha Roy. 2021. "Girl Child Is Adopted More in India: All You Need to Know on Adoption, from CARA." *Indian Express*, May 8. https://indianexpress.com/article /parenting/family/child-adoption-cara-india-girl-all-you-need-to-know-6153189/.

Cohen, Lawrence. 1998. *No Aging in India: Alzheimer's, the Bad Family, and Other Modern Things*. Berkeley: University of California Press.

Craig, Sienna. 2011. "Migration, Social Change, Health, and the Realm of the Possible: Women's Stories between Nepal and New York." *Anthropology and Humanism* 36(2): 193–214.

Dabas, Maninder. 2016. "Father's Name No Longer Mandatory on Passports, Sadhus Can Use Their Guru's Name Instead." *India Times*, December 23. https://www.indiatimes .com/news/father-s-name-no-longer-mandatory-on-passports-sadhus-can-use-their -guru-s-name-instead-268039.html.

Das Gupta, Moushumi. 2017. "More Single Women Coming Forward to Adopt Children in India, Shows Data." *Hindustan Times*, March 26. https://www.hindustantimes.com /india-news/more-single-women-coming-forward-to-adopt-children-in-india-shows -data/story-dgcvnQJoPFvkl6kqgC2bTK.html.

Das Gupta, Pranab Kumar. 1984. *Life and Culture of Matrilineal Tribe of Meghalaya*. New Delhi: Inter-India Publications.

Dasgupta, Rohit K., and Tanmayee Banerjee. 2016. "Exploitation, Victimhood, and Gendered Performance in Rituparno Ghosh's *Bariwali*." *Film Quarterly* 69(4): 35–46.

Datta, Romita. 2017. "Kolkata's Senior Citizens Find Love and Marry, Thanks to Thikana Shimla." *India Today*, July 24.

Dave, Naisargi N. 2011. "Indian and Lesbian and What Came Next: Affect, Commensuration, and Queer Emergences." *American Ethnologist* 38(4): 650–665.

———. 2012. *Queer Activism in India: A Story in the Anthropology of Ethics*. Durham, NC: Duke University Press.

Davidson, Joanna. 2019. "'People Insult Me—Oh My!': Reflections on Jola Women's Story-Songs in Rural West Africa." In Tracy Ann Hayes, Theresa Edlmann, and Laurinda Brown, eds. *Storytelling: Global Reflections on Narrative*. Pp. 165–174. Leiden: Brill.

Davidson, Joanna, and Dinah Hannaford, eds. 2022. *Opting Out: Women Messing with Marriage around the World*. New Brunswick, NJ: Rutgers University Press.

Dean, James Joseph, and Nancy L. Fischer, eds. 2020. *Routledge International Handbook of Heterosexualities Studies*. New York: Routledge.

DePaulo, Bella. 2007. *Singled Out: How Singles Are Stereotyped, Stigmatized, and Ignored, and Still Live Happily Ever After*. New York: St. Martin's Griffin.

————. 2017a. "6 New Things Researchers Learned about Single People in 2017." *The Cut*, December 28. https://www.thecut.com/2017/12/6-new-things-researchers-learned-about-single-people-in-2017.html.

————. 2017b. "The Urgent Need for a Singles Studies Discipline." *Signs: Journal of Women in Culture and Society* 42(4): 1015–1019.

DePaulo, Bella, Rachel F. Moran, and E. Kay Trimberger. 2007. "Make Room for Singles in Teaching and Research." *Chronicle of Higher Education* 54(5): 44.

DePaulo, Bella M., and Wendy L. Morris. 2005. "Singles in Society and in Science." *Psychological Inquiry* 16(2/3): 57–83.

Desjarlais, Robert. 2016. *Subject to Death: Life and Loss in a Buddhist World.* Chicago: University of Chicago Press.

Dewey, Susan. 2009. "'Dear Dr. Kothari . . .': Sexuality, Violence against Women, and the Parallel Public Sphere in India." *American Ethnologist* 36(1): 124–139.

Dhar, Shobita. 2017. "Adoption Made Easier for Single Women." *Times of India*, July 22. https://timesofindia.indiatimes.com/india/adoption-made-easier-for-single-women/articleshow/59708232.cms.

Dickey, Sara. 2013. "Apprehensions: On Gaining Recognition as Middle-Class in Madurai." *Contributions to Indian Sociology* 47(2): 217–243.

————. 2016. *Living Class in Urban India.* New Brunswick, NJ: Rutgers University Press.

Dommaraju, Premchand. 2015. "One-Person Households in India." *Demographic Research* 32: 1239–1266.

————. 2016. "Divorce and Separation in India." *Population and Development Review* 42(2): 195–223.

Driessen, Henk. 1998. "The Notion of Friendship in Ethnographic Fieldwork." *Anthropological Journal on European Cultures* 7(1): 43–62.

Dube, Leela. 1988. "On the Construction of Gender: Hindu Girls in Patrilineal India." *Economic and Political Weekly* 23(18): WS11–WS19.

————. 1997. *Women and Kinship: Comparative Perspectives on Gender in South and South-East Asia.* Tokyo: United Nations University Press.

Dutt, Shobhita. 2017. "8 Single Celebrity Mothers Who Are Setting an Example for Others." *Times of India*, July 4. https://www.indiatimes.com/entertainment/celebs/8-single-celebrity-mothers-who-are-setting-a-great-example-for-others-252742.html.

Eck, Beth A. 2013. "Identity Twists and Turns: How Never-Married Men Make Sense of an Unanticipated Identity." *Journal of Contemporary Ethnography* 42(1): 31–63.

Edelman, Lee. 2004. *No Future: Queer Theory and the Death Drive.* Durham, NC: Duke University Press.

Farvid, Panteá, Virginia Braun, and Casey Rowney. 2017. "'No Girl Wants to Be Called a Slut!': Women, Heterosexual Casual Sex and the Sexual Double Standard." *Journal of Gender Studies* 26(5): 544–560.

Fasula, Amy M., Monique Carry, and Kim S. Miller. 2014. "A Multidimensional Framework for the Meanings of the Sexual Double Standard and Its Application for the Sexual Health of Young Black Women in the U.S." *Journal of Sex Research* 51(2): 170–183.

Fernandes, Leela. 2006. *India's New Middle Classes: Democratic Politics in an Era of Economic Reform.* Minneapolis: University of Minnesota Press.

Fincher, Leta Hong. 2014. *Leftover Women: The Resurgence of Gender Inequality in China.* New York: Zed.

Fischer, Nancy L. 2013. "Seeing 'Straight,' Contemporary Critical Heterosexuality Studies and Sociology: An Introduction." *Sociological Quarterly* 54(4): 501–510.

Flood, Alison. 2014. "Indian Comic Creates Female Superhero to Tackle Rape." *Guardian*, 18 December. https://www.theguardian.com/books/2014/dec/18/india-comic-superhero -tackle-rape-women-priyas-shakti-parvati.

Friedner, Michele. 2015. *Valuing Deaf Worlds in Urban India.* New Brunswick, NJ: Rutgers University Press.

Gammeltoft, Tine M. 2014. *Haunting Images: A Cultural Account of Selective Reproductive in Vietnam.* Berkeley: University of California Press.

Ganguly-Scrase, Ruchira. 2013. *Global Issues, Local Contexts: The Rabi Das of West Bengal.* Hyderabad: Orient Blackswan.

Garber, Megan. 2016. "When *Newsweek* 'Struck Terror in the Hearts of Single Women.'" *Atlantic*, June 2. https://www.theatlantic.com/entertainment/archive/2016/06/more -likely-to-be-killed-by-a-terrorist-than-to-get-married/485171/.

Gawande, Atul. 2014. *Being Mortal: Medicine and What Matters in the End.* New York: Metropolitan.

Ghatak, Ritwik, dir. 1960. *Meghe Dhaka Tara* [A Cloud-Capped Star or Hidden Star]. Produced by Chitrakalpa.

Ghosh, Nandini. 2016. *Impaired Bodies, Gendered Lives: Everyday Realities of Disabled Women.* New Delhi: Primus Books.

———. 2018. "Experiencing the Body: Femininity, Sexuality, and Disabled Women in India." In Anita Ghai, ed., *Disability in South Asia: Knowledge and Experience.* Pp. 101–117. Los Angeles: Sage.

Ghosh, Rituparno, dir. 2000. *Bariwali* [The Lady of the House]. Produced by Anupam Kher.

Ghosh, Sayantanee. 2013. "Not Enough 'Room' for Single Women in Kolkata." *Times of India*, March 27. https://timesofindia.indiatimes.com/city/kolkata/Not-enough-room -for-single-women-in-Kolkata/articleshow/19233394.cms?utm_source=contento finterest&utm_medium=text&utm_campaign=cppst.

Ghosh, Shohini. 2010. *Fire: A Queer Film Classic.* Vancouver: Arsenal Pulp Press.

Gold, Ann Grodzins. 2010. "New Light in the House: Schooling Girls in Rural North India." In Diane P. Mines and Sarah Lamb, eds., *Everyday Life in South Asia.* 2nd ed. Pp. 80–93. Bloomington: Indiana University Press.

Goldstein, Joshua R., and Catherine T. Kenney. 2001. "Marriage Delayed or Marriage Forgone? New Cohort Forecasts of First Marriage for U.S. Women." *American Sociological Review* 66(4): 506–519.

Goli, Srinivas, Deepti Singh, and T. V. Sekher. 2013. "Exploring the Myth of Mixed Marriages in India: Evidence from a Nation-wide Survey." *Journal of Comparative Family Studies* 44(2): 193–206.

Gray, Catherine. 2018. *The Unexpected Joy of Being Single.* London: Aster.

Greenhalgh, Susan. 2012. "Patriarchal Demographics? China's Sex Ratio Reconsidered." *Population and Development* 38 (Supplement): 130–149.

———. 2015. "'Bare Sticks' and Other Dangers to the Social Body: Assembling Fatherhood in China." In Marcia C. Inhorn, Wendy Chavkin, and José-Alberto Navarro, eds., *Globalized Fatherhood.* Pp. 359–381. New York: Berghahn.

Grover, Shalini. 2009. "Lived Experiences: Marriage, Notions of Love, and Kinship Support amongst Poor Women in Delhi." *Contributions to Indian Sociology* (n.s.) 43(1): 1–33.

———. 2018. *Marriage, Love, Caste, and Kinship Support: Lived Experiences of the Urban Poor in India.* New York: Routledge.

Gupta, Poorvi. 2019. "13M Single Moms in India, Yet Taboo against Them Is Unchanged." *She the People.* July 18. https://www.shethepeople.tv/news/13-mn-single-moms-india/.

Hauser, Brooke. 2016. *Enter Helen: The Invention of Helen Gurley Brown and the Rise of the Modern Single Woman.* New York: HarperCollins.

Hindu. 2004. "Old Age Homes against Our Culture: Vaiko." Staff Reporter. *Hindu,* September 14. https://www.thehindu.com/todays-paper/tp-national/tp-tamilnadu/old-age-homes-against-our-culture-vaiko/article27668712.ece.*Hindu.* 2020. "Right by Birth: On Daughters and Hindu Succession Act." Editorial. *Hindu,* August 14. https://www.thehindu.com/opinion/editorial/right-by-birth-the-hindu-editorial-on-daughters-and-hindu-succession-act/article32347299.ece.

Horton, Brian A. 2017. "What's So 'Queer' about Coming Out? Silent Queers and Theorizing Kinship Agonistically in Mumbai." *Sexualities* 21(7): 1059–1074.

———. 2020. "Fashioning Fabulation: Dress, Gesture, and the Queer Aesthetics of Mumbai Pride." *South Asia: Journal of South Asian Studies* 43(2): 294–307.

Howlett, Zachary M. 2021. "Tactics of Marriage Delay in China: Education, Rural-to-Urban Migration, and 'Leftover Women.'" In Marcia C. Inhorn and Nancy J. Smith-Hefner, eds., *Waithood: Gender, Education, and Global Delays in Marriage and Childbearing.* Pp. 177–199. New York: Berghahn.

HuffPost. 2017. "Father's Name Should Be Optional on Degree Certificates, Maneka Gandhi Tells HRD Ministry." *Huffington Post,* April 17. https://www.huffingtonpost.in/2017/04/17/rule-of-fathers-name-on-degree-certificates-should-be-done-away_a_22042561/.

Inden, Ronald B., and Ralph W. Nicholas. 1977. *Kinship in Bengali Culture.* Chicago: University of Chicago Press.

Inhorn, Marcia C. 1996. *Infertility and Patriarchy: The Cultural Politics of Gender and Family Life in Egypt.* Philadelphia: University of Pennsylvania Press.

———. 2006. "'The Worms Are Weak': Male Infertility and Patriarchal Paradoxes in Egypt." In Lahoucine Ouzgane, ed., *Islamic Masculinities.* Pp. 217–236. London: Zed Books.

———. 2015. "New Arab Fatherhood: Male Infertility, Assisted Reproduction, and Emergent Masculinities." In Marcia C. Inhorn, Wendy Chavkin, and José-Alberto Navarro, eds., *Globalized Fatherhood.* Pp. 243–264. New York: Berghahn.

Inhorn, Marcia C., and Nancy J. Smith-Hefner. 2021. *Waithood: Gender, Education, and Global Delays in Marriage and Childbearing.* New York: Berghahn.

Jackson, Michael. 2012. *Lifeworlds: Essays in Existential Anthropology.* Chicago: University of Chicago Press.

Ji, Yingchun. 2015. "Between Tradition and Modernity: 'Leftover' Women in Shanghai." *Journal of Marriage and Family* 77(5): 1057–1073.

Jones, Gavin W. 2007. "Delayed Marriage and Very Low Fertility in Pacific Asia." *Population and Development Review* 33(3): 453–478.

Jordal, Malin, Kumudu Wijewardena, and Pia Olsson. 2013. "Unmarried Women's Ways of Facing Single Motherhood in Sri Lanka: A Qualitative Interview Study." *BMC Women's Health* 13(5): 1–12.

Jose, A. V. 2020. "How Can More Women Take Up Paid Employment?" *India Forum*, October 2. https://www.theindiaforum.in/article/how-can-more-women-take-paid-employment.

Joseph, Vanishree. 2016. *Methodology for an Evaluation Study: India's Working Women's Hostels Scheme*. London: Sage.

Joshi, Sonam. 2018. "Meet the Single DIY Moms." *Times of India*, August 26. https://timesofindia.indiatimes.com/home/sunday-times/meet-the-single-diy-moms/articleshow/65545871.cms.

Kaivanara, Marzieh. 2016. "Virginity Dilemma: Re-creating Virginity through Hymenoplasty in Iran." *Culture, Health and Sexuality* 18(1): 71–83.

Kala, Avaita. 2009. *Almost Single*. New York: Bantam Dell.

Karlekar, Malavika. 1986. "Kadambini and the Bhadralok: Early Debates over Women's Education in Bengal. *Economic and Political Weekly: Review of Women's Studies* 21(17): WS25–WS31.

———. 1995. "Reflections on Kulin Polygamy—Nistarini Debi's Sekeley Katha." *Contributions to Indian Sociology* 29(1–2): 135–155.

Khan, Fatima. 2020. "No Link between Marriage, Motherhood—Why More Single Women Are Opting for Adoptions." *The Print*. February 24. https://theprint.in/india/no-link-between-marriage-motherhood-why-more-single-women-are-opting-for-adoptions/369165/.

Khandelwal, Meena. 2004. *Women in Ochre Robes: Gendering Hindu Renunciation*. Albany: State University of New York Press.

Khazan, Olga. 2017. "We Expect Too Much from Our Romantic Partners." *Atlantic*, September 29. https://www.theatlantic.com/health/archive/2017/09/we-expect-way-too-much-from-our-romantic-partners/541353/.

King, Diane E., and Linda Stone. 2010. Lineal Masculinity: Gendered Memory within Patriliny." *American Ethnologist* 37(2): 323–336.

Kirmani, Nida. 2020. "Can Fun Be Feminist? Gender, Space, and Mobility in Lyari, Karachi." *South Asia: Journal of South Asian Studies* 43(2): 319–331.

Kislev, Elyakim. 2019a. *Happy Singlehood: The Rising Acceptance and Celebration of Solo Living*. Berkeley: University of California Press.

———. 2019b. "The Impact of Friendships on Single and Married People," *Psychology Today*, April 7. https://www.psychologytoday.com/us/blog/happy-singlehood/201904/the-impact-friendships-single-and-married-people.

Klinenberg, Eric. 2012. *Going Solo: The Extraordinary Rise and Surprising Appeal of Living Alone*. New York: Penguin.

Kowalski, Julia. 2016. "Ordering Dependence: Care, Disorder, and Kinship Ideology in North Indian Antiviolence Counseling." *American Ethnologist* 43(1): 63–75.

Krishnakumari, N. S. 1987. *Status of Single Women in India: A Study of Spinsters, Widows and Divorcees*. New Delhi: Uppal Publishing House.

Kundu, Sreemoyee Piu. 2018. *Status Single: The Truth about Being a Single Woman in India*. New Delhi: Amaryllis.

Kuriakose, Simi. 2014. "Meet the 5 Kinds of Single Women." *Times of India*, July 10. https://timesofindia.indiatimes.com/life-style/relationships/love-sex/Meet-the-5-kinds-of-single-women/articleshow/18848928.cms?

Lake, Roseann. 2018. *Leftover in China: The Women Shaping the World's Next Superpower*. New York: W. W. Norton.

Lal, Malashri, ed. 2015. *Tagore and the Feminine: A Journey in Translations*. New Delhi: Sage.

Lamb, Sarah. 1997. "The Making and Unmaking of Persons: Notes on Aging and Gender in North India." *Ethos* 25(3): 279–302.

———. 1999. "Aging, Gender and Widowhood: Perspectives from Rural West Bengal." *Contributions to Indian Sociology* 33(3): 541–570.

———. 2000. *White Saris and Sweet Mangoes: Aging, Gender and Body in North India*. Berkeley: University of California Press.

———. 2001. "Being a Widow and Other Life Stories: The Interplay between Lives and Words." *Anthropology and Humanism* 26(1): 16–34.

———. 2009. *Aging and the Indian Diaspora: Cosmopolitan Families in India and Abroad*. Bloomington: Indiana University Press.

———. 2013. "In/dependence, Intergenerational Uncertainty, and the Ambivalent State: Perceptions of Old Age Security in India." *South Asia: Journal of South Asian Studies* 36(1): 65–78.

———. 2014. "Permanent Personhood or Meaningful Decline? Toward a Critical Anthropology of Successful Aging." *Journal of Aging Studies* 29: 41–52.

———. 2017. "Ageless Aging or Meaningful Decline? Aspirations of Aging and Dying in the United States and India." In Sarah Lamb, ed., *Successful Aging as a Contemporary Obsession: Global Perspectives*. Pp. 230–242. New Brunswick, NJ: Rutgers University Press.

———. 2018. "Being Single in India: Gendered Identities, Class Mobilities, and Personhoods in Flux." *Ethos* 46(1): 49–69.

———. 2019a. "Interrogating Healthy/Successful Aging: An Anthropologist's Lens." *General Anthropology* 26(2): 1, 7–9.

———. 2019b. "On Being (Not) Old: Agency, Self-care, and Life-course Aspirations in the United States." *Medical Anthropology Quarterly* 33(2): 263–281.

———. 2020. "Old Age Homes, Love, and Other New Cultures of Aging in Middle-Class India." In Jay Sokolovsky, ed., *Cultural Context of Aging: Worldwide Perspectives*, 4th ed. Pp. 466–491. Santa Barbara: Praeger.

———. 2021. "Never-Married Women in India: Gendered Life Courses, Desires, and Identities in Flux." In Marcia C. Inhorn and Nancy J. Smith-Hefner, eds., *Waithood: Gender, Education, and Global Delays in Marriage and Childbearing*. Pp. 290–314. New York: Berghahn.

———. 2022. "Freedom to Choose? Singlehood, Gender, and Sexuality in India." In Joanna Davidson and Dinah Hannaford, eds., *Opting Out: Women Messing with Marriage around the World*. New Brunswick, NJ: Rutgers University Press.

Lamb, Sarah, and Iza Kavedzija. 2020. "Ends of Life: An Interview with Sarah Lamb." *Anthropology and Aging* 41(2): 110–125.

Lesch, Elmien, and Alberta S. J. van der Watt. 2018. "Living Single: A Phenomenological Study of a Group of South African Single Women." *Feminism and Psychology* 28(3): 390–408.

Levi-Strauss, Claude. 1969 [1949]. *The Elementary Structures of Kinship*. Translated by James Harle Bell, John Richard von Sturmer. Edited by Rodney Needham. Boston: Beacon Press.

Lewis, Helen. 2020. "What It's Like to Be a Leftover Woman." *Atlantic*. March 12. https://www.theatlantic.com/international/archive/2020/03/leftover-women-china-israel-children-marriage/607768/.

Linde, Charlotte. 2000. "The Acquisition of a Speaker by a Story: How History Becomes Memory and Identity." *Ethos* 28(4): 608–632.

Lomsky-Feder, Edna. 2004. "Life Stories, War, and Veterans: On the Social Distribution of Memories." *Ethos* 32(1): 82–109.

Luna, Sarah. 2020. *Love in the Drug War: Selling Sex and Finding Jesus on the Mexico-US Border*. Austin: University of Texas Press.

Maeda, Eriko. 2008. "Relational Identities of Always-Single Japanese Women." *Journal of Social and Personal Relationships* 25(6): 967–987.

Magnarella, Paul J. 1986. "Anthropological Fieldwork, Key Informants, and Human Bonds." *Anthropology and Humanism Quarterly* 11(2): 33–37.

Mahmood, Saba. 2005. *The Politics of Piety: The Islamic Revival and the Feminist Subject*. Princeton, NJ: Princeton University Press.

Majumdar, Rochona. 2004. "Snehalata's Death: Dowry and Women's Agency in Colonial Bengal." *Indian Economic and Social History Review* 41(4): 433–464.

Malhotra, Nishi. 2019. "Retirement Communities in India: An Idea Whose Time Has Come." *Silver Talkies*. January 23. https://silvertalkies.com/retirement-communities-in-india-an-idea-whose-time-has-come/.

Mani, Lata. 2014. "Sex and the Signal-Free Corridor: Towards a New Feminist Imaginary." *Economic and Political Weekly* 49(6): 26–29.

Manu. 1991. *The Laws of Manu*. Translated by Wendy Doniger with Brian K. Smith. New York: Penguin.

Marcus, Sharon. 1992. "Fighting Bodies, Fighting Words: A Theory and Politics of Rape Prevention." In Judith Butler and Joan Scott, eds., *Feminists Theorize the Political*. Pp. 385–403. New York: Routledge.

Mathew, Sunalini. 2019. "Meet the Choice Mothers: Single Women Who've Opted for Parenthood without a Partner." *The Hindu*, November 10. https://www.thehindu.com/society/meet-the-choice-mothers-single-women-whove-opted-for-parenthood-without-a-partner/article29920954.ece.

Mauss, Marcel. 1979 [1935]. "Body Techniques." In *Sociology and Psychology: Essays*. Translated by B. Brewster. Pp. 97–123. London: Routledge and Kegan Paul.

Mazumdar, Indrani, and N. Neetha. 2011. "Gender Dimensions: Employment Trends in India, 1993–94 to 2009–10." *Economic and Political Weekly* 46(43): 118–126.

McDermott, Rachel Fell. 2001. *Singing to the Goddess: Poems to Kali and Uma from Bengal*. Oxford: Oxford University Press.

———. 2011. *Revelry, Rivalry, and Longing for the Goddesses of Bengal: The Fortunes of Hindu Festivals*. New York: Columbia University Press.

McGinn, Daniel. 2006. "Marriage by the Numbers." *Newsweek*, 4 June.

Mehra, Nitya, Zoya Akhtar, Prashant Nair, and Alankrita Shrivastava, dirs. 2019. *Made in Heaven*. Mumbai: Excel Entertainment.

Mehrotra, Deepti Priya. 2003. *Home Truths: Stories of Single Mothers*. Gurgaon: Penguin Random House India.

Mehta, Deepa, dir. 1996. *Fire*. New Delhi: Kaleidoscope Entertainment.

Melkote, Rama, and Susie J. Tharu. 1983. "An Investigative Analysis of Working Women's Hostels in India." *Signs* 9(1): 164–171.

Mishra, Jayaprakash. 2020. "Queering Emotion in South Asia: Biographical Narratives of Gay Men in Odisha, India." *Asian Journal of Social Science* 48: 350–371.

Mishra, Neha. 2015. "India and Colorism: The Finer Nuances." *Washington University Global Studies Law Review* 14(4): 725–750.

Mishra, Paro. 2018. "Being 'Bare Branches': Demographic Imbalance, Marriage Exclusion, and Masculinity in North India." In Sharada Srinivasan and Shuzhuo Li, eds., *Scarce Women and Surplus Men in China and India: Macro Demographics versus Local Dynamics. Demographic Transformation and Socio-Economic Development*. Vol. 8. Pp 25–46. Cham, Switzerland: Springer.

Mitra, Durba. 2020. *Indian Sex Life: Sexuality and the Colonial Origins of Modern Social Thought*. Princeton, NJ: Princeton University Press.

Mokkil, Navaneetha. 2019. *Unruly Figures: Queerness, Sex Work, and the Politics of Sexuality in Kerala*. Seattle: University of Washington Press.

Morris, Wendy L., Stacey Sinclair, and Bella M. DePaulo. 2007. "No Shelter for Singles: The Perceived Legitimacy of Marital Status Discrimination." *Group Processes and Intergroup Relations* 10(4): 457–470.

Mukherjee, Amrita. 2015. "India's Single IVF Mums." *Friday Magazine*. https://fridaymaga zine.ae/life-culture/india-s-single-ivf-mums-1.1447869

Mukherjee, Srimati. 2016. *Women and Resistance in Contemporary Bengali Cinema: A Freedom Incomplete*. New York: Routledge.

Mukhopadhyay, Carol Chapnik, and Susan Seymour, eds. 1994. *Women, Education, and Family Structure in India*. Boulder, CO: Westview Press.

Mundhra, Smriti. 2020. *Indian Matchmaking*. Netflix.

Muñoz, José Esteban. 2009. *Cruising Utopia: The Then and There of Queer Futurity*. New York: New York University Press.

Myers, Robert. 2011. "The Familiar Strange and the Strange Familiar in Anthropology and Beyond." *General Anthropology* 18(2): 1, 7–9.

Nair, Anisha. 2018. "Single Parent Adoption in India: Rules and Eligibility." First Cry Parenting, October 1. https://parenting.firstcry.com/articles/single-parent-adoption-in -india-rules-and-eligibility/.

Narayan, Deepa. 2018a. *Chup: Breaking the Silence about India's Women*. New Delhi: Juggernaut.

———. 2018b. "India is the Most Dangerous Country for Women. It Must Face Reality." *Guardian*, 2 July 2018. https://www.theguardian.com/commentisfree/2018/jul/02/india -most-dangerous-country-women-survey.

Narayan, Uma. 1997. *Dislocating Cultures: Identities, Traditions, and Third World Feminism*. New York: Routledge.

Nath, Dipanita. 2016. "Keeping the Flame Alive: What Made Deepa Mehta's *Fire* Such a Pathbreaking Film." *Indian Express*, March 20. https://indianexpress.com/article/enter tainment/bollywood/keeping-the-flame-alive-what-made-deepa-mehtas-fire-such-a -pathbreaking-film/.

Ortiz-Ospina, Esteban, and Max Roser. 2020. "Marriages and Divorces." *Our World in Data*. https://ourworldindata.org/marriages-and-divorces.

Ortner, Sherry. 1984. "Theory in Anthropology since the Sixties." *Comparative Studies in Society and History* 26: 126–161.

———. 1996. "Toward a Feminist, Minority, Postcolonial, Subaltern, etc. Theory of Practice." In *Making Gender: The Politics and Erotics of Culture.* Pp. 1–20. Boston: Beacon Press.

———. 2005. "Subjectivity and Cultural Critique." *Anthropological Theory* 5(1): 31–52.

———. 2006. *Anthropology and Social Theory: Culture, Power, and the Acting Subject.* Durham, NC: Duke University Press.

———. 2016. "Dark Anthropology and Its Others: Theory since the Eighties." *HAU: Journal of Ethnographic Theory* 6(1): 47–73.

Parish, Steven M. 2008. *Subjectivity and Suffering in American Culture: Possible Selves.* New York: Palgrave Macmillan.

Patel, Bhaichand, ed. 2006. *Chasing the Good Life: On Being Single.* New Delhi: Viking India.

Patel, Geeta V., and Ravi Patel, dirs. 2014. *Meet the Patels.* Los Angeles: Alchemy.

Pathak, Sushmita. 2020. "Netflix's 'Indian Matchmaking' Is the Talk of India—and Not in a Good Way." National Public Radio, July 26. https://www.npr.org/sections/goatsand soda/2020/07/26/895008997/netflixs-indian-matchmaking-is-the-talk-of-india-and -not-in-a-good-way.

Perelli-Harris, Brienna, Stefanie Hoherz, Trude Lappegård, and Ann Evans. 2019. "Mind the 'Happiness' Gap: The Relationships between Cohabitation, Marriage, and Subjective Well-Being in the United Kingdom, Australia, Germany, and Norway." *Demography* 56(4): 1219–1246.

Phadke, Shilpa. 2020. "Defending Frivolous Fun: Feminist Acts of Claiming Public Spaces in South Asia." *South Asia: Journal of South Asian Studies* 43(2): 281–293.

Phadke, Shilpa, Sameera Khan, and Shilpa Ranade. 2011. *Why Loiter? Women and Risk on Mumbai Streets.* New Delhi: Penguin.

Phillimore, Peter. 1991. "Unmarried Women of the Dhaula Dhar: Celibacy and Social Control in Northwest India." *Journal of Anthropological Research* 47(3): 331–350.

Pinto, Sarah. 2014a. *Daughters of Parvati: Women and Madness in Contemporary India.* Philadelphia: University of Pennsylvania Press.

———. 2014b. "Drugs and the Single Woman: Pharmacy, Fashion, Desire, and Destitution in India." *Culture, Medicine, and Psychiatry* 38(2): 237–254.

Potash, Betty. 1986. "Preface." In Betty Potash, ed., *Widows in African Societies: Choices and Constraints.* Pp. v–vii. Stanford, CA: Stanford University Press.

Pothukuchi, Kameshwari. 2001. "Effectiveness and Empowerment in Women's Shelter: A Study of Working Women's Hostels in Bangalore, India." *International Journal of Urban and Regional Research* 25(2): 364–379.

Prajwal, N. 2018. "Cultural Differences and Negotiations in Inter-Caste Marriages: A Study in Bengaluru." *Artha Journal of Social Sciences* 17(2): 1–20.

Puri, Jyoti. 1999. *Woman, Body, Desire in Post-Colonial India: Narratives of Gender and Sexuality.* New York: Routledge.

Reddy, Gayatri. 2005. *With Respect to Sex: Negotiating Hijra Identity in South India.* Chicago: University of Chicago Press.

Ring, Laura. 2006. *Zenana: Everyday Peace in a Karachi Apartment Building.* Bloomington: Indiana University Press.

Robbins, Joel. 2013. "Beyond the Suffering Subject: Toward an Anthropology of the Good." *JRAI: Journal of the Royal Anthropological Institute* 19(3): 447–462.

Qamar, Maria. 2017. *Trust No Aunty*. New York: Simon and Schuster.

Qian, Yue. 2018. "Does Being Smart and Successful Lower Your Chances of Marriage?" *The Conversation*, 6 September. http://theconversation.com/does-being-smart-and-successful-lower-your-chances-of-getting-married-100169.

Rabinow, Paul. 2007 [1977]. *Reflections on Fieldwork in Morocco*. Berkeley: University of California Press.

Radhakrishnan, Smitha. 2009. "Professional Women, Good Families: Respectable Femininity and the Cultural Politics of a 'New' India." *Qualitative Sociology* 32: 195–212.

———. 2011. *Appropriately Indian: Gender and Culture in a New Transnational Class*. Durham, NC: Duke University Press.

Raheja, Gloria, and Ann Grodzins Gold. 1994. *Listen to the Heron's Words: Reimagining Gender and Kinship in North India*. Berkeley: University of California Press.

Rainbird, Sophia. 2014. "Asserting Existence: Agentive Narratives Arising from the Restraints of Seeking Asylum in East Anglia, Britain." *Ethos* 42(4): 460–478.

Raja, Vidya. 2019. "On Her Own: 3 Courageous Women Share What It Means to Be a Single Mother in India." *The Better India*. https://www.thebetterindia.com/174279/india-single-mother-inspiring-womens-day/.

Ramberg, Lucinda. 2014. *Given to the Goddess: South Indian Devadasis and the Sexuality of Religion*. Durham, NC: Duke University Press.

Ray, Raka, and Seemin Qayum. 2009. *Cultures of Servitude: Modernity, Domesticity, and Class in India*. Stanford, CA: Stanford University Press.

Raychaudhury, Anasua Basu. 2004. "Nostalgia of 'Desh,' Memories of Partition." *Economic and Political Weekly* 39(52): 5653–5660.

Raymo, James M. 2015. "Living Alone in Japan: Relationships with Happiness and Health." *Demographic Research* 32(2): 1267–1298.

Raymo, James M., and Miho Iwasawa. 2005. "Marriage Market Mismatches in Japan: An Alternative View of the Relationship between Women's Education and Marriage." *American Sociological Review* 70(5): 801–802.

Roy, Ananya. 2003. *City Requiem, Calcutta: Gender and the Politics of Poverty*. Minneapolis: University of Minnesota Press.

Roy, Sandip. 2008. "Be Gay, Be Anything—Just Not Single!" *Salon*, May 30. https://www.salon.com/2008/05/30/arranged_gay_marriage/.

———. 2015. What It's Like to Be Gay in Modern India." *Telegraph*, January 27. http://www.telegraph.co.uk/men/relationships/11365516/What-its-like-to-be-gay-in-modern-India.html.

Rubin, Gayle S. 1975. "The Traffic in Women: Notes on the 'Political Economy' of Sex." In Rayna Reiter, ed., *Toward an Anthropology of Women*. Pp. 157–210. New York: Monthly Review Press.

———. 2011a. "Introduction: Sex, Gender, Politics." In *Deviations: A Gayle Rubin Reader*. Pp. 1–32. Durham, NC: Duke University Press.

———. 2011b [1984]. "Thinking Sex: Notes for a Radical Theory of the Politics of Sexuality." In *Deviations: A Gayle Rubin Reader*. Pp. 137–181. Durham, NC: Duke University Press.

———. 2011c [1975]. "The Traffic in Women: Notes on the 'Political Economy' of Sex." In *Deviations: A Gayle Rubin Reader*. Pp. 33–65. Durham, NC: Duke University Press.

Sabbah-Karkaby, Maha, and Haya Stier. 2017. "Links between Education and Age at Marriage among Palestinian Women in Israel: Changes over Time." *Studies in Family Planning* 48(1): 23–38.

Sahlins, Marshall. 2011. "What Is Kinship (Part One)." *Journal of the Royal Anthropological Institute* (n.s.) 17: 2–19.

Samanta, Tannistha. 2018. "The 'Good Life': Third Age, Brand Modi, and the Cultural Demise of Old Age in Urban India." *Anthropology and Aging* 39(1): 94–104.

———. 2020. "Aging in E-Place: Reflections on Online Communities for the Aged in India." *Journal of Women and Aging* 32(1): 114–121.

———. 2021. "Aging, Housing Markets and Social Inclusion: Insights from India." *Journal of Aging Studies* 57. DOI: https://doi.org/10.1016/j.jaging.2021.100939.

Sandesara, Utpal. 2017. "'A Necessary Sin': An Ethnographic Study of Sex Selection in Western India." PhD diss., University of Pennsylvania.

Sangal, Aditi. 2020. "'Indian Matchmaking' Presents Painful Truths about Skin Color and Love in Indian Culture but Does Nothing to Challenge Them." CNN, July 22. https://www.cnn.com/style/article/indian-matchmaking-netflix-intl-hnk-beauty/index.html.

Sarkar, Tanika. 2002. *Hindu Wife, Hindu Nation: Community, Religion, and Cultural Nationalism*. Bloomington: Indiana University Press.

Sarkisian, Natalia, and Naomi Gerstel. 2016. "Does Singlehood Isolate or Integrate? Examining the Link between Marital Status and Ties to Kin, Friends, and Neighbors." *Journal of Social and Personal Relationships* 33(3): 361–384.

Satalkar, Priya. 2012. "To Marry or Not to Marry? Studying Others to Know Myself." *Medische Antropologie* 24(1): 207–224.

Sayer, Andrew. 2005. *The Moral Significance of Class*. New York: Cambridge University Press.

Sebastian, Aleena. 2016. "Matrilineal Practices along the Coasts of Malabar." *Sociological Bulletin* 65(1): 89–106.

Seizer, Susan. 1995. "Paradoxes of Visibility in the Field: Rites of Queer Passage in Anthropology." *Public Culture* 8: 73–100.

———. 2000. "Roadwork: Offstage with Special Drama Actresses in Tamilnadu, South India." *Cultural Anthropology* 15(2): 217–259.

Seligmann, Linda J. 2009. "Maternal Politics and Religious Fervor: Exchanges between an Andean Market Woman and an Ethnographer." *Ethos* 37(3): 334–361.

Seymour, Susan C. 1999. *Women, Family, and Child Care in India: A World in Transition*. New York: Cambridge University Press.

Sharma, Kalpana, ed. 2019. *Single by Choice: Happily Unmarried Women!* Delhi: Women Unlimited.

Shlam, Shosh, and Hilla Medalia, dirs. 2019. *Leftover Women*. Produced by Medalia Productions and Shlam Productions.

Shrivastava, Alankrita, dir. 2016. *Lipstick under My Burkha*. Mumbai: Prakash Jha Productions.

Singh, Bhrigupati. 2015. *Poverty and the Quest for Life: Spiritual and Material Striving in Rural India*. Chicago: University of Chicago Press.

Singh, Holly Donahue. 2016. "Fertility Control: Reproductive Desires, Kin Work, and Women's Status in Contemporary India." *Medical Anthropology Quarterly* 31(1): 23–39.

Singh, Parul. 2018. "8 Single Moms of TV Who Proved That They Do Not Need a Man to Raise Their Children." Bollywoodshaadis.com, May 13. https://www.bollywoodshaadis .com/articles/single-mothers-of-indian-television-4044.

Singh, S. Bachan Jeet. 2017. "Few Takers in Hyderabad for 'Single Woman' Pension." *New Indian Express*, June 1. http://cms.newindianexpress.com/cities/hyderabad/2017/jun/01 /few-takers-in-hyderabad-for-single-woman-pension-1611556.html.

Singh, Shiv Sahay, and Indrani Dutta. 2017. "Progress, One Girl at a Time." *The Hindu*. August 5. https://www.thehindu.com/society/progress-one-girl-at-a-time/article19433908.ece.

Sinha, Chinki. 2019. "Brave New Woman." *India Today*, October 11. https://www.indiatoday .in/magazine/cover-story/story/20191021-brave-new-woman-1607809-2019-10-11.

Slater, Mariam K. 1986. "Foreword: Sons and Levirs." In Betty Potash, ed., *Widows in African Societies: Choices and Constraints*. Pp. xv–xxii. Stanford, CA: Stanford University Press.

Sommer, Marni, Bethany A. Caruso, Murat Sahin, Teresa Calderon, Sue Cavill, and Therese Mahon. 2016. "A Time for Global Action: Addressing Girls' Menstrual Hygiene Management Needs in Schools." *PLoS Medicine* 12(2): 1–9.

Sridharan, E. 2004. "The Growth and Sectoral Composition of India's Middle Class: Its Impact on the Politics of Economic Liberalization." *India Review* 3(4): 405–428.

Stone, Linda, and Caroline James. 1995. "Dowry, Bride-Burning, and Female Power in India." *Women's Studies International Forum* 18(2): 125–134.

Sullivan, Nikki. 2003. *A Critical Introduction to Queer Theory*. Edinburgh: Edinburgh University Press.

Thapan, Meenakshi. 2003. "Marriage, Well-Being, and Agency among Women." *Gender and Development* 1(2): 77–84.

Tilche, Alice, and Edward Simpson. 2018. "Marriage and the Crisis of Peasant Society in Gujarat, India." *Journal of Peasant Studies* 45(7): 1518–1538.

Time. 2019. "School Has Been a Right for Girls in India Since 2009. So Why Aren't They Going?" June 27. https://time.com/5614642/india-girls-education/.

To, Sandy. 2013. "Understanding Sheng Nu ('Leftover Women'): The Phenomenon of Late Marriage among Chinese Professional Women." *Symbolic Interaction* 36(1): 1–20.

Traister, Rebecca. 2016. *All the Single Ladies: Unmarried Women and the Rise of an Independent Nation*. New York: Simon and Schuster.

Trimberger, E. Kay. 2005. *The New Single Woman*. Boston: Beacon Press.

Trivedi, Ira. 2014. *India in Love: Marriage and Sexuality in the 21st Century*. New Delhi: Aleph.

Twamley, Katherine, and Juhi Sidharth. 2019. "Negotiating Respectability: Comparing the Experiences of Poor and Middle-Class Young Urban Women in India." *Modern Asian Studies* 53(5): 1646–1674.

UNICEF. 2019. "Ending Child Marriage: A Profile of Child Marriage in India." New York: UNICEF. https://www.unicef.org/india/media/1176/file/Ending-Child-Marriage.pdf.

UN Women. 2019. "Progress of the World's Women 2019–2020: Families in a Changing World." https://www.unwomen.org/-/media/headquarters/attachments/sections/library /publications/2019/progress-of-the-worlds-women-2019–2020-en.pdf?la=en&vs =3512.

Vajpayee, Soumya. 2019. "Is It Easy to Be a Single Mother in India?" *Times of India*, March 28. https://timesofindia.indiatimes.com/life-style/relationships/is-it-easy-to-be-a-single -mother-in-india/articleshow/68356898.cms.

Vanita, Ruth. 2001. *Queering India: Same-Sex Love and Eroticism in Indian Culture and Society*. New York: Routledge.

———. 2012. *Gender, Sex, and the City: Urdu Rekhti Poetry in India, 1780–1870*. New York: Palgrave Macmillan.

Vijayakumar, Gowri. 2013. "'I'll Be like Water': Gender, Class, and Flexible Aspirations at the Edge of India's Knowledge Economy." *Gender and Society* 27(6): 777–798.

Wadhwa, Soma. 2007. "Caste Walls Divide Modern India." *Hindustan Times*, January 1. https://www.hindustantimes.com/india/caste-walls-divide-modern-india/story-OqHaQ Mu7rgBlcFBqmmZjaN.html.

Waldrop, Anne. 2012. "Grandmother, Mother and Daughter: Changing Agency of Indian, Middle-Class Women, 1908–2008." *Modern Asian Studies* 46(3): 601–638.

Walters, Kimberly. 2016. "The Stickiness of Sex Work: Pleasure, Habit, and Intersubstantiality in South India." *Signs: Journal of Women in Culture and Society* 42(1): 99–121.

———. 2022. "Pathivratha Precarity: Sex Work on the Other Side of Marriage in South India." In Joanna Davidson and Dinah Hannaford, eds., *Opting Out: Women Messing with Marriage around the World*. New Brunswick, NJ: Rutgers University Press.

Wangchuk, Rinchen Norbu. 2020. "Kolkata Single Mom Took on a Regressive System to Get Her Child an Education." *The Better India*, May 12. https://www.thebetterindia .com/226132/kolkata-single-mother-ivf-pregnancy-school-admission-education -inspiring-nor41/.

Weber, Rachel. 1995. "Re(Creating) the Home: Women's Role in the Development of Refugee Colonies in South Calcutta." *Indian Journal of Gender Studies* 2(2): 195–210.

Wekker, Gloria. 2006. *The Politics of Passion: Women's Sexual Culture in the Afro-Surinamese Diaspora*. New York: Columbia University Press.

Wilkerson, Isabel. 2020. *Caste: The Origins of Our Discontents*. New York: Random House.

Yengkhom, Sumita. 2015. "Mom by Choice, Not Wedlock." *Times of India*, March 7. https://timesofindia.indiatimes.com/city/kolkata/Mom-by-choice-not-wedlock/article show/46488575.cms.

Zehtabchi, Rayka, dir. 2018. *Period. End of Sentence*. Produced by Rayka Zehtabchi, Melissa Berton, Garrett Schieff, and Lisa Taback. Netflix. https://www.netflix.com/title/81074663.

INDEX

Aarini [Guha] (pseudonym), 1, 19, 102–3, 117, 162, 167; on confusion regarding changing mores on marriage, 122; on education and marriage, 28, 53; on hierarchy of Indian society, 1; on parents' failure to arrange her marriage, 38–39; in Silicon Valley, 38, 84; solo travel of, 117, 166

abandoned women, 6, 42, 83, 94, 194n2

abortion, 34, 94, 111

Abraham, Janaki, 113

Abu-Lughod, Lila, 9, 11

adoption, 2, 18, 143–47, 173; CARA (Central Adoption Resource Agency), 143, 144; Hindu Adoptions and Maintenance Act (1956), 143, 194–95n11

adult/adulthood, marriage as tied to, 7, 10, 34, 38, 152, 170, 173

agency, interplay with constraint, 9, 13, 14, 48, 111, 133, 176; overlap and blurring together of, 49; singlehood as, 25

Aging and the Indian Diaspora (Lamb, 2009), 190n12

Ajay [Nag] (pseudonym), 2, 7, 31, 100, 128, 131–33, 159, 184n12, 194n29

All the Single Ladies: Unmarried Women and the Rise of an Independent Nation (Traister, 2016), 14, 159, 169, 176

Almost Single (Kala, 2011), 110

alta (red dye on women's feet), 165, 196n6

Ambedkar, B. R., 192n11

Anindita (pseudonym), 2, 7, 100, 128, 131–33, 159

Anjaria, Jonathan Shapiro, 155

Anjaria, Ulka, 155

anthropology, 8, 33, 175; "dark anthropology," 11; of gender and kinship, focus on marriage, 33, 185n18; queer studies and, 10–11; widows and, 7

"anti-Romeo" squads, 56

arakshaniya (unmarried daughter no longer protected in natal home), 114

asexuality, 124, 133, 148, 192n3, 193n21

Asha (pseudonym), 37, 38, 114

Ashapurna (pseudonym), 158

Association of Strong Women Alone, 6

autonomy: aspirations for as presumed universal desire, 13, 14; as constrained within marriage, 28, 73; liberal, independent subject and, 13; singlehood and, 18, 19; US myth of in old age, 190n14

bachelors: *See* unmarried men

Bagchi, Josodhara, 74

Banerjee, Himani, 184n2

Banerjee, Mamata, 51, 187nn10–11

Banerjee, Tanmayee, 165

Bangalore, city of, 4, 57, 72, 162

Bariwali [*The Lady of the House*] (film, dir. Ghosh, 2000), 164–65

Basu, Hena, 16, 18, 83–84, 97

Basu, Srimati, 72, 85, 175

women and, 5, 72, 73, 76, 81–85,
  89–90
Kirmani, Nida, 156
Kislev, Elyakim, 12, 14, 159, 169
Klinenberg, Eric, 12, 92
Kolkata, city of, 1, 3, 21, 23, 39, 104, 128; Alipore
  neighborhood, 94; Ballygunge neighborhood,
  62, 66, 67, 147; in British colonial era, 29;
  cosmopolitan lifestyle of, 22; Dakshinapan
  Shopping Center, 70, 163; Deshopriya Park
  neighborhood, 15; elite families of, 53, 61, 158;
  friend groups in cafés, 162; Ganguly Bagan
  neighborhood, 62; Gariahat neighborhood,
  41, 82, 87–88, 99; High Court, 140; Hindu
  refugees from Partition in, 74, 76, 81–82,
  190n10; old age homes in, 94, 95, 96, 97, 98,
  190n5; outdoor markets, 19; Rabindra Sarobar
  Lake Park, 104; slums of, 66
Krishnakumari, N. S., 4
Kumkum (pseudonym), 135, 147–50, 167

Lake, Roseann, 169
Laws of Manu, 39, 186n30
"leftover women," in China, 53, 181n3
Leftover in China: The Women Shaping the
  World's Next Superpower (Lake, 2018), 169
lesbians, 2, 10, 16, 131, 167; legible to the public as
  homosocial friends, 131; lesbian identification
  as reason for not marrying, 26, 31; love
  and sexual relationships, 110–11, 128–33;
  in metropolitan areas, 18; prevented from
  marrying, 131, 173; self-care in old age, 100;
  "single women" category and, 6–7; support
  groups for, 48, 131, 159, 167; in Tamil Nadu
  state, 4. See also Fire (film)
Lévi-Strauss, Claude, 182n12
LGBTQ+ culture and movements, 6, 131, 152, 170.
  See also lesbians
Lipstick under My Burkha, 110
literature, love and romance in, 126
living alone. See solo living
"living in," outside marriage, 28, 127, 184n8
"loitering," 104, 161, 162, 163. See also Why Loiter?
loneliness, 88, 90, 109, 175
Losing My Virginity and Other Dumb Ideas
  (Banerjee, 2011), 110
love, 124–28; dating sites for elderly singles, 127,
  127; lesbian and queer love, 128–33; "love"
  marriages, 29, 121, 122–23

Made in Heaven (Indian web television series,
  2019), 32

Maity, Madhabi, 16, 31, 158
Majlis Legal Centre, 33
male chauvinism, 123–24
Malobika [Ganguly] (pseudonym), 95, 106,
  117–18, 158, 160, 163–64
Mani, Lata, 13
Manjuri [Karmakar] (pseudonym), 50–51, 74, 120
Marcus, Sharon, 115
marriage: age at, 1, 16, 35–36, 55, 188n19; age
  difference of brides and grooms, 36;
  arranged by parents/kin, 26, 29, 38–39, 64,
  121–24; being not married as a "defect," 33;
  child marriage rates, 185n25; class mobility
  and, 72; as compulsory norm, 3; decenter
  as unquestioned norm, 176; declining rates
  of, 7, 169; delaying and foregoing of, 48,
  51, 87; entailing the "exchange of women,"
  112, 182n12; gendered marriage imperative,
  33–39, 170; gender inequality intertwined
  with, 11, 174–75; global decline in rates of,
  169; importance in India, 3, 28, 174; legal
  minimum age, 36, 114; "love" marriages,
  29, 121, 122–23; patriarchy/patriarchal
  society and, 2, 113, 147; perceived as normal
  practice, 1, 173; as problematic, 174–75;
  range of attitudes toward, 18; reasons for not
  marrying, 25–32, 52, 124; as relation between
  families, 61; resistance to, 1; same-sex, 2, 13,
  43, 131; as representing a woman's "future,"
  76, 78, 85; sexual promiscuity discouraged
  by, 121; sexual relationships outside, 110,
  173; shakha pola bangles as symbol of, 138;
  sindur (vermilion) in part of hair as sign of,
  10, 24, 138, 148; social functions of, 5; uneven
  distribution of labor and care, 89; wives'
  break with natal families and, 72, 188n2.
  See also weddings
"Marriage Crunch, The" (Newsweek cover story,
  1986), 53–54
Martin, Rachel, 108
masculinity, 34, 52, 150–52, 186n29; lineal,
  150–152. See also men
Mauss, Marcel, 68
McDermott, Rachel, 189n11
Medha [Manna] (pseudonym), 10, 21, 32, 42,
  69, 90; Boudi as sister-in-law of, 70, 71, 135,
  154–55, 158; caste and class status of, 45, 48,
  186n1; choice of senior citizen residence,
  93, 96–97, 190n5; education of, 45–46,
  174; exercise routine of, 102; on fun and
  happiness, 168; gendered mismatch of class
  and, 61, 174; home decoration of, 167; on

sites of aspiration and care, 93–99, 190n5; percentage of participants in, *41*; as sites of abjection, 94–95; singlehood and, 94, 95, 96–98

old age care, 10, 38, 65, 92, 186n29; depleted savings and, 88; of elderly parents, 92, 132; of "elder orphans," 92; non-family forms of, 92–93, 189n1; plans and insecurities about the future, 91–93; rates of co-residence with children, 92, 189n4; as responsibility of daughters-in-law, 24; strategies for self-care, 99–103

Opting Out: Women Messing with Marriage around the World (Davidson and Hannaford, 2022), 169, 185n18

Pakistan, 74, 182n13, 192n13; East Pakistan, 76, 86
Patel, Baichand, 53
patriarchy, Brahmanical, 113, 121
Period. End of Sentence (documentary film, 2018), 55
personhood, 7, 11, 14, 152, 170; living solo as unusual form of, 14, 25, 39–43; marriage as central to visions of normal adult personhood, 7, 35, 152; new imaginaries of, 12; single personhood, 170
Phadke, Shilpa, 156, 161–63, 164
Phillimore, Peter, 4–5
Pinto, Sarah, 4, 14, 156, 175
pleasing syndrome, 156–59
pleasure, 6, 9, 11, 12, 155–159, 168; sexual pleasure as forbidden for single women, 109, 156; women's right to sexual pleasure, 110, 112, 156
Polly (pseudonym), 58, 60
poor, rural and urban, 17, 20, 73, 172
possibility, 49, 57, 175–76; expanding to say no to marriage, 179; intersecting conditions of possibility and constraint, 49, 133, 176; queerness and, 11
Poverty and the Quest for Life (Singh, 2015), 195n17
Pratima [Nag] (pseudonym), 27, 120
pregnancy, 32, 35, 112, 114–115, 142, 192n12, 194n8; risk/dangers of outside marriage, 25, 37, 112, 114, 151
privacy, 20, 43, 125
"Priya's Shakti" (comic book), 116, *116*
professionals, urban, 15, 16, 33, 125, 135, 145, 157, 173, 174, 183n33; professional success interfering with marriage, 28–29, 53–54; rising trend of professional women in China remaining unmarried, 181n3

pronouns, gendered, 2, 194n29
property inheritance, 84–85, 191n20

Qamar, Maria, 3, 182n11
Queer Activism in India (Dave, 2012), 128
queer studies, 10–11, 33, 69
queer theory, 9–10, 182n18

Rabindra Niketan Retirement Home (Kolkata), 96
Rachana [Sen] (pseudonym), 20, 38, 125
Radhakrishnan, Smitha, 157
Rajguru, Shaktipada, 188n4
Ramberg, Lucinda, 4
Ranade, Shilpa, 162–63
Rao, K. Chandrashekar, 191n20
rape, 25, 112, 113–14, 116, 184n2
recognition, 14, 132, 137, 183n27, 188n22; exclusion from, 111; of feminism and LGBTQ rights, 170; legal, 140; new forms of, 20
refugee status, 8. *See also* Kolkata, Hindu refugees from Partition in
reproduction, 5, 7, 35, 39, 157, 169–70; arranged marriages and, 39; expanding forms of gendered kinship and, 150; marriage as foundation for, 35; gendered marriage imperative and, 36; masculinity and, 152; patrilineal reproduction/reproductivity, 38, 150–52; "reproductive futurity," 10, 182n19; seed-soil metaphor and lineal masculinity, 150
respectability, gendered/feminine, 24, 35, 36, 111, 155, 156, 161–165, 173, 195n5; "anti-Romeo" squads and, 56; performance of, 25; in public spaces, 164; restricted access to, 133; "rules of the Indian morality," 47; strictures against fun and sexual activity for single women, 133, 155, 173; through marriage and childbearing, 4; women's access to non-privatized spaces and, 162, 165
"Retirement Communities in India: An Idea Whose Time Has Come" (*Silver Talkies* essay, 2019), 95
Reuters Foundation, 115
Rinku [Sen] (pseudonym), 108–9, 110, 114, 122–24, 133
"Romance of Resistance, The" (Abu-Lughod, 1990), 11
Roshan, Angad, 32
Roudri (pseudonym), 37–38, 163
Roy, Ananya, 62
Roy, Sandip, 43
Rubin, Gayle, 34, 112, 131

Founded in 1893,
UNIVERSITY OF CALIFORNIA PRESS
publishes bold, progressive books and journals
on topics in the arts, humanities, social sciences,
and natural sciences—with a focus on social
justice issues—that inspire thought and action
among readers worldwide.

The UC PRESS FOUNDATION
raises funds to uphold the press's vital role
as an independent, nonprofit publisher, and
receives philanthropic support from a wide
range of individuals and institutions—and from
committed readers like you. To learn more, visit
ucpress.edu/supportus.